Seriously!

~~Business & Social Sciences~~

CENTRAL LIBRARY OF ROCHESTER
AND MONROE COUNTY
115 SOUTH AVENUE
ROCHESTER, NY 14604-1896

SCIENCE & HISTORY

Pencil throughout
book upon checkout

ce sc
5/1

MAR 12 2014

Seriously!

*Investigating Crashes and Crises
as if Women Mattered*

Cynthia Enloe

UNIVERSITY OF CALIFORNIA PRESS

Berkeley   Los Angeles   London

University of California Press, one of the most
distinguished university presses in the United States,
enriches lives around the world by advancing
scholarship in the humanities, social sciences, and
natural sciences. Its activities are supported by the
UC Press Foundation and by philanthropic contributions
from individuals and institutions. For more information,
visit www.ucpress.edu.

University of California Press
Berkeley and Los Angeles, California

University of California Press, Ltd.
London, England

© 2013 by The Regents of the University of California

Library of Congress Cataloging-in-Publication Data

Enloe, Cynthia H., 1938–
    Seriously! investigating crashes and crises as if women
mattered / Cynthia Enloe.
        pages   cm.
    Includes bibliographical references and index.
    ISBN 978-0-520-27536-2 (cloth : alk. paper) —
    ISBN 978-0-520-27537-9 (pbk. : alk. paper)
    1. Feminism.   2. Feminist theory.   3. Women.
4. Male domination (Social structure).
5. Financial crises.   I. Title.
    HQ1155.E554 2013
    305.42—dc23

                                        2013015156

Manufactured in the United States of America

22 21 20 19 18 17 16 15 14 13
10 9 8 7 6 5 4 3 2 1

In keeping with a commitment to support environmentally
responsible and sustainable printing practices, UC Press
has printed this book on Rolland Enviro100, a 100%
post-consumer fiber paper that is FSC certified, deinked,
processed chlorine-free, and manufactured with
renewable biogas energy. It is acid-free and EcoLogo
certified.

For
Serena Hilsinger
and
Lois Brynes

/ - 5540

CONTENTS

ILLUSTRATIONS

I remember a friend several years ago deciding to use only her first initial in front of her family name when she published her debut book, a smart exploration into the workings of gendered militarism in four countries. At the time, she was working in a progressive think tank based in Europe. Most of her colleagues were men. I was puzzled. Why didn't she use her full name in print? She explained she was afraid that if readers saw her first name, an identifiably feminine name, they would not take her book seriously. Her worries were not unfounded: the men inside her own allegedly critical research organization did not take most women or any feminist ideas seriously. She was clearly unhappy, though, about having adopted this defensive tactic. All her writings since then have boldly carried her full name in print. That would be the last time that this feminist engaged in patriarchal erasure.

Many women have honed their tactics in the never-ending effort to be treated as serious thinkers in a world that continues to undervalue and marginalize any person or any idea imagined to be tinged with femininity. Just this past year one of American television's premier feminist news analysts published a new book about foreign policy. She used her full name on the cover, but as she dissected international politics in print, she also chose to apply little of her celebrated feminist-informed acuity. Despite her prime-time stature, when she delved into foreign policy—where so often masculinity masquerades as expertise—did she feel that she had to shelve most of her feminist understandings in order to be taken seriously?

Readers probably can tell their own stories of women (including themselves) adopting self-deprecating tactics in their quests to be taken seriously in a sexist world. These are stories worth telling. I have told some of my own embarrassing stories here. We must share our own experiences, even when we're embarrassed or ashamed. Hiding these privately honed tactics only helps perpetuate our underestimation of patriarchy's toll. Furthermore, if we muster the courage to tell these stories—of what we chose to wear to meetings, of why we lowered our voice registers when speaking in certain settings, of what topics we think a lot about but do not raise with professional colleagues—we will enable other women (and quite a few men) to see that they are not alone in erasing themselves. As we have learned over the years, realizing that one is not alone is a crucial first step in mobilizing to challenge an oppressive culture.

It was the international banking crash of 2008 that got me thinking about the masculinization of conventional seriousness and about what, alternatively, feminist serious analysis looks like. When news broke about the alleged sexual assault on a New York hotel housekeeper by the International Monetary Fund's managing director, I did what I often do: I started a file. I am never sure what will happen to my files. I just clip the newspapers, scribble notes, print out Internet reports, and let the file grow. Filing provides materiality to my ephemeral mulling. And so I began to ponder what feminists from Virginia Woolf onward have pondered: what's masculinity got to do with it?

What so many feminists, including Virginia Woolf, have taught me, however, is that this question will lead to a dead end if women are not taken seriously. It is the serious investigation of women's experiences of masculinity's diverse workings that shines a bright light on how and why patriarchal privileging of certain masculinities continues to flourish. So into my burgeoning file went any clues about where women were, not only in the IMF, but also in all the financial institutions that together bred the attitudes and spurred the actions that brought on the disastrous banking crash.

I like case studies. I always have. I want to know the minutiae of how things happen: who is at the table; who is stopped at the door; who laughs at what offhand joke; at whose expense is the joke; whose anxieties get top billing; whose proposals are treated as if they were irrelevant; who attends public rallies; who feels she has to stay home; who picks up a gun; who flees to the refugee camp. And why, always why. It is in case studies, in diving deep into the particular, that I gather the most valuable clues about the elusive big picture.

And so as I began to think more about the gendered politics of seriousness, I returned to my bulging file on Dominique Strauss-Kahn. And I pulled out the neighboring cabinet drawer that held my now-overflowing "Arab Spring" file. I started to wonder if some of the same patriarchal dynamics were at work in determining how both of these stories were being told—what was being featured, what was being left out. What would I find if I took seriously the workings of masculinities inside contemporary banking? What would be exposed if I took seriously Egyptian feminists' actions and ideas in the build up to and the aftermath of Cairo's Tahrir Square revolution?

I could not have filled my files and pursued these questions without the generosity of so many people who shared my curiosity and joined these investigatory journeys. Ngoc Du Thai Thi, Phuong Bui Tran, Xavier Guillaume, Jef Huysmans, Marsha Henry, Laura Sjoberg, and Rekha Pande encouraged me to write three of the chapters included here. For insights into the worlds of finance and economics, I have relied on Heidi Hartmann, Linda Basch, Sohaila Abdulali, Jane Knodell, Annadis Rudolfsdottir, Irma Erlingsdottir, Bob Benewick, Debbie Licorish, Amy Lang, and Ailbhe Smyth. For guidance in charting militarism's seemingly unending gendered twists and turns (including the militarization of revolutions), I have looked to Nadine Puechguirbal, Cynthia Cockburn, Madeleine Rees, Carol Cohn, Ayse Gul Altinay, Vron Ware, Ozgur

Heval Cinar, Andreas Speck, Aaron Belkin, Rela Mazali, Sandy McEvoy, Ann Tickner, Lisa Prugl, Karen Turner, Paul Amar, Terrell Carver, Tanya Henderson, and Sanam Naraghi Anderlini.

Serena Hilsinger, Lois Brynes, Ximena Bunster, Gilda Bruckman, Laura Zimmerman, Joni Seager—to you, my trusted early readers, friends who read keenly, each bringing to bear her own feminist thoughtfulness and gifts for language, I offer deep thanks. The two anonymous reviewers of my initial book proposal and the two anonymous reviewers of the later draft manuscript provided me with careful, knowledgeable suggestions. Serving as a reviewer for a publisher is work that is barely visible, but it is an act of genuine academic citizenship.

Julie Clayton of J.C. Consulting has been my superbly professional editorial teammate from start to finish of this book. She has tracked down photographers, formatted and then reformatted the manuscript, and kept the entire preprinting production on course through its multiple phases.

The pressures on publishers and booksellers grow more intense with each passing month. Hard-pressed university publishers can publish fewer books now than even five years ago. Painful choices are being made. If you hold a new book in your hands today, it is because an editor saw its merits, mustered support for its value and its salability, and went to bat in-house for its publication. I count it my supreme good fortune that I work with Naomi Schneider, executive editor of the University of California Press. This marks our seventh book together. Naomi has been rightly honored for her encouragement of, and commitment to, politically engaged scholarship. All of us, as readers and writers alike, are indebted to Naomi. Naomi's wonderful publishing colleagues have turned the manuscript into the handsome volume you are now reading. I so admire the remarkable skills of Kate Warne, production editor; Christopher Lura, assistant editor; Bonita Hurd, copyeditor; and the whole design department.

I love reading and scribbling in no-frills local eateries. Much of the work for this book, as for its predecessors, was done over tuna salad sandwiches and cups of black coffee at Annie's Clark Brunch in Worcester and the Newtowne Grill in Cambridge. Annie and Hafid and Kedar and the hardworking staffs of these two lunchtime oases have provided friendly democratic environments in which ideas can be nourished without anyone on either side of the counter imagining they have a corner on seriousness.

Joni Seager and I have forged a partnership over thirty years. It's a forging fused with laughter, curiosity, circles of friends, and love of adventure (though Joni's study is the one full of bears and rocks). I hope readers will see the influence of Joni's data savvy and her feminist irreverence in the face of orthodox authority, as well as her commitment to crisp syntax, throughout the chapters that follow.

CHAPTER ONE

Who Is "Taken Seriously"?

Let me start with a confession: I spent a long time—too long—*not* taking women seriously. That means I did not think I would gain anything analytically by paying close attention to women. I did not think that any explanation I could offer would be strengthened by my listening to women, observing women, or taking into explicit account the ideas and experiences of women. Furthermore, back then I did not think I would significantly deepen my understanding of men's ideas, men's decisions, and men's actions by taking women seriously.

Simply being a woman is no guarantee that you will take women seriously. In fact, as a woman, one might even imagine that one should avoid showing analytical interest in women so as not to be painted by others with a damning "feminine" brush.

For my doctorate, I chose to study the interplay of ethnicity and education politics in postcolonial, postwar Malaysia. This was during the 1960s. Malaysia was a country that only recently had gained independence from Britain and had come out of a prolonged civil war. Before leaving Berkeley, and then as I was settling into Kuala Lumpur, I read everything I could about Malaysian history and culture, about life on rubber plantations, about the British colonial strategy of co-opting traditional Malay sultans, about the Japanese wartime occupation, about both the insurgents and the Malaysian and British counterinsurgents during the years of civil war from the 1950s to the 1960s. I read novels, memoirs, ethnographies, political science studies, government reports, histories, and old newspapers. Most were authored by men. I scarcely noticed. Virtually all the featured actors portrayed in the books and articles were male. There were a handful of women characters in the novels, but many of them turned out to be the Malay mistresses of British colonial men. A notable exception were the more prominent women characters in Han Suyin's novel *And the Rain My Drink*.[1] Back then, I hardly paused to reflect on the oddity of these all-male casts of characters.

There was so much to absorb, I thought, such complex dynamics to grapple with. There were class differences—among the British expatriates, among the multiethnic Malaysians, and within each of Malaysia's three most prominent ethnic communities, the Malays, the Chinese, and the Tamils. Then there were the sources of interethnic mistrust to comprehend (mistrust fueled by the fact that each of the ethnic communities had its own daily newspaper, not only written in a distinct language but also published in a distinct script). On top of this were the complex and shifting political party alliances and electoral strategies, federal-state tensions, and multiple school systems, as well as the ups and downs of the rubber, palm oil, and tin industries. All together, the story seemed complicated enough. There was no room on my intellectual plate to add questions about gender. And, I imagined, to be taken seriously in my new academic career, I did not need to add such questions.

Back then, that is, investigating women's lives and the workings of masculinities and femininities seemed unlikely to tell me anything I really needed to know about British colonial rule, the Japanese wartime occupation, political economies, ethnic Chinese Malaysians' support for the guerrilla insurgency, the assumptions underpinning the authorities' counterinsurgency strategies, how wartime experiences were shaping postwar 1960s societal relationships, or even about how education policies were fueling the rising communal tensions. I was admitted to Kuala Lumpur's exclusive Selangor Club because I fit into the club's desirable expatriate category of "a woman without a husband in the country"—a membership I sought so that I could take male civil servants to lunch in the capital and sign for the bill without embarrassing them. I joined the all-women's (mostly Chinese and Indian) local field hockey team. I had Malaysian women colleagues at the University of Malaya. I became aware that many male officials talked to me precisely because they did not take seriously a twenty-six-year-old "girl" in sandals and a sleeveless cotton dress. Despite all this, the only people I chose to interview were men—male teachers, male civil servants, male politicians.

And because I did not take women seriously, I did not see these men *as men;* thus I did not try to investigate their diverse masculinities or the political consequences of their diverse masculinities. It was not as if I had made a conscious choice to interview only men. It just seemed normal.

It was only later, when I became a feminist, that I began to question this seductively powerful adjective, *normal,* the twin brother of *natural.* It was only later that I tallied up all that I had missed owing to my narrow vision, my shrunken curiosity. It was only later, too, after I had begun to ask feminist questions, that I realized my own gender-ignorant understanding of Malaysia's war and postwar eras was not simply incomplete; it was unreliable. Today, despite the wealth of feminist research and writing that has come out of Malaysia in recent years, there is yet to be written a thorough feminist analysis of the international politics of rubber (think Dunlop) or of the Malaysian armed guerrilla conflict of 1948–1960—and of its lingering postwar gendered consequences.[2] So because of our failing to take women seriously, we still do not know exactly what we have missed in our understanding of the emergent international political economy and of the Malaysian civil war and its long aftermath.

Not taking women seriously, not paying close attention to the subtle workings of gender, is not, however, simply a characteristic of the "bad old days." It characterizes most contemporary studies of economy, culture, society, and politics. We all are acutely aware that most social commentators, contractors, and policy makers still do not think deeply about women unless they are pushed to do it. And because most of these commentators do not take women seriously, they do not feel compelled to dig deeply into the often fraught dynamics of masculinities: that is, as a result of not taking women seriously, they do not see men *as men.*

It may not be mere coincidence, then, that on all three of the major American cable news channels—CNN, Fox News, and MSNBC—men (mostly white men) make up 65 percent or more of the "expert" guests chosen to appear on their prime-time news shows to discuss political issues. And in Britain too, feminist researchers monitoring nine of Britain's national newspapers found a similar gendered pattern: of the "experts" directly quoted in these influential papers' front-page stories, 76 percent were men; only 24 percent were women. Furthermore, as the British researchers from Women in Journalism found, women were most likely to be directly quoted in a newspaper account when they could be positioned by the journalists as victims. That is, these American and British media producers and editors see men as the ones best equipped to provide serious analysis of political questions facing their countries.[3]

We need to think collectively about what rewards are handed out for *not* taking women seriously—in research projects, in policy debates, in media discussions of the pressing issues of the day. This question has brought me to think a lot about the adverb *seriously.* To be taken seriously is a major reward that can be bestowed on a person. Sometimes the laurel bestowed is called gravitas. Few women are said by the architects of cultural pyramids to possess gravitas. Hannah Arendt and Susan Sontag were admired for possessing gravitas. But, then, often those generous bestowers treated both women as honorary men.

Conversely, as caveat or as punishment, seriousness can be withheld. During the 2012 phase of the uprising in Syria, a journalist briefly mentioned the only woman within the elite inner circle around Syria's besieged authoritarian ruler Bashar al-Assad. This was vice president

Figure 1. An all-male team of UN observers meets with an all-male group of Syrian rebels, Qusayr, Syria, May 2012. Agence France-Presse—Getty Images.

Najah al-Attar. Would she be a possible compromise candidate, various external observers were wondering, to replace President Assad? No, though she was in the regime's inner circle, she was deemed by these diplomatic calculators to lack gravitas.[4] To be taken seriously does not mean to be liked or to be admired. Rather, to be taken seriously means to be listened to, to be carefully responded to, to have one's ideas and actions thoughtfully weighed. It means that what one does or thinks *matters*—that is, significant consequences flow from it.

Propping up the phrase *taken seriously* is the presumption that one becomes worthy of being taken seriously if one is judged to be adult, rational, and able to wield meaningful influence. Those whose ideas are labeled "trivial" or "innocent" or "juvenile" or "shallow" or "silly" or "lightweight" or "pedestrian" will not be taken seriously. Those whose influence is "passing" or "parochial" will not be taken seriously. They will be dismissed. Their ideas will not need to be taken into account "when the chips are down"—that is, when the likely consequences are important, when "it matters." At best, if not taken seriously, these people will be listened to only later—that is, after the crisis has passed, after the crucial decisions have been made, when it no longer matters: after the new constitution is written, after the waters have receded, after the banks have been recapitalized, after the candidate lists have been finalized, after the electoral campaign funds have been raised.

The twenty-five women who in 1985 founded an American organization to raise money for those women candidates who would run on the Democratic ticket and who would support women's reproductive rights decided to name their new group "EMILY's List." *Emily* was not the name of a wealthy woman donor. EMILY, the founders explained, stands for: "Early Money Is Like Yeast." That is, these feminist strategists calculated, candidates who can raise money early in the prolonged, expensive American campaign season are the ones political insiders will take seriously.[5] Thus to be taken seriously in America's money-driven electoral politics, women would have to create a mechanism with which to raise that early money. Otherwise, their candidacies would be dismissed by power brokers as inconsequential.

At worst, people and their ideas that are *not* taken seriously will not be listened to at all, not now, not later. Instead, they will be exposed to ridicule. Their ideas will be called soft or naive or irrelevant or childish. It is not happenstance that conventionally minded people imagine most of these dismissive adjectives to be closely associated with the patriarchal notion of femininity. A gender-smart observer knows that in any masculinity-privileging society a person or an idea that can be feminized is a person or an idea that can be easily trivialized, dismissed. This provides an incentive for some men to try to feminize their male rivals. Feminization is a potent weapon in the masculinized contest between men over who will be taken seriously. If one is not attentive to the cultural politics of femininity, in other words, it is hard to make sense of the politics of diverse masculinities and the gendered rivalries between men.[6]

Who is taken seriously and by whom? These are not minor questions. The answers carry consequences, not only for the person who is dismissed but also for the hierarchies of influence, for the quality of the entire public conversation, and ultimately for the decisions that flow out of that conversation. If what is taken seriously is defined too narrowly—for instance, if feminist questions and feminist findings are dismissed as not serious—then the results can be inadequate explanations, poor decisions, flawed policies, failed efforts, and perpetuated injustices.

Most of us hope that we will be taken seriously. Yet, like beauty, seriousness is in the eye of the beholder. It is a status bestowed by someone else. Therefore, talking about being taken seriously in the passive tense is dangerous: it risks leaving the bestower invisible, unaccountable. You can try your best to be taken seriously, but it will be others who decide whether they will take you and your ideas seriously. This is why being taken seriously is held out as an inducement and reward—and is withheld as punishment. Rewards, inducements, and punishments, of course, shape behavior.

This is one of the reasons that one may feel "brave" when one insists on making women the focus of a doctoral dissertation, even though none of one's faculty advisors take questions of masculinity or femininity seriously in their own research or teaching. Those same well-meaning advisors may try to persuade the student that it would be "better for your career"—that is, one will be taken more seriously by future employers and colleagues—if instead one's research focused on, say, class relations in the copper industry or on the history of Twitter (each of which is, of course, presumably ungendered). Similarly, an ambitious journalist may steer away from proposing to her or his editor an in-depth investigation of factory women's lives or the workings of rival masculinities inside big banks. Better, the ambitious reporter calculates, to ask that editor—by whom one hopes to be seen as a serious journalist—if one can cover a territorial dispute or an oil drilling enterprise (again, each allegedly ungendered). Likewise, many elected women legislators resist being assigned to legislative committees that work on "women's issues." It is hard enough, they determine, to be taken seriously as lawmakers when, as women, they are trying to gain influence in a male-dominated institution, without also being assigned to a committee that specializes in issues that most of the male legislators do not consider serious.

The same inducement, reward, and punishment regime operates in today's international organizations. Sheri Lynn Gibbings tells a revealing story.[7] In 2003, she was working with and studying the New York–based women's advocacy groups that were the engines behind the United Nations Security Council's 2000 adoption of the groundbreaking UN Security Council Resolution 1325. This resolution requires all UN agencies and all UN member states to include women in peace negotiations and in all efforts to rebuild postconflict societies. The myriad impacts of armed violence on women living in war zones from East Timor to Congo and Afghanistan were thenceforth to be taken seriously by international and local actors. Moreover, according to 1325, women were not to be treated merely as victims in need of protection for which they should be silently grateful.[8] Local women in war zones were instead to be treated by national and international authorities as thinkers, strategists, and decision makers.

As the savvy women advocates behind the historic resolution knew, the proof of the international pudding was going to be in the eating—in the instance of 1325, the proof was going to be in the elite-level and ground-level implementation of all the provisions of the resolution. These UN-focused women activists had done so much to provide the evidence for, to draft the content of, and to mobilize Security Council delegations' support for 1325. To bring the international decision making to this point, these feminist-informed activists inside and outside the UN (from Oxfam, Amnesty International, Human Rights Watch, and Women's International League for Peace and Freedom, as well as from within UNIFEM, which is now incorporated into the new major agency UN Women) had created the NGO Working Group on Women, Peace and Security. In the wake of the historic passage of 1325, members of the NGO Working Group made their group's chief activity the monitoring of all agencies of the UN that should be implementing 1325's provisions to see if, in their daily actions, they indeed were taking the requirements of 1325 seriously. One of their monitoring devices was a monthly report on the UN's 1325-related actions, *Mapping Women, Peace and Security in the UN Security Council*.[9] The objective was to provide evidence of agencies taking the provisions seriously or, to the contrary, of their trivializing or ignoring those provisions; in this way they would hold the feet of the Security Council's state delegates and of the UN Secretariat to the bureaucratic fire. It takes a lot of strategic thinking and labor-intensive action to ensure that people inside any complex organization actually do take their commitments seriously.

According to Gibbings, in order to keep up the pressure, to ensure that the easily distracted UN delegates and officials remained attentive to the promises they had made in 1325, activists in the NGO Working Group tried to bring women from war zones to New York to meet with influential UN actors. They wanted to keep showing to the latter the women's realities on the ground. They also wanted to demonstrate that women active in women's groups organizing under duress in the midst of armed conflicts were sharp analysts of what was causing the violence, and that these women had ideas about what needed to be done to end it and to reweave their countries' shredded social fabrics.

In that spirit, in 2003, in the early months of the Iraq War, they invited several touring Iraqi women to come to New York to meet with key UN officials and government representatives. But the meetings did not go well. The Iraqi women were indeed sharp analysts. But they did not try to cover up their anger at what was happening to their fellow Iraqis in the wake of the U.S.-led military invasion. Furthermore, they framed their analysis in terms of "imperialism." Both their tone and their framing seemed to alienate a number of the UN insiders. The women activists who had set up the meetings were dismayed.

As Gibbings relates, members of the NGO Working Group later tried to figure out what went wrong. They were not going to stop bringing women from war zones face to face with UN people making decisions that were affecting those women's lives. But they concluded that, as they themselves had had to learn by years of trial and error, UN insiders would take seriously only those outsiders who would adopt UN-insider cultural practices. And those practices included the suppression of public anger and the usage of certain sorts of speech. Call them "speech norms." Moreover, when it came to talking about *women's* lives, and *women's* wartime proposals, the framing that the UN insiders found most "hear-able" was the sort that positioned women as the sources of hope. Being forthrightly feminist, a woman risked not being heard, not being taken seriously.[10]

The experiences of the NGO Working Group activists underscore a dilemma faced every day by feminists: how far does one go in trimming one's speech and one's concepts in order to be heard? How can one be taken seriously by people for whom talk of feminism, systematic rape, sex trafficking, misogyny, prostitution, sexual harassment, sexist humor, and patriarchy is deemed impolite or hysterical or extreme?

Feminists speaking to nonfeminists, often to antifeminists, about gendered violence or gendered impoverishment face a challenge: how do they speak realistically about the conditions of women, about the relationships between women and men, and about the relationships between states and women in a way that is taken seriously by their listeners *without* so diluting their message—in the name of adopting the insiders' bland speech norms—that the gendered realities of which they speak fade out of sight?

The unquestioned presumptions about what and who deserves to be rewarded with the accolade of "serious" is one of the pillars of modern patriarchy. That is, being taken seriously is a status that every day, in routine relationships, offers the chance for masculinity to be privileged and for anything associated with femininity to be ranked as lesser, as inconsequential, as dependent, or as beyond the pale.

Patriarchy cannot survive amid the current destabilizing changes— the end of colonial rule, the surge of foreign investment, the emergence of new industries, the spread of the Internet, the expansion of education, the influx of tourists, the toppling of oppressive regimes—unless ways are found by patriarchy's beneficiaries and supporters to nourish reward systems that (1) sustain the privileging of certain forms of masculinity, (2) treat most women as if they naturally lack autonomy, and (3) weigh all things deemed to be feminine as of lesser value than those deemed masculine when the discussion turns to topics that matter.

Any of us take something seriously when we begin to see that it *matters*. Something matters when we start to uncover its *consequences*. Thus, women are not taken seriously in large part because so many people (officials, sociologists, historians, economists, news commentators, bloggers) believe that whatever happens to women really does not have major consequences. This is a deeply held belief that has proved very hard to budge. It is a belief rooted in the patriarchal (that is, masculinity-privileging) presumption that women are fundamentally *dependent* beings.

As the following chapters reveal, in the narratives of economies and especially of finance, women typically are dismissed as not-serious actors or thinkers when their labor is (mistakenly) deemed inconsequential because it is so often part-time, low paid, or unpaid. Furthermore, as these same case studies show, women's political economies can be trivialized in public debates when the money they earn is (erroneously) trivialized as "pin money," as not the principal economic lifeblood of households, or when they are talked about solely as consumers (of groceries and clothes, not of construction equipment, bonds or real estate).

And as other chapters to follow demonstrate, in narratives of wartime and revolution, women are presumed to be confined to "the home front." They are (merely) "the protected." They are the (silent) "grieving." They are the (voiceless, idea-less) "victims." They are the symbols of "the nation," not its makers.

As these case studies reveal, women are mobilized, of course, for the revolution or for war-waging, but only by others (influential men and occasionally by a handful of women who have been deputized by men). Yet, when they are mobilized, it is only "for the duration," destined to be demobilized (by those same men)—sent back to their "natural" domesticated, unpaid, low-paid, dependent roles—as quickly as possible once the crisis has passed. In fact, women's return to domesticated dependency is often taken as proof—as in the United States of the late 1940s, and currently in Egypt—that a reassuring normalcy is being restored after the violence, after the turmoil.

If women are imagined to be basically dependents, these case studies show, then the people you should take seriously, by contrast, are the *independent* actors. They are the ones who strategize, who protect, who "don't have time to grieve," who take actions that shape history, who take risks that generate profits, who craft the lasting postcrisis lessons. It is the independent actors who confront the riot police, play hard, stay late at the office, eschew the domestic sphere. They are the "manly" ones. These manly independent actors, therefore, are the ones who can see "the big picture." The ideas, emotions, calculations, and actions that matter are those of the independent, autonomous actors—the bankers, the generals, the rebel commanders, the political party strategists, the diplomats, the editors. For good or for ill, it is their ideas, emotions, calculations, and actions, so the conventional thinking goes, that will have significant consequences, consequences that, supposedly, we all need to care about.

In patriarchal societies (including those that claim to be modern or even postmodern), to be feminized is to be made dependent; to be independent is to be masculinized. Thus it is no wonder that so many people—men and women—who believed that patriarchy was the natural and the best way to order societies fought so hard against women's suffrage. The battles waged intensely against women's right to vote—in Britain, in India, in Mexico, in China, in the United States, in Switzerland, in Kuwait—are as important to study as those campaigns that ultimately won women their suffrage rights, because those antisuffrage activists spelled out in often desperate clarity what they thought would be *lost* if women could cast their own ballots in public elections: the feminization of dependency.[11]

Figure 2. Indian suffragettes in the Women's Coronation Procession, London, June 17, 1911. © Museum of London.

The studies here of the 2008 financial crisis and subsequent recession, as well as the exploration of the still-evolving Egyptian revolution, demonstrate that it is no wonder those who value patriarchal social relations are made nervous when women in wartime and in other times of societal upheaval—after earthquakes, during financial crashes, in the midst of political revolutions—are revealed to have minds of their own. It makes those who cherish patriarchy anxious when women reveal their capacities for organization, strategizing, enterprise, and analysis. The eras commonly called "post"—postwar, postrecession, postdisaster, postrevolution—are usually eras marked by concerted efforts to put the independent woman back in her dependency bottle. That bottle is sometimes referred to as "the kitchen."

What does this mean for those of us working today to craft methods of gender analysis—especially feminist-informed methods of gender analysis, gender analysis infused with a curiosity about power? It means that we need to think carefully about how the rewards of being labeled as serious operate in all spheres of society. We need to be candid about how alluring those rewards can be for each of us. Patriarchy is stubbornly perpetuated because it is not simply oppressive; it is rewarding, it is alluring. It is reassuring to be protected. It is satisfying to be called respectable. It is pleasing to be labeled a good wife or a good mother. It can be a source of pride when the men in the room occasionally describe one's comments as rational.

To craft strategies and practices of feminist-informed gender research—and to get our findings taken seriously by diverse audiences— we need to directly challenge and dismantle the dismissive categories of "trivial," innocent," "naive," "sentimental," "soft," and "parochial."

The case studies that follow here are only contributions to a much broader, current transnational campaign by feminist analysts—of wars, of economic failures, of natural disasters. These studies provide examples of what feminist analytical seriousness looks like: they show what the workings of masculinities and femininities do to the economic, political, and cultural processes shaping our lives—and why they matter.

When we are investigating women's multidimensional and diverse relationships to conflict and economic turmoil, however, we must challenge those dismissive patriarchal categories in ways that do not turn women's liberation or women's rights merely into instruments in the hands of the powerful. Anything that is used instrumentally can be put back on the shelf once its users no longer find that instrument useful for their own ends.

An example: domestic violence against women often escalates in war zones and after wars in those households with returning male veterans (veterans of the government militaries or veterans of insurgent militias). If we argue that our research on war-related domestic violence should be taken seriously (by officials, by humanitarian-aid-group donors, and by social commentators) because the military's effectiveness is jeopardized if that violence by soldiers and ex-soldiers is ignored, then we imply that women's experiences of domestic violence by their male partners matters only insofar as it weakens that military—that it does not matter for its own sake, that women's physical integrity has little or no importance of its own. Using this instrumental argument, one may indeed catch the ear of officialdom, might persuade officials, donors, or militia leaders to pay more serious attention, but it will be at a steep price. It will mean that military priorities remain in the driver's seat. When any military strategist deems domestic violence a nonissue or "absorbable," findings about women's experiences of domestic violence will fall off the table.[12]

Likewise, today gender analysts have become increasingly interested in the poverty and accompanying homelessness experienced by many countries' women military and militia veterans after they leave their military organization. Frequently that poverty is accompanied by (or partly caused by) significant mental and physical disabilities that can be traced back to their specific wartime service.[13] In trying to get editors and officials to take seriously the impoverishment of women veterans, one might be tempted to argue that confronting those findings and taking steps to address them matters because neglecting or denying them tarnishes a patriotic or nationalist legacy. While, of course, this may be true, if that is the chief argument employed to gain serious attention, then, once again, the impoverishment and health problems of women veterans will, by implication, be seen to be important only insofar as they tarnish patriotism or the nation. They will not matter because women's well-being matters for its own sake.[14]

The trap—the dangerous temptation—here is to adopt other people's patriarchal criteria for what is worthy of serious attention as our own criteria. That is, it is tempting to believe that women matter only because they are somebody's wife, somebody's daughter, somebody's free or cheapened labor, somebody's unpaid caretaker, somebody's reproducer, somebody's emotional attachment, somebody's source of honor or shame, somebody's patriotic symbol.

At the very core of feminism is the conviction that women matter *for their own sakes*. As we will see, revolutionary feminist women have asserted that no woman's freedom of expression, or freedom from harassment, depends for its worth on its value to any man. This is a radical assertion. By *radical,* I mean it is an assertion that goes to the root of popular and official understandings.

It will be tempting to argue that we should have our gender analyses taken seriously because we are providing a useful instrument for those currently in power. We need to ask four questions as we weigh this temptation:

· What price are we paying when we use that instrumental argument?
· Is the price too high?
· Are there alternatives?
· Are there strategies by which we can get those alternatives taken seriously by the people we need to persuade?

One alternative to an instrumentalist argument is an explanatory argument: to argue that if we (and our hoped-for audiences) dismiss—shrug off—thoughtful, rigorous, carefully pointed feminist-informed gender analysis, we will fail to understand. That is, if anyone treats gender analytical findings as irrelevant or "soft," they will base their subsequent decisions on flawed explanations. This is my own argument in offering here feminist gender analyses of the 2008 banking crash, of the subsequent recession, of peacekeeping operations and peace movements, and of Egyptian women's experiences of the Arab Spring.

In other words, the case studies that follow here (all of which rely on other feminists' careful, often daring research) throw into sharp relief the amount of thinking—both individually and collectively—that diverse women do during crises and crashes, the thinking and acting that shape the contours and trajectories of current and future society. The result: those who ignore careful feminist-informed gender research will, first of all, naively imagine that women are merely dependent bystanders, victims without agency, inherently peaceful, domestically confined. They will erroneously imagine that women are passive, that they can be easily manipulated.

Second, those who ignore gender analytical findings that take women seriously will significantly underestimate the power wielded by governments, by state officials, by insurgents, by militias, by banking executives, by foreign forces both during and after crises, wieldings of power intended to influence women's behavior—women's relationships to men, their relationships to the economy, their relationships to the war's adversaries, their relationships to their own state. The result: they will imagine that wars are easier to wage, revolutions are easier to shrink or to roll back, and economies easier to repair than in fact they are. Likewise, those who dismiss feminist-informed gender analyses will naively imagine that it is easier to reestablish a patriarchal "normalcy" in the "post" era than in fact it is.

Third, if the findings of feminist-informed gender analyses of crashes and crises are treated as trivial, then the workings of, and impacts of, diverse masculinities will remain invisible. Taking women seriously always has the effect of enabling us to see men as men. That is, when only men are treated as if they matter, those men appear to be generals, authorities, activists, police, farmers, soldiers, managers, investors, economists, writers, and insurgents. That serves to hide their masculinities. It makes us incurious about how male revolutionaries, male budget directors, male soldiers, male bankers imagine their own manliness, worry about expressing their manliness, and make choices based on their efforts to prove their manliness to their male rivals and male superiors.

By contrast, as I hope the following case studies show, when we take women seriously we have to wonder about the pressures on them to be feminine—or sometimes to pass as manly. This curiosity motivates us to pay attention to how women craft their relationships to diverse men in their lives: their bosses, their clients, their allies, their husbands. That attentiveness, in turn, pushes us to pay closer attention to men as men. The result of not using gender analysis to carefully explore the workings of masculinities in economic crises, in revolutions, in wartime, and in the years following turmoil is this: one will mistakenly presume that all men are attracted to soldiering or banking, and that leaders do not have to use power to persuade many men to fight, or they do not have to press male bankers to adopt new risk-taking, masculinized identities. In turn, one will naively ignore the reality that many men's traumatic wartime experiences, or their exhilarations in a banking boom or in a revolution, are converted into postwar, postboom, postrevolution worries about their status as manly. One will underestimate the number of the decisions made leading up to, during, and after crises that are made by men in order to prove their manliness in the eyes of other men. One will underestimate women's resistance to being turned into postwar, postcrash, postrevolution fodder in the contest between masculinities.

The conventional politics of seriousness is a series of personal and public dynamics that, if unchallenged, serve to reinforce patriarchal structures. The politics of seriousness can allow patriarchy to be sustained even when dramatic social changes, such as those marking today's world, are occurring. The case studies that follow are feminist investigations of particular crises—economic, militarized and political—but, simultaneously, they are feminist investigations of workings of seriousness. These investigations flow from a conviction that we need to monitor gendered seriousness on large stages and small, in the public arenas and in private spheres.

The gendered politics of seriousness is serious.

CHAPTER TWO

Launching and Naming

Sexual Harassment and One Women's-Studies Story

I had never heard the word *feminist,* certainly not *patriarchy,* or even *suf-fragettes.* This was the late 1960s, and my ignorance was not only stunning but also, given my upbringing, downright odd.[1]

My California-born mother had been a teenager when women won the vote, among the first generation of American women who came of age having the right to vote, won only in 1920. Once she could vote, she never missed an election. She was also among the small proportion of American women of her generation who had the chance to attend college. She chose an all-women's college, Mills College, across the bay from San Francisco. In the 1920s Mills had a dynamic woman president, Amelia Reinhardt, whom, years later, my mother still talked about admiringly. Mills College faculty in the 1920s presumed that their women graduates would be able to earn their own livings. Among the courses my mother took was criminology—not exactly the sort of training designed for mere brides-to-be.

More than three decades later, after going to coed public schools in post–World War II suburban New York, I too chose to attend an all-women's college, Connecticut College, founded by a group of progressive women and men to educate young women after nearby Wesleyan University decided in the early 1900s to drop women from its student

Figure 3. My mother, Harriett Goodridge, as a Mills College graduate in her cap and gown, California, 1928. Courtesy of the author.

body.[2] I was at "Conn" in the years before women's studies was imagined and launched. Many of our women professors had overcome formidable barriers to gain their doctorates and achieve prominence in their male-dominated fields. But we students never asked them about their experiences. They taught us the theories of Locke and Hobbes, the works of Chaucer and George Bernard Shaw, and the politics of Franklin Roosevelt, Joseph Stalin, and Konrad Adenauer. No mention was ever made of Mary Wollstonecraft, Aphra Behn, Virginia Woolf, Alexandra Kollontai, or Alice Paul. Occasionally, though, these women professors did drop hints that they were discontented with the canons with which they packed their own course syllabi. For, when I was a senior, it was they who chose to bring Eleanor Roosevelt to campus. It was they too who insisted that we all go to hear Hannah Arendt when she spoke on campus. Afterward, we, however, still failed to ask our professors more questions. They dropped hints, but we did not pick them up.

For graduate school, I returned to my mother's home state to attend the University of California, Berkeley, where I pursued a doctorate in political science, focusing on Southeast Asia. Joining others at Berkeley, I went on strike in 1966, carried picket signs, heard Joan Baez sing on the steps of the administration building, and switched my adolescent-chosen political affiliation from the Republicans to the more (I hoped) progressive Democrats. Still, I never thought to ask any of my Berkeley professors about how women had won the vote or, even more revealing, why it had been denied for so long. I studied the Chinese revolution but never heard anything about Chinese women revolutionaries. I barely noticed that all fifty of my political science professors at Berkeley, the allegedly "radical" university, were men.

It is embarrassing to think back now on how incurious I was during all these years. Yet keeping in mind my own prolonged ignorance of women's subjugation—and of women's activism to roll back that subjugation—has provided me with a valuable starting point from which to teach women's studies. It has stoked my curiosity: how has knowledge of women's lives been kept so well hidden, even from the girls and women one might expect to have had the best chance of gaining that knowledge? Students who come into an Introduction to Women's Studies class never having heard of Virginia Woolf or knowing nothing of women's roles in the Chinese, Russian, Vietnamese, or Algerian revolutions are not empty-headed. Remembering my own ignorance, I realize that they are products of a sprawling, loose-jointed patriarchal effort to make women's lives appear—even to women themselves—unserious, trivial, irrelevant, and boring.

By the early 1970s, I was teaching in Ohio. As a Southeast Asian politics specialist, I had opposed the U.S. war in Vietnam, though some of my colleagues at the time were seduced into lending their regional expertise to the U.S. government's war operations. To be candid, I do not think I actually was terribly smart about the workings of government co-optation, so today I wonder how I managed to avoid the considerable temptations dangled before Southeast Asia specialists by the

U.S. government during the 1960s and 1970s. After all, to be invited to offer one's expertise to a government is often held out as a token of being taken seriously.

Having recently returned from doing research in Malaysia, I was then living in southern Ohio, on the borders of Kentucky and Indiana. Miami University (the Miami, I learned, originally were a local Indian tribe whose members were driven out of Ohio in the nineteenth century by white settlers) was a large state university; its political science department never before had had a woman faculty member. My fifteen male colleagues were welcoming, however, and taught me the academic ropes. Though I was a "first" at Miami, my feminist consciousness was still unformed: I did not assign my students to read a single woman social science author (I am not even sure I knew of any, aside from Arendt); and my courses were silent on women's politics. It was while at Miami that I wrote my first book, *Ethnic Conflict and Political Development.*[3] I learned so much doing that research, about the dynamics of ethnic politics in colonial rule, in revolutions, in political party rivalries, in state policy making, and in economic development. But it was men who populated the pages of my book. I concentrated on their complex ethnic identities and strategies, not knowing to pay any attention to their problematic masculinities. Women remained mere ghosts on the page.

During 1971–1972, I taught as a Fulbright scholar in the Caribbean country of Guyana. I was drawn to Guyana because it shared with Malaysia a legacy of British colonial rule, an economy dependent on the export of raw materials (bauxite and sugar), and, of special interest to me, a divisive, racialized ethnic politics. My seminar at University of Guyana was held at night on the edge of a sugar plantation. Large beetles flew through the open windows to join our class. The students were civil servants, both Afro-Guyanese and Indo-Guyanese. They were all men. In fact, all my friends that year in Georgetown were men; several of them were involved in risky opposition politics. Focusing so hard on ethnic politics continued to blind me to the crucial gender dynamics both within and between these two communities. Only later would I wonder where women were in sugar, bauxite, and banana politics; where they were too in electoral politics and in the cultural politics of West Indian literature.

Today, as I continue to try to make sense of the ongoing, complex politics of wartime and postwartime Iraq, I keep recalling how easy it was for me then—and, it still is for most commentators today—to award ethnic and sectarian politics intellectual seriousness, to give them analytical primacy over gendered politics. Who can bother with women's relationships to men in political parties and militias, when the ethnic and sectarian tensions are so acute? So goes the conventional reasoning. Looking back now at how narrow my own questioning was then in both Malaysia and Guyana, the lesson I have drawn is this: always pay very close attention to ethnic, racial, and communal politics, but never imagine that one can fully understand those politics unless one simultaneously and vigorously investigates the politics of femininities and masculinities inside and between classes, and inside and between ethnic groups.[4]

The first feminist publication I ever subscribed to was *Ms. Magazine.* This was in the spring of 1971. I had never heard of Gloria Steinem, I did not know anything about abortion rights, and had never heard the phrase *domestic violence.* But as I read that first issue of *Ms.*—a special insert published inside *New York Magazine*—I was excited. Here was a whole world of political thinking and political action that was new to me.[5]

It was the students at my new university who woke me up to women's studies. In the fall of 1972, I began teaching at Clark University in Worcester, Massachusetts, a mill town that continued to attract scores of immigrants from every continent. Once again, I had the dubious distinction of being a "first" in a political science department. Luckily, though, this time I shared that distinction with another woman, hired into the department faulty at the same time. Sharon Krefetz was an American politics specialist, while I focused on comparative politics. Sharon and I did not look at all alike, yet in those early years male

Figure 4. Meeting of early *Ms. Magazine* editors, New York, 1972. © Nancy Crampton.

faculty colleagues routinely called each of us by the other's name. Women had not been admitted to Clark as undergraduates until World War II (to make up for the absent young men, who had been drafted to fight), but it did enjoy several attributes that made it hospitable to unconventional ideas. For a start, unlike most New England colleges, Clark was thoroughly secular; it had no Christian chapel on campus. The masculinization of campus culture was diluted by the fact that Clark did not have a football team and fraternities were peripheral. Moreover, Clark's two most influential departments, geography and psychology, had European intellectual roots. Together, these attributes made Clark especially attractive to postwar American Jewish students and their parents. When I arrived in the fall of 1972, Jews were a mere 2 percent of the total U.S. population but they constituted 68 percent of Clark's undergraduates. While teaching at Clark, there was little chance that one could slip into a lazy presumption of American cultural homogeneity.

It was students who initiated the launch of women's studies at Clark. In 1974, a group of undergraduate women went to the dean, the university's first woman dean, and said that they had heard from friends at other colleges that there was this new academic field called women's studies. They were not quite sure what it was, but it sounded exciting.

The dean, Marcia Savage, called together all the women faculty on campus (less than a dozen of us) to have a lunchtime conversation with students about this surprising new field, women's studies. That modest noontime meeting marked a turning point. The students' eagerness was infectious. None of us faculty members had been trained to teach about or to conduct research on women, but with the dean's support and students' excitement, we plunged in. Sharon Krefetz developed a new course, Women in American Politics (at the time, women were a mere handful of U.S. congressional representatives and senators and were barely visible as governors or mayors). Serena Hilsinger, a professor of English, daringly offered to create a pioneering course that explored fiction by English and American women writers from the seventeenth through the twentieth centuries. Aphra Behn would finally get contemporary readers. Both new courses became instant hits with students.

I promised to work up a new cross-national course, Comparative Politics of Women (whatever *that* was!), to start a year later. Developing that course changed my entire understanding of what was political and of what I needed to take seriously. In the mid-1970s there were scarcely any books by political scientists on the comparative politics of women, so I drew heavily on wonderful new books being published then by young feminist historians—on women as textile and garment workers in the early decades of the industrial revolution, and on the nineteenth-century origins of British, Chinese, and Russian women's political organizing and theorizing. This early reliance on feminist historians has had a lasting impact: I have learned never to imagine that focusing on present-day events is sufficient; causality has deep roots. Still today, I avidly read publishers' catalogues devoted to books on history. Moreover, it has been my teaching about diverse women's politics that has continued to shape my own research on women's politics. I do love teaching. I am still learning from students.

By the 1970s, I was spending several weeks a year doing research in London. At first, I continued to concentrate on ethnic politics. At that point, my research interest lay particularly in those ethnic and racial politics that shaped both colonial and postcolonial state elites' strategies for creating and manipulating militaries. I tracked Muslims in the Soviet military, Scots in the British military, Sikhs in the Indian military, indigenous soldiers in the Australian and New Zealand militaries, Francophones in the Canadian military, Alawites in the Syrian military, Kurds in the Iraqi and Iranian militaries, whites in the Rhodesian and South African militaries, Kikuyus in the Kenyan military, and of course Native Americans, Chinese, Japanese, Filipinos, Latinos, and African Americans in the U.S. military. I tracked states' recruitment strategies and their deployment formulas; I delved into regimental mutinies, coup d'état attempts and elites' nervousness about each of these. It was all absorbing.

Out of this work came what would be (though I did not know it then) my last nonfeminist book, *Ethnic Soldiers*. It was published first in Britain.[6] Despite my glaring lack of gender analysis, publishing this book initially outside the United States had the positive effect of making me think of non-American readers as the book's first readers. I began consciously trying to avoid making all-too-easy America-centric assumptions. Being a cross-national analyst was not enough: I had to try to be a transnational thinker and writer as well. That involved not denying my U.S. location but admitting it and then trying to stretch beyond it.

Ethnic Soldiers—or, rather, working with the British trade market editors of Penguin—did something else for me: it made me imagine that my books might be available to readers outside of academia. I had become a fan of Penguin paperbacks during my time in Malaysia. So I could picture those tantalizing green- and orange-covered Penguin paperbacks lining shelves in British and Commonwealth bookstores, places where all sorts of readers browsed. That vision was thrilling, but it also made me worry. If *Ethnic Soldiers* was coming out in a Penguin paperback, I would have to learn how to write accessibly; I could not hide behind arcane "insider" academic language, the sort of obscure language that passed as serious within academia. In fact, I would have to apply to my writing the lessons I was learning about how to teach effectively. My sense of myself as a teacher and as a writer could not be split in two.

Women friends in London soon started drawing me into the exciting new circles of feminist research and activism. I was introduced to a feminism that sprang out of socialist labor politics (while also critical of masculinized labor union politics and of sexist interpretations of Marxist thinking). I listened to British feminists in standing-room-only halls dissect heterosexism and patriarchy (in 1980 I never had heard either term). I added to my subscriptions two British publications, the feminist research journal *Feminist Review* and the feminist news magazine *Spare Rib*. I met Jane Hawksley, a young British feminist editor then at a labor union–supported small publisher, Pluto Press, who urged me to take a fresh look at all the militaries I had been investigating and to start looking for women in those militaries.

From these London encounters came my first feminist book, *Does Khaki Become You?* which compared the diverse roles of women in the ranks of, and serving as, civilian supporters of the American and British militaries.[7] For the first time, I delved into the history and current politics of prostitution, gendered arms manufacturing, nursing, and marriage, topics no political science professor in 1960s Berkeley ever had suggested I consider. Once again, I was writing for a British publisher and one whose editors conceived of their potential readers as including more than academics. I had begun to realize, too, that to be feminist a book had to be useful to both researchers (students and faculty) and activists. More than that, while writing *Khaki* I began to see that to be feminist a writer had to be not only accessible to but also accountable to readers—and that one could not be held accountable to one's readers unless those readers could figure out exactly what one was saying. This seemed a daring idea.

During 1981–1982, as I wrote *Khaki,* I also suddenly realized that in my earlier books (six of them, none of them gender-curious) there were scarcely any voices of "ordinary" people—of women and men who did not wield either intellectual or official authority. The burgeoning feminist histories (and, increasingly, ethnographies) I was then devouring were chock full of women's voices—voices of textile workers, plantation workers, nurses, and labor organizers, of women as writers, wives, and reformers. So I deliberately began to look for first-person accounts, newspaper interviews, diaries, and memoirs. I reread my mother's own diaries. And I conducted more interviews myself. Women, I thought, should have the chance to speak for themselves in my books, whether or not I found what they had to say uncomfortable or disquieting.

Publishing *Does Khaki Become You?* expanded my feminist engagements exponentially. It turned out that in the 1980s, scores of women in countries as different as Finland, Israel, Canada, Sweden, Japan, Korea, India, Chile, Australia, and Turkey were becoming alarmed not only by rising militarism but also by women's complicity in militarization and by male peace activists' refusal to take seriously feminists' analyses of militarism. As *Khaki* took on a transnational life of its own, I had the opportunity to trade hunches with feminists in more and more countries. And that, of course, made me ask more and more new questions. Those questions prompted me to wonder about how all sorts of dynamics in international politics might be better understood if women's lives were made visible and taken seriously as a source of international analysis.

This was when I began asking, "Where are the women?"—in the history of colonialism and anticolonialism; in the international textile industry; in the political economies of rubber, sugar, tea, and bananas; on and around military overseas bases; in the growing tourism industry; and in globalized domestic work. All of that asking and the resultant digging led to my writing *Bananas, Beaches, and Bases.* It too first appeared in Britain, published by Pandora, a daring small feminist press, though soon after in the United States as well, by University of California Press, whose editor, Naomi Schneider, promised to keep Carmen Miranda on the book cover.[8]

Bananas was published at exactly the moment when more women were entering the academic field of international relations, one of the most thoroughly masculinized fields of social science. Some of those women academics—for instance, Ann Tickner, Spike Peterson, and Jindy Pettman—were courageously starting to ask explicitly feminist questions that would challenge the masculinist assumptions that, until then, undergirded the study of international politics. In universities the study of international politics was commonly called international relations, or simply IR. The fact that this gutsy band of feminist IR academics embraced *Bananas* would give that book a wider readership than I could ever have imagined.

Though I found researching and writing energizing, I was still, happily, first and foremost a teacher. Back at Clark, in the fall of 1975 women's studies was off and running. But we became a women's studies faculty group—and more important, a women's studies faculty community—only three years later, when Ximena Bunster arrived on campus from Chile as a visiting professor of sociology and anthropology. Ximena had been one of the last doctoral students trained by famed American anthropologist Margaret Mead. She had studied the roles of Chile's Mapuche women leaders in that indigenous community's politics. Returning home to Santiago with her doctorate, she had introduced feminist ethnographic research methodologies and soon rose to become Chile's youngest-ever full professor.

A military junta's brutal authoritarian rule can transform even an accomplished academic into an exiled, short-contract, nontenured, visa-dependent, visiting professor. Driven into exile by the dictator Augusto Pinochet, that is what Ximena Bunster had become in the late 1970s. Despite the insecurity of her position in the United States and at Clark, Ximena took on the job of transforming the women's studies faculty group into a genuine community.

Figure 5. Ximena Bunster (right) as a graduate student, with a Mapuche woman, Chile, 1963. Courtesy Ximena Bunster.

Even though they have proved hard to sustain in practice, Ximena's feminist academic community-building strategies are ones I still admire. First, she opened up our fledgling faculty group to all those interested in developing a women's studies course, even if they were not quite sure when or how they might do it. Second, there were no cookie-cutter definitions of who would be deemed a "real feminist." Our personalities and styles were varied, but there were never ideological factions among the wonderfully diverse faculty group who came together.

Third, from the outset Ximena insisted that there be no status distinctions among us. Visiting faculty, tenure-track untenured faculty, tenured faculty, full professors (a few of us had by then climbed up the ladder), all shared laughs, interests, strategies, and gossip. We titled our first modest, occasional, women's studies newsletter, edited by Lois Brynes, *Gossip,* after the word's original old English meaning, "god sister": a woman who sponsored a child at his or her baptism—that is, a nurturing supporter.

Fourth, Ximena, with her feminist, anthropologically wide-ranging curiosity, invited women on the staffs of the library, the school of continuing education, the admissions office, and the health and counseling services to join in the women's studies faculty discussions and meals. As a result, we all became a lot more realistic about students' lives and about all the skills and all the women's labor it takes to run a modern university. I think one of the reasons so many members of Clark's women's studies faculty have gone on to become effective department chairs, program directors, and deans is those inclusive lessons we taught each other in the early years of our women's studies faculty group.

Fifth, Ximena built bridges to the campus's new student-run Women's Center. We held occasional joint discussions on issues such as pornography—meeting in the women's students' own space (a basement room in a men's dormitory!). In the 1970s, many colleges around Boston had student-run, administration-allowed "porn nights"; they were ended only when women students, campus by campus, organized protests against them. It was a small band of undergraduate women's-studies students who successfully petitioned to end Clark's "Porn Night." Not long after, a duo composed of an undergraduate woman, Beth Herr, and a untenured sociology professor, Betsy Stanko, launched the Worcester's first shelter for battered women, Daybreak. Later, another feminist duo, Gabrie'l Atchison, a women's studies doctoral student, and Jody Emel, a professor of geography, started All Kinds of

Girls, a program linking undergraduate women students to local girls aged seven to eleven, designed to build girls' self-esteem in the face of the intense pressures on them to internalize the false values of thinness, heterosexism, competition, and consumerism. It was this early alliance between the women's studies faculty and those students active in the campus Women's Center that kept the academic program connected to the wider city. But these connections have had to be continuously reenlivened. I am indebted to several generations of undergraduate women students for keeping me locally connected.

Sixth, Ximena looked around the ethnically diverse, industrial city of Worcester, saw other colleges, and reached out to their faculty women, who also were taking early steps to create women's studies programs. We on the Clark women's studies faculty got to know women faculty at nearby schools (on whose campuses most of us had never set foot), among them two Catholic colleges, Holy Cross and Assumption, as well as Worcester State College, Worcester Polytechnic Institute, and, later, the University of Massachusetts Medical School.

In the late 1970s, Clark's women's studies program had no budget, not even a budget line. Not until the 1980s would we acquire a part-time secretary and a closet-size office. We were intellectually engaged with each other and with our students, but the senior administration did not take women's studies seriously. We failed to meet the three criteria of alleged academic seriousness: we were not seen by other faculty as a "real" discipline; we were just a mere program, not an established department with its own budget, tenure track lines, and clout in university affairs; and, finally, we did not attract major external donors.

Any feminist analyst knows that not only culture but also *structure* matters. All of us on the Clark women's studies faculty (including the program director) were under full-time contractual obligations to the "mainstream" departments; it was our colleagues in those "home" departments, not those in women's studies, who voted on whether any of us would get reappointed or promoted. It took work by a number of us on influential campus committees finally to get interdisciplinary contributions taken seriously as a promotion criterion when a faculty member came up for tenure.

Furthermore, it was the chairs of our "home" departments who decided whether any of our individual proposals for a new cross-listed course—on women and psychology, on women in French (or Spanish or Chinese) literature, or on the history of African American women—would "fit" that department's own needs. Thus bargaining with and, even better, forging alliances with department chairs became crucial to the development of the women's studies program. Along the way, we won many department chairs over to seeing both the intellectual and budgetary value of women's studies: cross-listing any course with women's studies made a department look more intellectually adventurous and almost guaranteed that that course would have high enrollment.

Despite our structural limitations, our meetings were lively and often irreverent. Word soon got around campus that the women's studies faculty group was where the intellectual action was. New Clark faculty—including, by the early 1980s, more and more young women—began to seek us out. By then, we each were doing more teaching, more research, more advising, and more administering. So to keep stressed-out faculty engaged, a women's studies faculty group needed to provide real camaraderie and genuine intellectual excitement. That's still true.

The annual event that cemented our women's studies friendships, not only among us as Clark colleagues, but also as women's studies faculty on Worcester's several campuses, was a sumptuous annual autumn dinner at the colonial-era farmhouse home of Serena Hilsinger and her partner, science educator Lois Brynes. Sitting there on the floor and on easy chairs, we ate, drank, and talked together those fall evenings, and we offered encouragement as we expressed genuine interest in each other's research. One can feel pretty lonely as the only feminist in a patriarchal or dysfunctional department—one hooked on hierarchy, plagued by bizarre faculty behavior, or hobbled by disciplinary parochialism. But over delicious food and among convivial, bright feminist colleagues, one could be reminded that one's genuine intellectual community is far larger—and far more supportive—than just the department or even the institution where one toils every day.

Now, before any reader thinks that Clark's women's studies in the late 1970s and early 1980s was idyllic, let me tell you what happened to Ximena Bunster—and how our women's studies faculty as a group stood ineffectually on the sidelines. It was in trying to support Ximena, though, that I became a fully practicing feminist and learned to take feminist gendered analysis seriously, to see how and why it mattered.

First, a brief detour. In the late 1970s, I knew more about British women's activism than I did about women's activism in Cambridge, an hour away on the Massachusetts Turnpike. Then a friend took me to New Words, the Cambridge feminist bookstore. Launched by four women in 1974, New Words had become a regional hub of intellectual and activist feminism. I was nervous going through the door. What would it be like? What should I be like when I was there? Well, it was friendly, welcoming—and exciting. All those books and journals by and about women. Feminist magazines from Mexico, Canada, and India. Postcards, posters, and buttons. I felt as though I had been living on another planet. Here was real life. New Words became part of my expanding feminist world. I went to poetry readings and talks by novelists and historians there. I found books there to assign in my Clark courses. I began to seek out women's bookstores everywhere I went—in Toronto, Amsterdam, London, Dublin. And, when Ximena needed support, I would find it at New Words, my local women's bookstore.

Ximena Bunster and I had offices across the hall from each other at Clark, and we had become friends through women's studies and our shared interest in Latin American politics. I think it was in the fall of 1979 when Ximena came into my office, shut the door, and asked, "Cynthia, is it usual for a department chair to invite you to his family's house and then to expose himself to you?" Ximena went on to describe her sociology chair's bizarre and intimidating sexualized behavior, including his suggestion that her contract renewal (and thus her U.S. visa, and thus her safety) would be at risk if she did not accept his advances. Having, by then, served on a number of university committees, I naively suggested that she file a formal charge with the administration and the faculty tenure and promotion committee, whose mandate included responsibility for "faculty morale." But I had underestimated the passivity of the then-all-male senior administration, as well as the stark inadequacy of the university's conceptual and structural capacity. They tied the hands of even those conscientious fellow faculty members who tried to be of assistance behind the scenes.

Faculty members active in Clark's women's studies group were confused. What exactly was at stake? Was flirting in the office or dating colleagues to be banned? For all the talk that was generated by Ximena's filing her charge—much of that talk anxious, some of it impassioned—the women's studies group, still in its early years, could not come to a collective agreement about what the issue was or what should be done.

At this point in the story, I suspect readers will be shouting at this page: "Sexual harassment! Didn't you see it was sexual harassment?" But there was scarcely any recognition of that brand-new feminist concept on any college campus or in any workplace in 1979. Without a concept, we all know, it is hard to reach a consensus and is difficult to act, even for a group of thoughtful, generous colleagues. That, for me, has been one of the lasting lessons of what many of us around Boston still refer to as "the case": it takes activist feminist analysis to produce feminist concepts; without activist thinking—and without the results of that thinking, without activist-derived conceptualizations—we all would be stymied.[9]

Tensions spiraled on campus. Four more Clark women bravely joined Ximena in her charge against the department chair (the foursome included a Puerto Rican graduate student in geography, the sociology department secretary, an untenured sociology professor, and an undergraduate woman student). Ximena wittily labeled her chair "the equal opportunity harasser." In reaction, the accused sociology chair called on his networks (men and women, many of them well-known figures) in local and national peace organizations to support and validate him. He claimed that it was impossible for a man such as himself, a man so involved in a peace movement, to be guilty of an abuse of power, and that, therefore, Ximena must be merely a pawn of the conservative university administration, in collusion, he claimed, with the CIA. This man had delusions of grandeur. As patently absurd as his claims were, given that Ximena had been driven out of Chile after risking her life to oppose the CIA-backed Pinochet, his preposterous accusations meant that those of us who were trying to support Ximena could no longer imagine that we were dealing with simply a campus issue.

I turned to Gilda Bruckman at New Words. She introduced me to a small group of five Boston feminists who called themselves the Alliance Against Sexual Coercion. Ximena and I drove into Boston to meet one of the AASC activists. After listening attentively to Ximena's description of her department chair's advances, his intimidating suggestions, and the administration's ineffectual response, she said to us, "There is a new term for this combination of actions by a superior toward an employee and an employer's negligence. It's called 'sexual harassment.' It's less about sex and more about power." She then went further, tutoring us in the innovative feminist analysis that members of AASC and the labor lawyers and feminist advocates they were working with had, step by thoughtful step, hammered out. Sexual harassment, she explained, needed to be taken seriously, understood as a violation of an employee's labor rights by not only the man who engages in sexual harassment but also by any of his superiors who refuse to take a woman's complaints seriously or who retaliate against her for filing such a complaint.

Neither Ximena nor I had ever before heard *sexual* and *harassment* put together in the same phrase. This was feminist theorizing at its most radical and its most valuable.

This new feminist concept and its crafters were rowing against a popular (and often self-serving) cultural tide, the widespread presumption that what the activists of AASC and feminist lawyers and labor advocates saw as an infringement of women's rights was, instead, not to be taken seriously. After all, these deniers argued, this workplace behavior was merely "harmless flirting," or it was "only joking around," or it was a benign "compliment."

Over the next three years, Ximena and I, along with the four other Clark women, their supporters among undergraduate and graduate students, and a growing number of women (and some men) within the American Sociological Association, the Association of American Geographers, the American Anthropological Association, and the large Boston-area peace movement and women's movement argued, strategized, hired feminist lawyers, lobbied Clark's trustees, and tutored journalists to get sexual harassment to be taken seriously. We held fund-raisers. Adrienne Rich, who publicly turned down a Clark honorary doctorate after she learned of the sexual harassment controversy, came to Boston to do a benefit poetry reading to help pay for the four women's legal and medical bills.

These years were exhausting; they were exhilarating.

Eventually, Ximena and her four co-complainants won. Ximena left Clark and returned to Chile to take part in the movement that overthrew Pinochet. The Chilean women's movement would pave the way for Michelle Bachelet to be elected president of Chile and later the first head of the new UN Women.[10]

The university agreed to pay the four Clark women's remaining legal and medical fees, and, at the women's insistence, the trustees authorized the hiring of the school's first sexual harassment grievance officer. The harassing professor lost his position as chair and went into early retirement. His influence inside the peace movement waned. More important, many (not all) peace movement activists came to understand that patriarchy and genuine peace could not coexist.

Among the members of our campus women's studies faculty group, even though we failed to act together we each individually, I think, absorbed profound lessons about the complex workings of institutionalized sexism and about the paralyzing consequences of our own anxieties.

Those three years we spent coming to grips with the feminist concept of, and daily implications of, sexual harassment were both painful and clarifying. For me, women's studies could never again be, if it indeed ever had been, strictly academic. The experience also brought home to me the truth of a grittily profound theoretical assertion: the personal is political. That feminist insight makes the complicated lives we lead more understandable, but absorbing its truth does not necessarily make living our lives simpler.

CHAPTER THREE

The Mundane Matters

Why Feminists Take Daily Life Seriously

By definition, the "everyday" appears inconsequential. It appears not to *matter.* How could paying attention to who makes breakfast add to our analytical powers? How could monitoring laundry take us deeper into causality? Surely, assigning weight to casual chats in the elevator or the banter before a meeting begins would be a waste of precious intellectual energy. The everyday is routine. It is what appears to be unexceptional. Devoid of decision making. Seemingly prepolitical.

For an embarrassingly long time, I did not pay attention to the everyday. I, of course, lived it. My relationships with others—parents, friends, colleagues, interviewees—depended on my everyday routines somehow meshing with theirs. But I did not think to spell them out when I engaged in formal analytical efforts. I presumed that my task was to reveal the workings of—and consequences of—power, and that those workings would manifest themselves by standing out from the mundane. If this were true in my attempts to understand ethnic politics in Malaysia (my initial research), it would be, I imagined, all the more true when I began to investigate the causes and consequences of international politics.

I was wrong.

It was feminist analysts who opened my eyes to how wrong I was and what exactly I was missing in the dynamics of international politics by naively imagining that the everyday was prepolitical, analytically trivial, causally weightless.

The most famous late-twentieth-century feminist theoretical pronouncement is: "The personal is political." Its crafters were calling on women (and any men who had sufficient nerve) to look into the everyday dynamics of their lives to discover the causes of patriarchal social systems' remarkable sustainability. This feminist call would have profound implications for understanding the flows of causality. Taking seriously everyday routines and relationships would alter our understandings of how political cultures were constructed and enforced. And eventually, listening to this feminist call—to investigate the personal as if it were political—would turn a bright new light on the interlocking structures of relationships between those actors we so simplistically call "states."

The sites for research, these pioneering feminists argued in the 1970s, 1980s, and 1990s, were not just states' corridors of power, not just political parties' or insurgents' strategy sessions, not just corporations' board rooms. The sites where we would have to dig for political causality were kitchens, bedrooms, beauty parlors, and secretarial pools; they were pubs, squash courts, factory dormitories, golf clubs, and strip clubs—as well as village wells and refugee camp latrines.

By turning these overlooked places into sites for doing serious research, feminist-informed investigators made an astounding discovery: *power was deeply at work where it was least apparent.*

This finding proved disturbing for many social scientists. They had long found alluring the challenge of (and built their professional careers on) revealing the "Big Picture" of the international system. They certainly had not been initially attracted to their scholarly professions by images of themselves taking notes in a brothel, a kitchen, or a latrine.

In asserting that "the personal is political," feminist analysts were claiming that the kinds of power that were created and wielded—and legitimized—in these seemingly private and trivial sites were causally connected to the forms of power created, wielded, and legitimized in the national and interstate public spheres. Moreover, state and economic elites each knew it, even if they rarely openly admitted it. That was why those with their hands on the levers of state, cultural, and economic institutional control were so preoccupied with designing and promoting certain sorts of regimes of marriage, prostitution, child care, and reproduction. They were driven to exercise that control because they believed that patriarchal domestic hierarchies had to take a particular shape if they were to support public patriarchal hierarchies. Yet (and here was the tricky part) policy makers knew that they needed to exercise this control without upsetting the supremely useful myth that private and public spheres were structurally and morally separate.

State elites' preoccupations? Oh, surely, the conventional thinking went, they were preoccupied with taxation, labor unrest, trade imbalances, the next election, possible rebellions, national sovereignty, and militarized security! Look again, warned the feminists. Feminist analysts were not contending that state elites were unconcerned about these headlined issues. Rather, they revealed, state elites and their economic allies were convinced that sovereignty could not be guaranteed without state control over women's sexuality and women's labor; likewise, these decision makers believed that interstate militarized and economic rivalries could not be managed effectively without particular groups of male citizens becoming personally invested in distinct but complementary modes of manliness.

Novelists had realized this for more than a century, especially writers of "domestic" novels. These were not stories of grand adventure or elite machinations. Rather, they were stories of the hearth, parlor, and dining table. Any reader of Jane Austen's or George Eliot's astute novels learned that the maintenance of interclass and gendered power in Britain's rapidly changing nineteenth century relied on the day-in, day-out "below-the-radar" reinforcements of particular domesticated sentiments and expectations—and that they, in turn, formed the pillars of a distinctive sort of imperial state. But most scholars of international politics, unfortunately, have not been in the habit of recommending that their students read *Mansfield Park* or *Middlemarch*.

In my fledgling attempt to test the analytical usefulness of "the personal is political" as I explored international politics, I was not sure where to look. Where was the mundane, the personal, the private, the domestic in the politics of militarized international politics, in the politics of globalized trade? Weren't international politics as far from the domestic as one could get? And to be honest, I was afraid that I would lose my tenuous hold on my credentials as a serious political scientist if I let it be known that I was becoming interested in what went on in the parlor. Nobody, furthermore, had until then encouraged me to think that taking the lives of ordinary women seriously or that plunging into the daily workings of femininity would earn me professional respect.

Then, of course, there was the problem that, as a mere political scientist, I had not been equipped to investigate the domestic sphere, much less intimate relationships, even if I could figure out where those sites were in international politics. In my conventional kit were tools to observe and make sense of policy processes, institutional structures, formal ideologies, public rivalries, and social mobilizations. Each of these tools seemed too blunt or out-of-scale for pursuing my new feminist-informed questions. But I had to begin somewhere, so I started reading a lot more fiction, a lot more feminist histories, and a lot more ethnographies. Today, I would still put books and articles from all three of these genres on the top of my recommended readings list.

Gradually, I started thinking about two sites simultaneously, not sure what I would uncover or whether anyone would recognize either investigation as serious, or as political, or as international. My first site was the assembly lines of multinational corporate export factories. The second was the private households of male soldiers. Both of these ongoing investigations would have lasting effects on how I explored the ideas, rituals, players, stakes, structures, and formal policies whose interactions made and remade international politics. But along the way, I would have to muster the intellectual stamina to follow what I soon discovered were much more extended chains of causality, from the micro to the macro, from the mundane to the dramatic. Perhaps more challenging, I would have to overcome a sexist cultural assumption pervading most social sciences: whatever was tarred with the brush of femininity was intellectually trivial, was not worth taking seriously.

While initially I investigated the international politics of gendered export assembly lines and gendered military households separately, the two investigations eventually converged. National state officials and corporate managers were relying, I gradually realized, on masculinized militaries (and militarized police) to keep their feminized garment, sneaker, and electronics assembly lines profitably rolling.[1]

It was feminist-informed labor organizers of women in multinational factories who initially showed me the way. Women organizing export factory women workers in Hong Kong, South Korea, the Philippines, and Mexico in the 1980s had discovered through trial and error that the orthodox—that is, masculinized—formulas for organizing male factory workers would not work for women. Concentrating on issues arising solely from within the factory (e.g., the speeding up of the assembly line) and on salary-focused demands derived from presumptions about paid work and workers' lives were, they discovered, out of sync with the everyday realities of women factory workers. Thus, these women organizers decided, organizing strategies that gave only these issues center stage would be ineffective.

That is, to be successful as a labor organizer, one had to start from—not treat dismissively, not treat as trivial, not treat as merely private—the mundane dynamics of most women's wall-to-wall, dawn-to-dark lives. To challenge the international alliances between local state and economic elites and the executives of Apple, Nike, Walmart, Gap, Sony, Philips, Motorola, or Levi's, activists would have to not only "think big" but also "think small." And they would have to do both simultaneously. This intellectual strategy adopted by feminist activists—thinking small in order to think big—would guide me to a new analytical approach to international political economy.

A woman working in a sneaker factory in South Korea (or later, in Indonesia and Vietnam) or in an electronics factory in southern China or in a garment factory in Bangladesh, Los Angeles, or Mexico did not enjoy the masculinized luxury of imagining herself first and foremost to be a paid employee of a particular export-oriented company. She usually had to keep clearly in mind that, if unmarried, she must meet her own, her parents', and the state's expectations of her as a "dutiful daughter," a young woman who would prioritize her responsibilities to her parents back in a poor rural village. If unmarried, she simultaneously (she, her parents, and male government officials all hoped this fit neatly with her personal, daughterly goals) would have to be daily aware of her need to act in ways that kept her feminized respectability intact—that is, that kept her "marriageable."

If the woman factory worker were already married, then she had to be sure that she behaved in everyday ways that put her marriage first, that sustained her public reputation as a "good wife," and that did not embarrass or anger her husband. The threat of a husband's domestic violence against a wife displaying autonomy served not just the husband but also the foreign-investment-dependent state and its multinational corporate allies. If labor organizers remained uninterested in the minutiae of domestic violence, then, these women organizers concluded, they would stand little chance of successfully unionizing women factory workers.

As a newly feminist-informed researcher, I began to take seriously these organizers' analyses, and as a result, I slowly came to the realization that only if one investigated popular ideas about the good daughter, feminine respectability, marriageability, and the practices of domestic violence could one make realistic sense of the contemporary international political economy. Taking seriously the myriad everyday realities shaping factory women's ideas and practices has had strategic implications for feminist labor organizers. For instance, they cannot unthinkingly call after-work meetings as male organizers usually did, certainly not evening meetings, since merely attending an after-hours gathering could jeopardize many women's social standing as respectable young women or responsible wives. If such meetings at some point did become essential, then the organizers and the women workers themselves would have to confront explicitly the popular definitions of "dutiful daughter," "respectable woman" and "good wife." Those three ideas were too potent—in the minds not only of women but also of men, neighbors, and media commentators—to be treated as mere side issues. Furthermore, together the women workers and feminist organizers would have to politicize women's everyday understandings of feminine respectability and women's everyday experiences of domestic violence. Unionizing might have to extend to holding community-wide conversations and running child care centers, health clinics, and shelters for abused women.

Marriage, the local cultural constructions of "good" and "bad" women, the "honorable" man able to "control" his wife, and men's violence against women—not only decent wages and shop-floor hierarchies—had to become integral to women's organizing strategies in multinational export factories. In other words, the beliefs, practices, and policies that were bricks in the wall separating women workers from their ability to organize were thicker, and the resultant walls higher, than most nonfeminist observers had wanted to admit. To ignore men's wielding of domestic violence, to treat women's and men's ideas about the "good woman" as if they were "just" local culture, was to severely underestimate what it was taking to maximize globalized profits. Still, for many of those observers and critics who lacked a feminist analysis, who preferred to see only the workings of class, not of gender, it was easier to simply fall back on blaming women for being "women"—that is, to explain women's seeming lack of successful unionizing as a result of their being "naturally" cautious, parochial, and apolitical.

Yet when organizers did take women factory workers' mundane realities seriously, when they did carefully analyze them, and when they did weigh possible strategies to offset them, it was possible to craft demands that could be made in solidarity, to organize strikes that were more likely to succeed, and to mobilize wider community support that strengthened the protesting women workers.[2] Any of these successes would alter the four-sided alliance on which today's global trade has come to rely—that is, the alliance (often fraught with tension) between (1) local government officials, (2) local joint venture capitalist partners, (3) local and foreign factory-owner contractors, and (4) executives in the foreign corporation whose brand-name products were rolling off the assembly lines, generating revenues for all four sets of players. Most of these key players controlling each corner of this dynamic, often unstable square were men. But if their female employees (especially those in the most feminized assembly factories, producing electronics, toys, processed foods, textiles, and garments) could find ways to organize and assert their rights, this four-sided global production alliance would be shaken by the tremors.

Listening to feminist labor organizers and women factory workers producing goods for overseas markets who joined their efforts led me to pay attention to what was going on outside the factory gates. Feminist labor activists underscored the importance in women workers' lives of the relationships outside the factories. Those relationships generated expectations, constraints, worries, hopes, and support. Consequently, to be realistic about what sustained—or challenged—the present international political economy, I would have to follow these women workers home, to their crowded dormitories, to their distant home villages, even go along when they went shopping.[3] I would have to take into account their often uneasy relationships with their mothers and fathers, as well as their sisters (whom they urged to migrate to the city) and brothers (whose school fees they often paid). I would have to consider their anxieties about relationships with their husbands and boyfriends. If I were to make feminist sense—that is, more reliable sense—of the international politics of the trade in privatized goods and of states' stake in that trade, I would have to start giving serious (sustained, careful) thought to the gendered politics of marriage, the constructions of femininities and masculinities, and the strategies women use to avoid violence.

Nowadays, I think that one aspect of factory women's lives that I still have paid too little attention to is friendship—friendships that factory women form with the women who are their workmates. Perhaps giving their complex family relationships their due has blinded me to their friendships—or their lack of friendships, or the quality of those friendships, or the political consequences of those friendships. Are women who are assembling Apple's iPads or stitching Levi's jeans able to make friends with their fellow workers? How do those friendships influence how they think about taking the risk of making demands, of joining an organization, or of actually protesting against their employers' practices? I had never before asked myself these questions. I had known that webs of friendships have been crucial to the creation of women's movements in Serbia, Chile, the United States, and Sweden, but still I treated friendship as too mundane to help explain what was going on in the international political economy.

Then I read Leslie Chang's fascinating account of the stress-filled lives of young Chinese women working in the globalized factories of Guangdong, southern China's hyperindustrialized province. Chang's account made me pause and think about how these young women thought about friendships, how they worked to sustain them.[4] Just because you share a factory dorm room with eleven other women, just because you have in common the long work hours, the loneliness, and the distance from your families in rural villages, this does not mean you and your workmates will become friends. In fact, the very structure of today's globalized factory life may make forging and sustaining friendships especially hard. And as Leslie Chang (who speaks fluent Chinese) found out during her months of spending time "hanging out with" a number of young rural-to-urban migrant factory women, if you are an ambitious young woman factory worker in Guangdong, you quickly realize that staying in one factory will ensure that you are stuck in a dead-end job. So, in order to get ahead, to earn better pay, to rise above the lowest status in the world of today's frantic—and profoundly gendered—factory work, you will have to hone the art of jumping from job to job, from employer to employer. The young women told Chang that this was the only way for a factory girl to get ahead. That does not leave much chance to make and keep friendships.

What do the difficulties in building friendships mean, then, for creating solidarity among the women who assemble iPads in the sprawling Chinese factories of Apple's giant Taiwanese contractor Foxconn? Organizing is hard to do when the common mantra adopted by savvy young Chinese women workers is: "You can only trust yourself."

I could not answer any of the hard questions about globalized political economies unless I treated the mundane as though it were serious. I would get an analytical grip on the current international political economy, I gradually realized, only if I devoted careful, sustained attention to women factory workers' everyday lives, before dawn until long after dusk. If I shrank from this task, I would risk underestimating the amount and kinds of power shaping international politics—and what it takes to upset those power relations. It was, I learned, a risk too big to take.

CHAPTER FOUR

DSK, Vikings, and the Smartest Guys

Masculinities in the Banking Crash of 2008

An internationally powerful banker is accused of sexually assaulting a hotel maid. A year later prosecutors charge him with organizing a prostitution ring during his years at the bank. Women working inside the same bank strategize to fend off unwanted sexual advances by their male colleagues. Simultaneously, inside other too-big-to-fail banks, women are made to feel like outsiders while cults of particular masculinities flourish. What is going on?

Feminist-informed investigations expose some of the crucial dynamics that brought the banks crashing down in 2008. They reveal, too, the dangers of prematurely imagining that in the wake of the crash we have learned the lessons that will stave off a disastrous repeat performance. A feminist investigator is equipped with a bright searchlight with which to expose the everyday cultural workings of masculinities and femininities inside large financial institutions—cultural workings that have been largely treated by observers, bankers, and banking reformers as trivial. What follows is not the end of the story, but it may provide a useful beginning.

THE DSK AFFAIR

Let's start with the International Monetary Fund. Greece, Iceland, and many of the other governments trying to climb out of the postcrash Great Recession have appealed to the IMF for loans. This is not the first time the IMF has attracted serious attention. Over the six decades of its existence, most of that attention, nonetheless, has focused on the IMF's policies, little on the workings of its internal culture.

Feminist analysts, especially those working in poor countries, have written extensive critiques of the official strings that IMF officials have tied to its emergency loans to indebted governments. These researchers have exposed the negatively gendered consequences of the IMF's favored "structural adjustment" anti-inflationary formula: cut government spending and attract foreign capital investment. In practice, fulfilling the IMF's loan requirements has entailed national governments maximizing local citizens' unpaid and low-paid labor while firing thousands of publicly employed state workers (teachers, nurses, accountants) and rolling back publicly funded social services (health care, public transport, postal delivery, and schooling, as well as subsidies for food and fuel).

Employing a feminist curiosity, these gender-aware monitors of the IMF—from the Philippines, Jamaica, Barbados, Peru, Mexico, India, Kenya—have asked a simple but potentially revealing question: Do women and men in the loan-receiving countries experience the IMF formula identically? Over and over again, their findings have pointed to one answer: "No." These analysts have found that it is women, especially poor women, even more than their male fellow citizens, who have been marginalized in the lowest-paid informal sector and recruited into the low-paid (usually nonunionized) export manufacturing sector, and who, at the same time, have taken the brunt of public layoffs and social service cuts when their government officials have accepted IMF loans with these gendered "structural adjustment" strings attached.[1]

So when the managing director of the IMF, the prominent French politician Dominique Strauss-Kahn, initially was accused of sexually assaulting a housekeeper in New York's Sofitel hotel in the spring of 2011, it was not the first time that feminists had had good reason to pay serious attention to the IMF. But it was the first time that its internal culture caught the attention of feminists. The sexual assault charge against its senior executive prompted an array of questions and attracted the attention of many feminists who previously had paid scant attention to international finance. Some feminists investigating the charges against Strauss-Kahn questioned whether he represented a common masculine mode of behavior in French political life, where sexual harassment often has been dismissed as merely an "American" concept. Other feminists focused their attention especially on the vulnerable position in which women working as hotel housekeepers are placed by their hotel managers with respect to the hotels' male guests. Thanks to their questioning, we learned that the right to keep hotel room doors open while they were inside cleaning was a political demand of unionized housekeepers.

Other feminists used well-honed gender analyses to examine how immigrant women working in low-ranking feminized jobs are made particularly vulnerable when lodging a workplace charge of sexual harassment or sexual assault. Still other feminists, long attentive to local police and judicial systems' mishandling of women's rape accusations, turned a spotlight on the New York City police department's and the New York district attorney's office's processes of collecting evidence and weighing trial strategies.

Yet, as accusations of sexual misconduct in this incident (popularly known as the "DSK affair") tumbled out, Christine Ahn, a Korean American feminist analyst who had followed the IMF for years, wondered aloud whether there might be a causal link between (1) an organizational culture that evidently had tolerated such sexist behavior by its senior executive, and (2) an organization that generated policy decisions that left poor women carrying the bulk of the burden for their governments' debts.[2] That is, Ahn was asking us to connect the dots leading from the dominant organizational culture shaping everyday lives of women and men inside the IMF to its policies that were shaping women's and men's lives globally.

As we try to make sense of any organization—the National Hockey League, the British House of Commons, Apple Corporation, the Chinese Communist Party's Politburo, Walmart, Rupert Murdoch's News Corporation, the Egyptian military—we should take steps to answer this question: If members of any organization permit an internal culture to take root that validates certain sorts of abusive or exclusivist masculinity, and that marginalizes most women and most forms of femininity, will that same culture help produce sexist policy decisions and actions when that organization deals with the external world?

Even to start answering this question, we will have to use feminist questions and feminist methodologies to systematically investigate the in-house cultural history and current dynamics of that organization. This means taking seriously the contested workings of ideas about masculinities and about femininities inside any organization, as well as paying close attention to women, even when they are pushed to the organization's periphery.

During the early days of the DSK affair, only a few observers devoted attention to the gender climate inside the Washington headquarters of the International Monetary Fund. Yet what they uncovered there was tantalizing. Binyamin Appelbaum and Sheryl Gay Stolberg, reporters for the *New York Times,* looked at the gender-disaggregated data for employees of the Washington-based IMF and interviewed women working as professionals inside the Fund.[3] They discovered that, in 2011, a mere one-fifth (21.5 percent) of all of the IMF's managers were women; four-fifths (78.5 percent) were men. Better than the U.S. Congress, but not by much.

The two inquisitive journalists pushed their investigation beyond the numbers. They interviewed women professionals inside the IMF headquarters, many of them economists, about what it was like to live their daily work lives inside the IMF during the directorship of Dominique Strauss-Kahn: "Some women avoid wearing skirts for fear of attracting unwanted attention. Others trade whispered tips about overly forward bosses."[4]

When mapping the gendered culture of any workplace, it is useful to be curious about what women employees on each rung of the ladder feel comfortable wearing to work. If they want to be taken seriously by their clients, peers, and superiors, what clothes do they avoid wearing to work? Why? Men's attire is never as fraught with personal risk. Steve Jobs famously encouraged a fashion culture at Apple's California corporate headquarters that eschewed the conventionally masculine attire of suit and tie, favoring for male employees the more informal but equally masculinized black T-shirts and jeans. But much more often it is women whose workplace clothing is the subject of cultural policing (and possible ridicule), because it is women—at all levels of an organization—who are more likely to be physically objectified by their male clients, workmates, and superiors. If women are a minority of employees and placed in subordinate positions, that policing can be intimidating.

The IMF's women professionals went on to describe to the journalists the long workdays and the intense overseas missions, both of which, they said, blurred the lines between professional and private relationships among the Fund's employees. And because most of the Fund's senior posts were held by men, those relationships were usually between women and men of unequal status. The IMF's internal culture that tolerated intimate though unequal relationships between women and men stood out in part because the IMF, headquartered in Washington but an international agency, was exempt from the U.S. anti-sexual-harassment laws and rules—laws and rules created in the 1980s and 1990s as a result of concerted women's advocacy.[5]

Still, there had been an awareness in at least some corners of the Fund that the gendered culture that had come to dominate their workplace was sliding toward a zone of ethical compromise. Just three years prior to the DSK affair, authors of the Fund's internal review warned that the behavior of senior managers (of whom men constituted over

78 percent) was largely unrestrained. They concluded, "The absence of public ethics scandals seems to be more a consequence of luck than good planning and action."[6] In 2011, that luck ran out.

Members of the IMF's governing board were sufficiently embarrassed by the global headlining of misbehavior by the Fund's managing director's to ask Dominique Strauss-Kahn to resign. In the glare of 24/7 media coverage, the board chose as his successor Christine Lagarde, then the finance minister of France. Taking up the post in the summer of 2011, Lagarde became the first woman ever chosen to direct the IMF. Lagarde, however, was not chosen solely because she was a woman. Since its founding in the aftermath of World War II, the IMF always had been headed by a European (while the World Bank's senior post always had gone to an American). Moreover, Lagarde, who spoke fluent English and had worked for years in the United States, was backed by the U.S. government. At least as important in influencing the IMF board members' choice was the fact that, in mid-2011, Europe's Euro zone economic crisis was a major preoccupation of the Fund. Deep knowledge of European finance and her strong working relationship with Angela Merkel, chancellor of Germany, the Euro zone's economic engine, also was high on the list of Lagarde's advantages in the eyes of the Fund's male-dominated board as they sought to "get beyond" the DSK affair.[7]

While the internal gendered culture of the Fund was not explicitly addressed by the members of its governing board, they seemed to hope that replacing a man with a woman atop the organization would have some palliative effect. The board members, nonetheless, did introduce one explicit change: the addition of a new formal condition to the managing director's contract. The IMF contract that Christine Lagarde signed in mid-2011 contained, for the first time, a section on conduct and ethics, requiring the managing director to "strive to avoid even the appearance of impropriety."[8]

On the eve of her appointment, Lagarde returned to a theme she had introduced earlier: the masculinized environment that has dominated both the IMF and the European Union's banking elite (the European

Figure 6. Group of Seven finance ministers and governors, and Christine Lagarde (far right), the recently appointed IMF managing director, Marseilles, France, September 2011. Bloomberg—Getty Images.

Central Bank's twenty-three-member governing council is an all-male affair), as well as the globalized financial world more generally, telling reporters: "If I were elected as managing director I would stand on my feet as a woman, not necessarily with a pair of trousers, and certainly with a level of testosterone that would be lower than [that which characterizes] many in the room today."[9]

The prolonged DSK affair rolled on, as French prosecutors charged Strauss-Kahn with complicity in an international prostitution ring, as France's new president, François Hollande, pledged to support a new law on sexual harassment, as the New York hotel housekeeper filed a civil suit against Strauss-Kahn, and as he retaliated with a civil suit of his own against the housekeeper.

What we still do not know, however, is whether the day-to-day informal relations, presumptions, and practices that shape the IMF's gendered organizational culture have significantly changed since Christine Lagarde stepped into its top post. Has the formerly blurred line between professional and private relationships now become clearer in the minds of both men and women working inside the Fund? Is women economists' work now taken more seriously, so that they are more likely to get promoted to senior positions? Are women at the Fund less nervous each morning when they choose what to wear to work?

We also have not yet tried to answer an even more ambitious question: If Lagarde's leadership of the IMF has altered the gendered culture reigning inside the IMF, has that, in turn, had any significant effect on the ways in which the Fund assesses and acts toward the women and men in those countries whose governments come to it in search of loans?

WALL STREET'S "SMARTEST GUYS"

Linda Basch, an anthropologist and until recently the director of the highly respected National Council for Research on Women, monitored the experiences of women in investment banking.[10] The council had its own offices in lower Manhattan, the hub of the private international banking world, perfectly placed to collect gender-disaggregated data on who has held leadership posts in the multistranded financial services industry—and why, and with what consequences for women, for the industry, and for the country's economic well-being. That is, Basch and her colleagues were not only intent upon mapping the sexist glass ceiling that prevented talented women inside the financial services industry from climbing the company ladders but also curious about what such a privileging of masculinity meant for society at large.[11]

Feminist monitors from the National Council for Research on Women revealed that in 2009, owing to what they saw as a hostile work environment, including a culture that made long working hours the norm, a mere 10 percent of U.S. mutual fund managers were women. They found that, underscoring the masculinization of the fastest-growing sector of the financial services industry—hedge funds—only a tiny 3 percent of the money invested in U.S. hedge funds was managed by women.[12] While people inside the American financial services industry might think of themselves as agents of change, researchers for the U.S. Government Accountability Office paint a picture of them as resisting substantial change: "Overall diversity at the management level in the financial services industry did not change substantially from 1993 through 2008, and diversity in senior positions remains limited."[13] Things had not changed much inside the U.S. financial services companies. What this meant was that in 2008, as the industry reached its peak of prestige, profits, and political influence, men and women from racial minorities, who together make up a third of the total American population, held only 10 percent of senior-level positions in the industry: minority men holding 6 percent and minority women holding 4 percent.[14] These low proportions were not the result of old-fashioned sexism. They were produced by glossy, high-speed, postmodern racialized patriarchy.

Basch took her findings on the road, speaking to numerous financial industry groups. She knew that, for the research findings of the National Council for Research on Women to have an impact, people needed to know about them, needed to take personal possession of the information. "Of course," she recalls, "only women came to the talks." Yet, as interested as these women were in her data-based description of banks' glass ceilings, when it came time for open discussion most women hesitated to say anything at the open mike. They would tell their stories to her only in hushed tones, privately, after the talk. They came up one by one. She was right, they told her. The atmosphere on the trading floors of the investment banks where they worked was hostile to women. No doors on the bathroom stalls, strippers at office parties. Oh, and the lewd jokes, the foul language ... These women were angry, but they were cautious. Still trying to make careers inside the financial industry, they calculated that if they told their own stories publicly, they would hurt their own professional standings. As Basch recalls, "They were afraid that they wouldn't be taken seriously."[15]

In the aftermath of the global economic crash of 2008, there has been a torrent of books and articles seeking to explain what happened—what caused the crash. Many financial experts have pointed to the widespread banking practice of concocting financial instruments so opaque that even their own traders could not adequately understand them—and thus could not realistically weigh the risks embedded in them. Informed commentators also cited industry executives' widespread practice of offering incentive packages that, unwisely, heaped extraordinary rewards upon those employees who took the greatest risks and who maximized short-run profits. Complementing this already dangerous duo, banking strategists' deliberately created "credit default swaps," selling these in marketing campaigns that targeted deeply indebted, desperate public authorities (including money-strapped American municipalities and the government of Greece). Moreover, they crafted mortgage sales campaigns that targeted individuals who had weak credit ratings, people with low-paying jobs, people already burdened with debt, people having little or no savings. These sales campaigns often were supported by an insider banking culture that fostered traders' (and their superiors') outright disdain for their companies' own clients.[16]

To complete the picture of the irresponsible formula that fueled the bubbling boom of 1990–2008, postcrash critics pointed to the calculated lobbying effort by bankers to prevent the extension of public regulation into the newest sectors of investment banking and to roll back existing government regulation of the galloping financial industry. As financial affairs investigative reporter Gretchen Morgenson has described in excruciating detail, during these two decades members of both American political parties holding key positions in Congress and in several presidential administrations joined hands with ambitious entrepreneurial leaders of banks, mortgage sellers, and investment traders to loosen—or decimate—public regulation of the banking industry. They framed their campaign in terms of promoting the "free market" and the "American Dream."[17]

Structure matters. That is, who owns what, which regulations determine who is required to do what, who has the authority and tools to enforce those regulations—these matter. And so do the organizational charts that determine who has to answer to whom and who can promote or demote whom. But so too do collectively shared conscious beliefs, implicit assumptions, commonly held (and fostered) selective memories and forgettings, insider jokes, widely experienced levels of comfort and discomfort, unexamined criteria for trust and distrust, and notions of who is an insider and who an outsider, as well as collective worries, hopes, and fears. Together, these constitute culture.

Feminist-informed gender analysis pays attention to both structure and culture—and the relationships between them. Cultures shape structures (what lines of authority are effective because they feel "natural," what proposed rules are resisted because they are branded "alien"). Likewise, structures shape culture (lawmakers hope that passing new laws making sex, age, and race bias in hiring illegal and punishable will, over time, alter most people's understanding of what constitutes "fairness" and what constitutes the grounds for workplace "trustworthiness").

Both cultures and structures are human-made and thus the products of decisions—including the decision to remain passive, to not intervene. Both are the subjects of debates, confusions, resistances, subversions. Both cultures and structures become building blocks for shared identities. When trying to make full and useful sense of what brought about the financial tsunami of 2008, one needs to fire up one's curiosity to investigate particular structures and cultures and the dynamic interactions between them—not only at national levels (e.g., distinctive U.S., Icelandic, British, Irish, Greek, Norwegian, German, Canadian, Chinese, and Indian political cultures and political economic structures of 1990–2008), but also at the level of the financial industry and of particular powerful companies within that industry.

For instance, at the national level, given the dominant American political culture's susceptibility to any policy choices couched in terms of "free market" and the "American Dream," it proved nearly impossible for anyone warning of the dangers lurking underneath the U.S. regulation rollbacks from 2000 to 2008 to gain traction. Those in Washington who hoisted warning flags of caution—for instance, Sheila Bair, then chair of the Federal Deposit Insurance Corporation—were not taken seriously. In part this was because they were feminized and in part because, in the American political environment of the 1990–2008 boom, they sounded to their boosterish listeners as though they were pouring cold water on the American Dream of universal home-ownership.[18]

The postcrash exposure of the recipe for financial disaster—obscure financial instruments, employee incentive packages that rewarded extreme risk taking, pursuit of short-term profits, targeting vulnerable institutions and individuals in the selling of high-interest loans, contempt for one's own clients, and rolling back state regulation of the financial industry—has been enormously useful. These careful dissections of the misguided formula that made a bubble look like a boom and caused that bubble to burst have informed the proposals for economic financial system reform.

A few of those analysis-based proposals have become law. A few of those new regulatory laws, in turn, have started to be enforced by new and revitalized government regulatory agencies. Yet some of the loopholes that were deliberately written into those postcrash laws, at the behest of banking lobbyists and their congressional supporters, were stretched open even more widely in order to allow the bubble-era practices to persist after the crash. This political reality was thrown into sharp relief in May 2012—four years after the crash, two years after the U.S. reforms were legislated. At that time the financial giant JPMorgan Chase, after its senior executives—including Ina Drew, one of the few women to overcome the Citigroup's masculinized clubbiness to reach a senior bank position—dismissed early warnings, finally admitted that the company had suffered a stunning six billion dollar loss on its traders' extremely risky investments.[19]

The legal reforms have been aimed at changing the structures of the financial industry—that is, introducing new rules and new authorities for government regulators. By contrast, there have been only limited efforts to excise the bubble's cultural ingredients.

One major effort to change national cultures operating outside the industry was mobilized in 2011–2012 by the Occupy Wall Street movement. From Wall Street to Detroit, from London to Reykjavik, "Occupy" activists employed vibrant creativity to change the economic expectations, values, concerns, and bases of trust held by their fellow citizens. They challenged officials' argument that some banks were "too big to fail." They called for more public alarm at the widening gaps between the hyperwealthy and everyone else. It is thanks to the Occupy activists in tents and online, for instance, that outsized bankers' bonuses have taken on the public aura of the bizarre, and that so many of us now talk about our countries' economic elite as "the 1 percent."[20]

But what of the culture of risk taking and the cultural penchant for shortsightedness that were hallmarks of the banks' internal cultures during the bubble/boom era?

An energetic British reporter read all 662 pages of the U.S. Treasury's postcrash report, *The Financial Crisis Inquiry Report*. It was the work of experts, appointed members of the Inquiry Commission, instructed to track down the causes of the 2008 U.S. economic crisis. What the reporter, Tim Adams, found was that "the words 'she,' 'woman' or 'her' do not appear once in its 662 pages."[21]

Feminists always pay attention to pronouns. More than that, feminist analysts exploring any workplace culture have learned that explaining how certain cultures are seeded and sustained requires taking seriously—paying sustained attention to—the workings of particular sorts of masculinities. While in today's popular discourse the hormone testosterone has become a common shorthand for a certain kind of aggressive masculinized performance, feminist investigators are wary of biological determinism. They know that it is a way of thinking that historically has been wielded to institutionalize women's subordination, as if relegating women to the unpaid, politically peripheral domestic sphere were biologically inevitable, "natural." Instead, using a feminist investigatory approach, these investigators start with questions, not predetermined answers. It means asking about the subtle and blatant workings of any culture's notions and practices of masculinities and femininities as they are made, unmade, and remade daily by scores of people interacting unequally with each other.

Feminists have learned, too, that the valorizing of particular breeds of masculinity cannot be effectively explored unless one pays careful attention to, is persistently attentive to, the daily operations of feminization and to the experiences of women—women who try to pry open the organizations' closed doors, women who work on the peripheries of each organization (as secretaries, as cleaners, as hired strippers), and to women who are outside the formal organizations but are involved with the men making their lives on the inside: wives, ex-wives, girlfriends, and daughters. That is, just because Wall Street became masculinized in distinctive ways during the late twentieth and early twenty-first centuries does not mean one should limit one's investigation to the beliefs and practices of men.

Feminists' cultural investigatory questions directed at organizations include: Where are women visible in the organization? Where are they virtually invisible? What has the "one" or the "first" woman had to do to reach her position? Has she been left there in splendid isolation, or has her ascendancy signaled a widening of the whole organization's formerly masculinized career path? What rumors and jokes circulate among members of the organization about the few women who have reached the top?

To fathom an organization's internal culture, the feminist-informed investigator has to listen. One needs to pay attention to the stories that employees tell each other about women who used to be at the top but now are gone. One has to listen for beliefs expressed over coffee or beer about the women who currently are climbing the rungs up to the top. That is, one's ethnographic days "in the field" have to be as long as those of the people whose microculture one is trying to understand. And one's research field site has to be as wide as the relationships that help shape the organizational culture. Thus the investigator may have to ride the crowded subways to and from work, go along to the pub after work, attend basketball games or holiday parties with the bank's employees, and spend time with the friends and family members when the banking employee finally gets home.

Along with Linda Basch, two other feminist-informed anthropologists have made the world of high- and fast-paced finance their field. The first is Gillian Tett, managing editor of the *Financial Times*. She currently covers Wall Street, but during the height of the boom she had her sights set on London's financial district, "the City." She drew on her anthropological training, she said, to delve into the culture that had come to dominate the London offices of the American giant JPMorgan Chase. Out of her anthropologically minded journalist's questioning came Tett's much-discussed book *Fool's Gold*.[22]

In print and in lectures, Tett has argued that to adequately explain why the bubble happened and why it burst, one has to be serious about investigating that workplace culture. Chief among the prevailing cultural tendencies she uncovered was investment bankers' refusal to share information with anyone outside their own narrow "tribe." Tett uses *tribe* to mean something quite particular: a kind of community that encouraged competition-driven social isolation that created a "silo effect," preventing knowledge from being usefully shared, knowledge that, if shared, might have warned more people that the financial risks being taken were dangerous. As an anthropologist, she explains, one is trained "to look at how societies and cultures operate holistically." Referring to London's financial center, Tett continues: "And most people in the City don't do that. They are so specialized, so busy, that they just look at their own little silos."[23]

Katherine Ho is another feminist-informed anthropologist who chose the banking industry as her field. Ho studied the deeply gendered, racialized, and classed cultures of New York investment trading firms in the years of the 1990–2008 bubble/boom.[24] When she launched her investigation, Ho was on leave from her graduate studies at Princeton. She was conscious of her location in contemporary U.S. society as an Asian American woman. Together her several locations, she tells us, made her simultaneously an insider and an outsider in the booming world of high finance—often an advantageous combination for a researcher looking into the cultures of any organization or industry. On the one hand, Ho soon discovered that nonwhites constituted a mere handful of Wall Street's traders, and that women of all races were a distinct minority in this masculinized, highly charged world. The white male insiders nonetheless managed to deny their complicity in institutional sexism, she discovered, by embracing the comforting belief that women would not want to live this sort of work-obsessed life. At the same time, they denied any complicity in racism by internalizing the belief that their workplaces were strict meritocracies, often asserting that "the only color that Wall Street sees is green" and that "money does not discriminate."[25]

Princeton, on the other hand, was Ho's admission ticket to the world of high finance, since the white men running the American investment houses, she learned, presumed that only graduates of Ivy League colleges were "smart" enough to succeed in the fast-paced, ruthlessly competitive world of financial trading.[26]

Karen Ho conducted her ethnographic research in two phases. First, she worked for a year as an employee in the trading department of Bankers Trust of New York Corporation (commonly referred to as BT). While there, she kept a journal recording her own experiences and feelings, but she deliberately did not record anything about her coworkers, since she had not formally asked them if they were willing to be part of her study. It was only in the second phase of her careful investigation, after she had been laid off by BT and returned to her status as a full-time doctoral student, that Ho conducted a series of in-depth confidential interviews with men and women of diverse races and ethnicities working inside several big New York financial firms.

Phase one of her research experience left a lasting impression on Ho. During her year as a trader she began to get a sense that was confirmed later in her scores of interviews: these banking insiders were thoroughly convinced that they deserved the high salaries and annual bonuses they were paid, that this money came to them simply as a result of their own hard work (*hard work* to them—and their superiors—meant "over-work") and as a consequence of their being "the smartest guys."[27] This dedication to overwork was gendered. Ho's male coworkers believed that "normal" women had "another life," that they thus would not want, or could not afford to want, a job that was so life-consuming. Getting home before nine on a workday evening was looked on with some sus-picion by masculinized coworkers. If male traders had children, it was assumed by them and their superiors that someone else, not "the smart-est guys," were looking after them.

Assumptions about marriage, like assumptions about attire, are usu-ally gendered and always useful to investigate when seeking to describe and explain any organization's culture. It takes a feminist curiosity and a feminist investigatory strategy to question the causal links between marital relationships and global banking.

That year spent on the inside also gave Ho a visceral sense of the physical and emotional toll it took to adopt Wall Street's boom-era cul-tural practices: "Toward the end of my time at BT, I was hitting my stress limit at work. Under constant pressure to vie for more and more projects in order to demonstrate my smartness, my capacity for hard work, and my ambition for deal-making responsibility, I was expected to demonstrate the desire for more money as evidence that I had prop-erly imbibed these new sensibilities."[28]

Karen Ho's multiyear ethnographic study exposes what sort of mas-culinity was used by executives as a criterion when they recruited, socialized, and rewarded their employees. It was not enough to be a man. The sort of masculinity they were looking for and nurturing was a kind of manliness that exuded competitiveness, that was capable of quick and agile decision making, that tolerated endless pressure, that courted high risk. It was a kind of masculinity that, at least on the sur-face, could absorb the roller-coaster experiences of success and failure, that wove overwork into personal identity, and that took pleasure in the rough sociability among similarly driven men.[29] That is, it was a dis-tinctive form of masculinity among myriad forms of masculinities.

Within the culture of these Wall Street firms during the boom years, male traders were derisive of other modes of masculinity. They held in contempt what they saw to be the ineffectual, indecisive masculinities dominant in the managerial ranks of manufacturing corporations. That is, while people outside their world might imagine that capitalist men admire other capitalist men, inside BT, Citigroup, Morgan Stanley, Lehman Brothers, and Goldman Sachs the landscape of masculinities that Ho mapped was far more hierarchically differentiated.

Another sort of capitalist masculinity that the high-flying "smartest guys" disparaged was the kind of masculinity dominant among earlier generations of male bankers—the conservative, slow-to-make-risky-loans sort of manliness. These earlier masculinized American bankers were commonly portrayed as conservative, pin-striped, well-fed, and "solid." By contrast, male investment bankers in the years 1990 to 2008 might have portrayed themselves as fast, risk taking, shirtsleeved, jokey, sleep deprived, and caffeine fueled.

Erin Duffy was not an anthropologist, but she was an observer. She worked in the Wall Street investment firm of Merrill Lynch for ten years, turning to fiction writing only after she had been laid off during the crash. Duffy says that, while the central character of her novel, *Bond Girl*, is also a woman trader, she crafted her hero to be "more fearless" than she herself had been. However, Duffy has explained, her descriptions of life on the Wall Street trading floor during the boom years matched her own experiences and those of other bankers she knew.[30] She describes her character's first day at work:

> I could hear screams on the trading floor from the elevator vestibule and felt my hands begin to sweat. It seemed like total chaos. People—nine out of ten of them men—raced through the hall, their loafers crushing the once-plush carpet fibers flat and thin, talking, laughing, cursing. Some wore ties and jackets. Most wore khakis and their moods tattooed on their foreheads.... I could see huge banners hanging from the ceiling marking the accolades the division had earned over the years, the way the championship banners hung in Madison Square Garden. The room was enormous.[31]

Yet Erin Duffy, like her main character, learned how to handle the cascades of data falling onto her several computer screens; she learned how to keep working the phones to make deals while eating the next round of take-out fast food. Also like her main character, she survived the initial culture shock and came to internalize the firm's daily norms and expectations. Working in the huge open space without even cubicle walls to provide a modicum of privacy, Duffy learned to shake off the casual sexism that flowed like the endless cups of coffee: "There are always going to be certain guys who don't want to take a phone call from a woman or don't want to take advice from a woman, but they would probably be like that if they were doctors or lawyers or anything else."[32]

Central to this dominant mode of investment-banking masculinity was the avoidance of anything the investment bankers presumed to be feminized: for instance, leaving work at 5 P.M. to spend time with a partner or care for children, maintaining a tidy work station, abstaining from alcohol, being indifferent to sports, eschewing crude language.

And one more cultural hallmark: the contempt for caution. Inside these boom-era American banking firms, caution became feminized.

Caution, of course, is not always associated by sexists with feminization. If caution can be dressed up as manly responsibility, if it can be presented as sophisticated, multivariable, "facing the facts" analysis, then caution can be celebrated as distinctly (even uniquely) masculine, something that manly men do better than all women and certain men. But on Wall Street during the booming bubble years, acting fast in the face of extreme uncertainty was proof of one's own qualification to join the insider club of "the smartest guys." In that particular Wall Street gender climate, exercising caution was typically deemed by insiders to signal a lack of manly daring, an unwillingness to tolerate instability, and an inability to take the sort of risks that profit maximization required.

These distinctive masculinized cultural norms that were being entrenched inside Wall Street firms were reinforced by these men's participation in several industry-wide exclusive organizations. There is

Kappa Beta Phi. This little-known Wall Street fraternity was launched in 1929—a fateful year in the history of American finance. Its events are "cloaked in secrecy." Its members "include big-name bankers, hedge fund billionaires and private equity titans." At its 2012 annual induction dinner, tuxedos prevailed among the two hundred diners. Few women were visible. New inductees were required to "don wigs, gold-sequined skirts and skin-tight tops," thus efficiently sending out twin messages: only men would be the inductees, and femininity was funny.[33]

A second group that has helped sustain Wall Street's masculinized industry culture goes without a name and is even more exclusive. It has only nine members, all male, drawn from the most senior executive offices of New York's largest financial firms, including JPMorgan Chase, Goldman Sachs, and Morgan Stanley. Their meetings are held in secret; no minutes are recorded. While its alleged purpose is to look after the well-being of the entire financial services industry, its priority is to "defend the dominance of the big banks."[34]

There is no report of this handful of men dressing up for each other's amusement in sequined skirts. In fact, these elite-banking men's mundane practices at their respective firms' offices may not include shouting, fast food, or crude jokes. Yet their success—and their calculations of what has brought and will sustain their banks' success—may rely on the trading floor's brand of masculinity. That is, in any large organization's culture, there is likely to be operating a diverse set of masculinities. What deserves investigation is how each mode of masculinity is fostered at each rung of the organizational ladder in ways that ensure that the whole complement of masculinities "works" for that organization's goals. This is as true in a bank as it is in a university, in a sports league, or in a military: the most visible, most blatant form of masculinity at work in an organization may not be its sole masculinized microculture. Thus, while the investment traders' masculinized culture calls for critical attention, a feminist light needs to be shined as well on the less accessible, more discreet dark-suited masculinized cultures operating at the pinnacle of the financial services firms.

In the early 2000s, a small number of women financiers began to desert the big masculinized firms and start up financial companies of their own. According to the women interviewed by researchers from the National Council for Research on Women, those women chose to craft new organizational cultures that valued financial caution. They tended to weigh a wider array of factors when assessing the investments of their clients' funds, and they judged potential investments using a longer-term time frame. These women-managed financial firms, while controlling only a small proportion of Wall Street's total capital, tended on average to fare much better than the bigger firms when the crash came; their firms lost proportionately less and also experienced less turmoil. As she studied the data from the 2008 financial crash, professor of business Michel Ferrary concluded, "The more women there were in a company's management, the less the share price fell in 2008." She continued: "Feminization of management seems to be a protection against financial crisis."[35]

Economist Jane Knodell has raised a fruitful question for our ongoing monitoring: If the relative security of investing with women-managed firms is widely recognized, will more major investors start to redirect their funds to those firms? That is, even if these investors (e.g., pension fund managers) never publicly criticize the dominant masculinized banking culture, will they simply "march with their dollars" away from the most dysfunctionally masculinized banks?[36]

Alternatively, the cultural devotion to the bubble era's distinct form of trader masculinity may not be undone. Gendered organizational cultures are stubborn. They cannot be transformed until they have been systematically investigated. And, even after such explicit gender analyses have been conducted, it still requires a lot of candor, energy, and fresh consciousness to mobilize the kind of collective will to uproot an entrenched organizational culture so that new notions about masculinity and femininity can be planted and allowed to thrive.

In the wake of the 2008 crash, many women inside the U.S. financial services industry hoped that the evidence of the economic advantages of a less masculinized organizational culture, plus the general shakeup coming with the failures of Lehman Brothers and Merrill Lynch, would together inspire new thinking and new cultural practices that would roll back institutionalized sexism. But as the recovery seemed to be taking hold within the industry in 2010, there were signs that professional women's "career paths are narrowing again even as the business picks up."[37] Simultaneously, while more women were entering business schools (constituting 39.3 percent of U.S. business school students in 2010), the proportion of those who were pursuing careers in finance or accounting was dropping.[38]

The U.S. financial industry's 2008 crash was caused by a convergence of several dysfunctions, structural (the government deregulation of the banking industry, the merging of traditional banking with high-risk trading and the onset of silo compartmentalization) and cultural (overconfidence, pursuit of extraordinary wealth, and shortsightedness). But I have become convinced that if we leave it at that, if we ignore the U.S. financial industry's deliberate cultivation of a particular kind of masculinity on the trading floor and its disparagement of femininity inside its most influential workplaces, we will see another financial crash in our near future. We refuse to take feminist investigatory findings seriously at our peril. For too many people working in these large American banking firms today, the dominant, gendered workplace culture still feels rewarding and comfortable.

THATCHER'S CHILDREN

Britons refer these days to "Thatcher's children." These are the young men and women who came of age during the nearly twelve years (1979–1990) Margaret Thatcher was prime minister. Thatcher was more than just Britain's first woman prime minister and the first twentieth-century British prime minister to win three consecutive national elections. She also was the national leader who successfully promoted a new dominant mode of British masculinity. "Thatcher's children"—those

Britons of this late-twentieth-century generation who came to absorb her values and expectations—no longer had any use either for the working-class coal miner or for the tweed-clad country squire, two iconic British masculinities that operated in tandem to sustain Britain's famed class system. Margaret Thatcher, though herself an Oxford graduate and a Conservative Party loyalist, came to believe that this particular gendered class system was incapable of generating the sort of competitive postcolonial capitalist growth that her country required in order to thrive in the late twentieth century. Thus she led a government that closed the mines and brutally quashed a miners' strike, while rolling back the post–World War II welfare state, turning a deaf ear to the country's energetic women's movement, and dismissively pushing aside some of the privileged male grandees who, until then, had controlled the Conservative Party.[39]

The sort of British masculinity that Thatcher's government promoted through its policies of aggressive privatization was a masculinity that reveled in individualism, risk taking, and profit maximization. Whereas in the United States this gendered package was only a step further along an already established national cultural spectrum, in Britain the gendered package was designed to mark a sharp break with the past.

It was "Thatcher's children," especially the men of that generation, who pursued jobs in the City, London's financial hub, and crafted the gendered culture that came to dominate British banking during the financial boom of 1990 to 2008. Although the Labor Party, led by Tony Blair, came to power in 1997, that particular sort of Thatcherist masculinity was not displaced; it continued to shape the workplace assumptions and values that guided British banks and the London branches of American banks for the next decade.

Britain's banking industry remains the largest in Europe. Successive governments, Conservative and Labor, have seen the interests of the country's banking industry as requiring the government's promotion and protection.[40] This has added to the significance of the financial industry's distinctive masculinization. That is, it is an industry that not only employs thousands of people, not only makes a lot of money for certain Britons, not only embodies Thatcher's gendered legacy. It is also a sector of the British economy whose well-being senior politicians perceive as being essential to the whole society's well-being.

The first woman permitted on the trading floor of the London Stock Exchange was Susan Shaw, and she did not gain entrance until 1973.[41] In 2009, within Britain's top 350 corporations, a mere 3 percent of executive directors were women, and 130 of these most powerful companies had not even a single woman on their boards of directors.[42] Within the British finance industry today, women remain a minority, though a growing minority. By 2010, within British financial institutions, women were 40.1 percent of all managers. But that figure comes with a caveat: this seemingly high proportion gives a misleading impression, since it includes managers of departments that are removed from the "main action" of the banks and investment houses, distant from those departments where profits are made. Thus the managerial posts that women hold are not where the highest salaries and biggest bonuses are paid.[43] In fact, according to a study by Britain's Equality and Human Rights Commission, in 2009 women earned 80 percent less than men in performance-related pay (often in the form of commissions and bonuses) at the country's largest finance companies.[44]

Digging deeper into the prevailing British banking workplace cultures, researchers found that a large majority (72 percent) of women inside the financial services industry agreed that "the attitudes of senior male managers were a barrier to women progressing into senior roles." Many of them pointed to the culture of their own firms as the chief culprit. As a result, when asked where they pictured themselves to be in the firm ten years ahead, 36 percent of the women surveyed said that they expected to be in the same position they currently held; only 14 percent of the men had these same low expectations.[45] The researchers concluded that this disparity was evidence less of women bankers' lack of ambition, and more of women's accurate analyses of their firm's masculinized workplace cultures that would hold them back in their careers. As one senior British woman banker explained about her senior male colleagues' sense of discomfort working with women as their peers: "I wonder sometimes, quite honestly, when a role comes up and you get a woman going for it ... whether they would just err more to the male application. It's just that kind of unconscious bias."[46]

When the banking crash hit Britain in 2008, a leading journalist, Ruth Sunderland, the financial affairs editor of Britain's national Sunday paper *The Observer,* decided to interview six leading British women working in the City. Together, they traced the workplace cultural assumptions and practices inside Britain's financial firms that, they were convinced, had led to disastrous external consequences.[47]

> ROS ALTMAN, INDEPENDENT INVESTMENT BANKER: I have absolutely no doubt that a significant factor in all of this [financial chaos] is excess machismo; the idea that you always have to be one step ahead, that you always have to beat your rivals. There was not the cooperative thinking that there would be in a female environment; it was about how to be the best, the first, almost irrespective of the risks. I certainly wouldn't argue that if women had been in charge, everything would have been different, but if there had been a greater female contribution to the running of businesses, there would have been a natural tendency for a woman to say, "Let's take a bit of a longer-term view."

> RUTH LEA, ECONOMIC ADVISOR, ARBUTHNOT BANKING GROUP: I half agree with that. I used to work at Lehman Brothers and there was a huge atmosphere of machismo.... It reminds me of going on a far eastern trip with a male colleague and it was totally wearing. Every time we got to another financial centre he would be off to the gym. I thought, "I can't bear this," and I would be off to the mini bar. At the end of the week I was the one still standing, though not totally sober! It was macho, risk-taking, and a sales culture that I won't say was immoral, but it was buccaneering. The problem is that buccaneering spirit migrated from the investment banks into general banking and infected the whole financial system.... It is quite clear that the awful macho risk-taking has got into the bloodstream.

> EMMA HOWARD BOYD, DIRECTOR, JUPITER ASSET MANAGEMENT: I don't think it is about men and women. Paul Moore [a whistleblower whose banking superior ignored his warning of the dangerous investments

being made] blew the whistle. It is about diversity of attitudes towards risks. We need broader ways of looking at investment and risk-taking.

CHARLOTTE CROSSWELL, CHIEF EXECUTIVE, NASEEQ OMX EUROPE: I think women do have a different attitude to risk, but you need to take some risks in business. I believe in the diversity argument, that you need a balance....

ROS ALTMAN: You need a moderating influence to all that testosterone, and there wasn't that influence, or certainly not sufficient of it.

TONI EASTWOOD, TRAINING DIRECTOR, EVERYWOMAN: You don't have that balance at the top of the banks. The higher you go up, the less you see women.... Their views are being lost at the top.

CARY MARSH, CHIEF EXECUTIVE, MYDEO.COM: ... My personal experience starting up a technology business is successful firms are the ones with a diversity of thinkers. They would have a live-wire entrepreneur who is gung-ho and a risk taker, but you would have calmer people who temper the risk takers. There is a pack mentality in the City. It is about people who want to run with the pack. This whole crisis is caused because people were all taking risks at the same time.

ROS: It is about not wanting to be a wimp. Everyone is taking risks and if I don't do that I am going to be the wimp. What man would sign up for that? ...

TONI: But what woman in that environment would sign up to be a wimp either? Even if there were more women, the ones in that culture are very similar. They might not be comfortable, but they either have to run with the pack or leave.

JANICE WARMAN, DEPUTY EDITOR, SPECTATOR BUSINESS MAGAZINE: There is the Thatcher factor, where you have to behave like a man to get ahead and that is a negative thing. In fund management, for instance, a lot of firms like women because they are better at client relationships, better at treating their staff, but longer term a lot more women left because they found it hard to have a domestic or social life.

TONI: ... They [women] see these testosterone-filled environments and they don't want a career in that.

Headlines that turned gender gaps at the top of British firms into news have sparked political debate over whether Britain should follow Norway. The Norwegian government escaped the financial crash. Was it not simply because Norway had North Sea oil but also because the Norwegian government had passed an innovative law requiring all Norwegian corporations to have at least 40 percent women on their corporate boards, and those boards had been more cautious in their attitudes toward investments? At least one British Member of Parliament, Caroline Lucas, a vocal critic of Parliament's own "schoolboy culture," wondered in print whether the chances of the British House of Commons passing such a quota law were slim, given the fact that the percentage of women MPs in the Commons was a pale 22 percent.[48]

THE VIKINGS

Icelanders were hit early and hard by the 2008 financial crash. There was as much surprise as alarm that Iceland was pushed to the brink of national bankruptcy. Few outside of the arcane world of international finance had even noticed that during the 1990's, and up until 2008, Reykjavik, Iceland's small capital city, had become an international financial hub. Most people, if they gave thought to Iceland at all, imagined active volcanoes spewing clouds of ash, and hot springs in which one could take a relaxing sulfur bath.

The other hallmark of contemporary Iceland had been its gender politics. By the opening of the twenty-first century, Iceland had gained the reputation of apparently creating near-equality between women and men. In the midst of the boom, 80 percent of Icelandic women had paid jobs; in the national parliament, women held 33 percent of the elected seats.[49]

In 2006, as the boom bubbled, the World Economic Forum ranked Iceland number four in the world in terms of the narrowness of its national gender gap. That is, when comparing 130 countries across regions and across levels of economic development according to how equal men and women were in their respective access to political influence, paid labor, educational opportunities, and health care, only Sweden (number one in 2006), Norway (number two), and Finland (number three) had been more successful than Iceland in shrinking their respective gender inequalities. In 2006, Britain ranked number nine in comparative national gender gaps, and the United States ranked an embarrassing number twenty-three.[50]

The relative success of Icelandic women in gaining influence and access to resources did not prevent Iceland from blowing its own dramatic financial bubble. This suggests that, for all its success, the Icelandic women's movement in the 1990s had not yet transformed (and Icelandic feminists never have claimed that they have managed to transform) the patriarchal internal cultures of political parties' leaderships and of the country's banking establishment. The sophisticated local women's movement did not claim that its relative success had inoculated Icelandic society against the capitalist manipulations of a masculinized national myth.

Yet, as we will see, despite these shortfalls, what the Icelandic women's movement had achieved by 2008 was enough mobilization and enough gender equality that Icelandic women would be positioned in the postcrash years to respond to the bubble's disastrous burst far more forcefully than could the more marginalized American or British women.

Ruth Sunderland, the British financial affairs journalist, decided to follow up her postcrash conversation with British women in finance with a trip to Reykjavik. On dark northern winter days early in 2009, she talked with Icelandic women who had witnessed from the inside how their country's elite bankers and their male political allies had created Iceland's boom, step by risky structural and cultural step.[51]

For instance, Joanna Waagfjord, chief executive of an independent investment firm, explained that during Iceland's boom years young, inexperienced men became "too dominant." She soon discovered that they scarcely understood the complicated derivatives they were selling so aggressively. Other women executives warned, however, that, while men were the central creators of this new masculinized culture in Icelandic banking, some Icelandic women adopted those young men's cultural attitudes and practices in order to be seen as players during the boom.[52]

Because Icelandic women had won so many victories on the road to gender equality in the years before the boom reached its peak, there did exist a distinctive cultural backdrop against which Icelanders could view the ascendancy of both these aggressive male bankers and masculinized business practices between 1990 and 2008. In the United States and Britain, the dominance of men in the world of finance may have looked almost normal, even if the brash masculinized microculture of trading floors was distinctive. That was not true in Iceland. By 2000, to most Icelanders, male dominance in any sector of Icelandic society looked weird. Elin Jonsdottir, the managing director of an investment firm, explained to Sunderland: "We all feel it is strange when you looked at the banks and the directors were all male, and this is Iceland where female participation in the workplace is higher than anywhere else in the world. We are beginning to look at companies as old-fashioned if they have only male directors. There is still a bit of a boys' club, with women as outsiders—people know the rules and are comfortable with that—no one was asking difficult questions. But the boardroom should not necessarily be too comfortable."[53]

What looks strange, what seems normal, what produces a sense of comfort, what feels awkward: these are the makings of a culture. Icelanders, by 2000, had so drastically refashioned their national political culture that all-male groups of bankers may have existed, but to many Icelanders they looked odd.

Precisely because the gendered cultural dynamics that helped produce the boom and the crash looked odd to so many Icelanders, the emergence of the boom-era masculinized banking culture needed to be investigated and explained. If something does not look odd, it is less likely to be investigated. That is precisely why "normalcy" serves as such a protective covering for so many patriarchal institutions.

In the wake of the crash, many Icelandic feminists, to whom the bankers' boom culture had looked so odd, began to craft precisely this sort of gender analysis. The newly elected Icelandic parliament (whose

Figure 7. Vikings landing in Iceland, a popular representation. Myths of the Norsemen come from the Eddas and Sagas. London Harrap. By H.A. Guerber (Helen Adeline), 1909.

proportion of women had climbed from a precrash 33 percent to a post-crash high of 39 percent) commissioned two Icelandic scholars to conduct an explicitly gendered analytical study, as well.[54]

What these analysts concluded was that, from the 1980s through the 1990s and into the first eight years of the new century, Icelandic men in the center-right Independence-Party-led government allied with men in Reykjavik's banks to successfully press for Iceland's banks to be privatized, and then for those privatized banks to be deregulated, all in the name of national modernization and rapid economic growth. No more would Iceland be merely a remote, cold volcanic island dependent on fishing, sheepherding, and hardscrabble farming. It would become a respected player on the world stage of finance. But Icelandic feminists did not stop at this structural analysis. They made gender politics of culture a topic of investigation. Thus the Vikings.

The Vikings were Norwegian maritime male conquerors who, along with women they abducted from the northern islands of Scotland, settled what was to become Iceland in the ninth and tenth centuries. Against the odds, they carved out a sustainable economy and a sturdy social system in a land seemingly inhospitable to humans. Even during the centuries of Norwegian and then Danish colonial rule (Icelanders declared their independence in 1944), Icelanders made images and stories of the Vikings central to their construction of a national identity. Giving primacy to their Viking heritage, they saw themselves as a people who were distinct, tough, egalitarian, and resilient. Icelanders did not create a landed aristocracy, yet the hardy fisherman was to the pre-financial-boom-era Icelanders what the coal miner was to many pre-Thatcher Britons: a masculinized model of national strength, pride, and identity. The fisherman and his sheepherding and farming cousins—along with their reputedly long-suffering, uncomplaining, hardworking, loyal, and god-fearing wives—seemed to be direct cultural, as well as biological, descendants of the Vikings.[55]

But in the 1990s, Iceland's feminist researchers found, the men in government and the men in banks who joined together to put Iceland's economy on a new, more-profit-generating path employed a new version of Viking masculinity to legitimize their policies and cultural practices. With the collusion of the country's influential media editors and commentators, these men argued that Iceland's speculating, risk-taking bankers navigating the high seas of global finance were the genuine descendants of those ninth-century Viking adventurers. But whereas the Vikings of old had prized thrift and egalitarian solidarity, their investor descendants shamelessly indulged in luxurious consumption out of the reach of most of their fellow citizens. The local media christened these men "business Vikings" (in Icelandic, *utrasarvikingur*).[56]

Thus, while Wall Street's "smartest guys" and London's "Thatcher's children" were heralded as new, or at least relatively new, national breeds, Iceland's risk-taking male bankers were celebrated by the country's elites as a new incarnation of an ancient national breed.

As in the United States, so too in Iceland: the masculinized culture that drove the banking firms to dangerous excess was promoted at the top by particular exclusivist masculinized groups. In Iceland, the most influential of these was the Locomotive Group. The all-male membership of the Locomotive Group collectively convinced themselves that pushing aside state regulators, maximizing short-term profits, and thinking little about long-term ramifications was the formula for success. Halla Gunnarsdottir, a member of the Feminist Society of Iceland, which conducted a study of the Locomotive Group, explained: the Locomotive Group's modus vivendi was not simply a capitalist ideology; it was a culture. These men presumed that women did not have the bravado to engage in short-term high-risk profit making; they announced their success by buying fast cars and dressing in expensive suits; they spent time together in bars and strip clubs.[57]

In the aftermath of the autumn 2008 crash, Icelandic women began to reassert their influence. Coming from a position of relatively greater strength than their American and British counterparts, Icelandic women ran for parliament in even higher numbers, they helped elect the world's first prime minister who was an "out" lesbian feminist, they campaigned for a woman candidate—a prominent television journalist—for president (she lost to the longtime male incumbent), they commissioned a gender-explicit investigation of the crash, they empowered the new Green/Socialist ruling coalition to craft further women-friendly social policies, and they offered new gender models for business firms that made maternalist values central to company practice and promoted middle-aged women as especially valuable to firms' performance.[58] At the same time, many Icelanders became self-reflective, calling not simply for new laws but also for constitutional reform to make the still inbred political system more transparent, and criticizing their own brief love affair with hyperconsumerism. In the wake of the crash, Icelanders, hearing of friends' expensive purchases, labeled them "so 2007."[59]

The 2011 World Economic Forum's *Gender Gap Report* showed some of the consequences of Icelandic women's postcrash mobilization: whereas in 2006 the gender gap in Iceland ranked fourth-narrowest in the world, by 2011 Iceland had jumped up to first place, having the narrowest gender gap of all nations. That same year, Norway became number two, Finland number three, and Sweden number four. Britain, which had ranked number nine during the boom, slipped to number sixteen in 2011. The United States, number twenty-three in 2006, had, since the 2008 election of the Obama administration, climbed up to number seventeen in the world rankings, though it still had a wider gender gap than did the Philippines (number eight), Lesotho (number nine), and South Africa (number fourteen).[60]

TAKING WOMEN SERIOUSLY IN THE POLITICS OF BANKING

Canadians, like Norwegians, escaped the worst fallout from the 2008 international banking crash in large part because they had crafted—and maintained—a more attentive public regulatory structure. But when explaining their success in skirting the crash, Canadians did not cite only structure; they pointed to culture. Many Canadians spend substantial energy distinguishing themselves from the domineering Americans to their south. They like to remind their southern neighbors that they have produced many of their neighbors' professional ice hockey players, as well as best-selling authors such as Margaret Atwood and Michael Ondaatje. They point too to their more prominent roles in UN peacekeeping, their wider health insurance coverage, and their lower homicide rates. With the financial crash, Canadians also talked about their different cultural attitudes toward banking, though it was not clear that anyone south of the border was listening.

A Canadian professor of business explained why no Canadian banks had had to be bailed out during the in 2008: "We are 'peace, order and good government.' They [Americans] are into the pursuit of happiness. The U.S. banks were pursuing their own happiness, with the sort of assumption that it would all work out fine."[61] Another Canadian, a male executive of the Royal Bank of Canada, described the difference between the two neighboring banking cultures this way: "The US system is less risk-averse than the Canadian system."[62] The Canadian banking industry is male-dominated and patriarchal, and Canadian feminists express alarm at the Conservative government's rolling back of gender equity gains made over the last three decades.[63] On the other hand, the masculinized culture that does prevail inside Canada's major banks appears to have produced attitudes that not only have generated less frustration in the face of state regulation but also have framed the exercising of caution as unthreatening to their particular brand of patriarchal masculinity.

That is, the internal cultures of finance industries can differ from one country to another and from one generation to the next, even within a globalized capitalist economic system. Neither structural analysis nor ideological analysis, even when joined, is sufficient for making useful sense of any country's bankers and banking system. The prevailing national and workplace cultures of masculinities and femininities need to be taken seriously, to be investigated as if they have consequences that matter.

In particular, the welding of risk taking and short-term-goal-seeking to the most organizationally prized version of masculinity—especially when it is combined with a misogynist denigration of caution—can so warp any country's financial system that the economic security of an entire society is jeopardized. Therefore, in each international agency, in each firm, in each network of firms that constitute a nation's finance industry, feminist questions must be posed and investigatory strategies honed to answer these crucial feminist questions:

- Is the firm's or the industry's working culture masculinized? How did it become masculinized in this particular way?
- What decisions (including the decision to remain passive) have been taken to create and entrench that particular version of a masculinized organizational culture?

- How do women working inside the finance industry experience their workplaces and daily cope with the prevailing cultures in those workplaces? What are the consequences for them and for the industry of their chosen coping strategies?
- What do the lives of women outside the industry, but implicated in its daily operations—women who are wives, partners, cleaners, strippers, prostitutes, clients—reveal about how that internal masculinized culture is sustained?
- How does the agency's, firm's, or industry's prevailing internal gendered culture help generate its external policies—toward its clients, allies, investors, borrowers, and regulators?
- How does the marginalization of women in the wider society blind us to the prevailing dysfunctional masculinized organizational cultures? How does sexism in the country at large subvert efforts to dismantle those harmful cultures?

We have models for this sort of feminist investigation. In addition to Karen Ho's Wall Street ethnography and the Icelandic feminist's investigation of the Viking banking culture, there are other cogent feminist analyses of workplace cultures we can turn to for guidance: Cynthia Cockburn's investigation of a London printing company, Hugh Gusterson's of a California nuclear weapons science laboratory, Carol Cohn's of a network of American civilian defense intellectuals, Ann Allison's of a Tokyo nightclub, Robin LeBlanc's of Japanese local political party organizations, Nan Robertson's of the *New York Times,* and Lynn Povich's of *Newsweek.*[64]

The genderings of politics inside institutions cannot be fenced off from the politics outside those institutions. They have to be investigated together. Twelve months after Dominique Strauss-Kahn was charged with sexual assault, a new Socialist government under a new Socialist leader was elected in France. The newly elected president, François Hollande, announced that, for the first time in French history, 50 percent of the president's cabinet would be composed of women.

Figure 8. French president François Hollande (second from right) with the women he selected to head ministries in his new cabinet, 2011. Christopher Karaba/EPA.

The women would be racially diverse, reflecting the realities of contemporary French society.

Hollande further acknowledged the post–DSK affair political dynamics by reestablishing the Ministry of Women's Rights and appointing a thirty-four-year-old Morocco-born local councilor, Najat Vallaud-Belkacem, to head the revitalized ministry. She, in turn, announced that she would act quickly to reinstitute a national law against sexual harassment, which the country's Constitutional Council had previously repealed. French feminists had been outraged, energized, and mobilized by the DSK affair. They had insisted that sexual harassment in French workplaces no longer be treated as a puritanical delusion, and that women have a stronger voice in political party, electoral, and government decision-making. Now, in May 2012, these activists turned their attention to the new government. They noted that at the time of Hollande's victory the French parliament's membership was a lowly 18.5 percent women (a mere percentage point higher that of the U.S. Congress). Furthermore, they criticized the parliament's current gendered environment, noting that some women delegates were made to feel uncomfortable wearing skirts to work. French feminists expressed satisfaction with President Hollande's cabinet appointments but offered a warning: only when the new president made women the heads of the French state's most powerful ministries would they judge him to be taking women's ideas, women's issues, and powerful men's sexual behavior seriously.[65]

CHAPTER FIVE

Women in Recession

Austerity and Misogyny

Four years after the spectacular international banking crash of 2008, upbeat commentators were talking about the "recovery." The Great Recession of 2008 was officially declared over by the end of 2012. For many women and men—in the United States, Ireland, Iceland, the United Kingdom, Greece, and Spain—the economic pain, however, was still acute. Joblessness and home foreclosures remained historically high. Loans were still hard to obtain. Pensions were uncertain as employers reneged on retirement pledges and stock markets continued their roller-coaster rides. And the effects of drastic national and local government budget cuts had just begun to be felt.

Taking feminist analysis *seriously* means asking where women are in each corner of each recession and why—and *then* continuing to ask those questions month after month, as the economy takes its twists and turns—and *then* translating the investigatory findings into a basis for realistic economic policies. Feminist economic analysts monitored the International Monetary Fund's loan conditions to poor countries, revealing the gendered consequences of the 1997 Asian economic crisis; they charted the distinct impacts of the international economic sanctions imposed on 1990s Iraq. They have taught us that to discover where the women are—and how they got there, and what the costs of their being stuck there are—requires investigating how spoken and unspoken ideas about masculinities and femininities push some concerns about women to the top of the public agenda (e.g., their reproductive activities), while other concerns about women (e.g., their unpaid caring work, their low wages) are allowed to sink to the bottom of that agenda or to slide off the public table altogether.[1]

Economic hardship and a resultant pervading sense of insecurity can make many people receptive to conspiracy theories and scapegoating. Racism and xenophobia often thrive during hard times. So does misogyny. Consequently, taking feminist economic analysis seriously requires keeping a sharp eye not only on private employers and public economic officials but also on the purveyors of meanness and their often seductive rationales.

ROADS AND BRIDGES ARE GENDERED

Let's start with a graphic American example of what happens when feminist questions are *not* asked in the throes of a recession, the results of that failure—and how some feminists have effectively responded to that official failure.

Barack Obama came into office in January 2009 with tremendous fanfare. He was the first African American to be elected to the U.S. presidency. As the economy had tumbled, the Obama campaign had called for "hope" and had promised "change," not just for African Americans but for all Americans. When Obama took his oath of office in January 2009, the banking crisis was at its peak. Uncertainty and fear were rife. Yet beyond crafting a plan to save the banks, Barack Obama, a Democrat, and his new White House policy team already were focusing on jobs. Just days after Obama's historic election, even before he was inaugurated and as he was still making Cabinet appointments, the president-elect's economic transition team was hard at work drafting an economic stimulus package, a plan the president could send to Congress shortly after his inauguration.

As women's advocates in every country have learned, "transitions" are times filled with gendered promise but are also fraught with gendered danger. Whether in the immediate aftermath of a war, or in the wake of deposing a dictator, or during the weeks between an election and the inauguration of a new governing administration, transitions are times of fluidity. Yet crucial decisions are being made during those weeks, decisions that can harden as soon as the transition morphs into established, formal relationships. Transitions, consequently, are times during which feminists have learned to stay alert, to stay mobilized, to keep mustering evidence, sharpening arguments, and cultivating access to decision makers. This is never easy. It is especially difficult for those citizens who do not make careers out of full-time lobbying. For ordinary citizens, winning an election, toppling a dictator, or pushing all warring sides to the peace table will have taken months of exhausting collective effort. It will have required neglecting personal relationships, postponing daily chores. It will be tempting, therefore, for most people to relax, to demobilize, to return to pressing personal concerns as soon as the transition is under way.

A network of American feminist historians and feminist economists decided in postelection November 2008 that such a demobilization would be a mistake. Their decision to stay alert and connected would have a significant impact on what the Obama White House would eventually propose to stimulate the broken U.S. economy in 2009. But this feminist impact would not be felt until the Obama transition team came to the brink of making a profoundly patriarchal economic mistake.

In the weeks after Obama's election, his transition team continued work on a federal spending plan designed to fulfill the president-elect's promise to get America back to work. Both chambers of Congress, whose members also were elected in November, would be returning to Washington in January with Democratic majorities—affording the new president a political luxury he would enjoy only for the next two years. Time was of the essence.

"We'll put people back to work rebuilding our crumbling roads and bridges, modernizing our schools that are failing our children, and building wind farms and solar panels; fuel-efficient cars; and alternative-energy technologies that can free us from our dependency on foreign oil and keep our economy competitive in the years ahead."[2] This was Barack Obama's vision for a jobs-generating stimulus package. Not surprisingly, key people around the president-elect looked to the last American economic crisis for lessons: Franklin Roosevelt's renowned 1930s New Deal. As a result, the initial stimulus package to come off the Obama team's drawing boards was a classic New Deal–inspired public works jobs program: invest federal dollars in buildings, roads, rails, and bridges, though with an added Obama innovation, investment in new "green" energy technology. The stimulus focus would be on what is called "infrastructure."

While the Obama transition team's formula followed a well-trodden public investment path, it also addressed a current public problem: America's infrastructure was old and crumbling. Anyone who saw rusting and peeling bridges on their daily commute could see the evidence of the country's infrastructure neglect. Infrastructure projects translate into a lot of jobs. So, the Obama team reasoned, their proposed stimulus plan would achieve two goals at once: investing federal dollars in infrastructure improvements would enhance the country's commercial competitiveness for years to come; simultaneously, thousands of people would be put back to work immediately in skilled, decently paid construction jobs.

No one on the Obama transition team, apparently, had paused to consider gender. That is, the question that the architects of the transition team's stimulus package apparently did not ask themselves was: Who exactly would be the "people" most likely to be put back to work, to get a much-needed paycheck, if building and repairing roads and bridges were made the focus of an Obama stimulus package?

Why? Did they simply forget? Or did they imagine that jobless women could just slip back into the "kitchen"—that is, into their "natural" unpaid, dependent, domestic roles—and so did not really need paid employment? Or perhaps the president-elect's stimulus crafters were well aware of who a roads-and-bridges stimulus plan would favor, but they were more afraid of the anger of unemployed men than they were of the anger of unemployed women.

No matter which reasoning was at work inside the transition team during these crucial days of November and December 2008 and January 2009, their drafting of such a masculinized stimulus plan was odd. After all, for the preceding two years the Obama election campaign team had assiduously courted women voters, and on election day women's votes indeed had been decisive. In November 2008, within every racial group—especially among white voters—more women than men had turned out to vote; and within every racial group (even though a slim majority of white women voted for McCain), more women than men cast their ballots for Barack Obama than for his rival, Republican John McCain.[3]

If the Obama stimulus drafters had asked civil servants in the federal Bureau of Labor Statistics, they would have learned that, in 2009 America, women held a puny 2 percent of electricians' and 2 percent of carpenters' jobs.[4] Infrastructure jobs, if left narrowly defined, would translate into men's jobs.

Moreover, they would have known that the gendered U.S. economy had changed remarkably since the 1930s, that as much as they might admire Franklin Roosevelt's New Deal, they should approach that model with caution in 2008. Had they done even a beginner's gender analysis, the Obama economic team would have known that by the time the post-2008 Great Recession was strangling the economy, American women had become almost half of the country's total paid employees. The old portrait of the U.S. economy—one in which men were the family breadwinners while most women worked at home without pay, contentedly dependent on their husbands or fathers for their economic security—may have been false even in the 1930s; it was glaringly outdated when the economic crisis of 2008 hit. Furthermore, by 2008, not only were most American women in the paid labor force, but also millions of women had become the sole or chief income earners in their households.

Every economic crisis happens at a particular moment in the ongoing evolution of a country's gendered politics. This is as true of Ireland, Iceland, the United Kingdom, Greece, and Spain as it is of the United States. The 1930s Great Depression had hit the American society less than a decade after women had won the right to vote and while Jim Crow laws still trapped most African American women and men in low-paid, unskilled jobs. Although a core of women activists had remained engaged in politics after winning the right to vote in 1920, many women, having spent almost fifty years mobilizing to win that right, had partially demobilized by the time of the 1929 stock market crash. Despite the efforts of Eleanor Roosevelt and other feminists in the 1930s, pressures to enact policies favoring men as the "family breadwinners" were almost irresistible, in part because there was then no legal prohibition on the books against sex discrimination in hiring and firing. As feminist historians revealed, most of the men hired to build the New Deal's major projects such as the Triborough Bridge and the Hoover Dam were white men. And a mere 18 percent of the precious New Deal jobs went to women.[5]

By contrast, when the Great Recession hit American society eighty years later, more women than ever needed their own paid employment, even if they continued to do most of the unpaid work of caring for children and the elderly, cleaning, preparing food, and doing the laundry. At least as important, this latest economic crisis occurred after the Second Wave of the American women's movement had pushed open the creaky doors of paid employment to more women of all races— widowed, married, single, and divorced women. Activists of the 1970s, 1980s, and 1990s had successfully lobbied for legislation to make workplace sex-discrimination illegal. Enforcement remained problematic, but at least the legal structures had been put in place.

The Great Recession of 2008 also came after women's studies had been created in scores of colleges and universities across the country.

Within women's studies, feminist historians and sociologists studied women's past and present gendered patterns of paid and unpaid labor, while feminist economists developed innovative research agendas inside and outside the walls of academia. *Feminist think tank* was not an oxymoron in 2008. Some members of this generation of feminist labor analysts were explicitly interested not only in analyzing private and public economic policies but also in having an impact on those policies.[6]

Thus the Obama White House team's initial proposal for a federal job-creating stimulus package set off alarm bells among a network of feminist historians, economists, and policy experts, as well as among leaders of the now-established women's rights organizations such as the National Organization for Women, Feminist Majority, and the Institute for Women's Policy Research, each of which had its headquarters in Washington and closely monitored public policy proposals and legislative politics. Their collective warning: bridge and road repairs would translate into jobs almost exclusively for men, even if now for a more racially and ethnically diverse group of men.

Feminist historians such as Linda Gordon, Alice Kessler-Harris, and Eileen Boris warned against using the 1930s New Deal jobs programs as a simplistic model for the 2008–2009 Obama stimulus plan. Feminist economists such as Heidi Hartmann and Randy Albelda alerted policy makers to two prominent realities of the American gendered economy: first, in twenty-first-century America, despite concerted efforts to make them more diverse, many job sectors remained masculinized (e.g., construction, engineering); other job sectors remained feminized (e.g., nursing, child care, elder care, elementary education, clerical work); and second, in twenty-first-century America, jobs in the masculinized sectors paid better than jobs in the feminized sectors.

Feminist historians, economists, and policy analysts activated networks they had built up over the previous thirty years in universities, academic associations, and policy research institutes. They published joint statements online and in print calling on the Obama team to rethink its stimulus package before it was too late. They coordinated efforts between women's advocacy groups and researchers. They ensured that everyone was sending Obama's advisors the same clear message combined with focused recommendations. They used their carefully nurtured political Washington contacts to arrange meetings with midlevel officials and advisors on the transition team and, soon after, inside the new Obama administration. They provided the policy makers with evidence of how an infrastructure-only stimulus package would bypass economically distressed women—and why that mattered both economically and politically, not only to women, but also to the country as a whole.

This strategically minded feminist network of researchers and advocates went further. They offered the Obama stimulus crafters an expanded vision for how they could publicly frame a more inclusive stimulus plan: to get the American economy back on its feet for the long haul, physical infrastructure repair and innovation had to be combined with steps to strengthen the country's "human infrastructure." Efforts to construct bridges, roads, and green technology would falter if American society continued to neglect the education, care, and health of all its citizens.

Their feminist analytical message made an impact within the administration. Soon the Obama administration officials were revising their description of where in the economy the proposed federal stimulus spending package would be spent—on roads and bridges, yes, but also on health care and education. That redesigned plan—which was passed into law as the American Recovery and Reinvestment Act of 2009—dramatically increased the likelihood that many women would benefit alongside their husbands, brothers, and fathers. This mattered because in the 2009 American labor force, women were 98 percent of early-education teachers and 92 percent of registered nurses.[7]

Three years later, Heidi Hartmann reconvened members of the earlier network for another analysis and a follow-up strategy session. They had stayed attentive to what was happening to women's employment as the Great Recession turned into a wobbly recovery. The Obama stimulus infusion of funds had run out, and the Republicans in Congress had refused to renew it. What Hartmann's network had noted was that some men and women were beginning to regain jobs lost at the outset of the economic crisis. For example, Latino men were slowly regaining some construction jobs as the construction industry was beginning to resume building houses; women of all races working in the health care industry were holding on to their jobs, even if low paid, since private-sector health care was one of the few economic sectors that had continued to grow despite the recession.

Nonetheless, in this early stage of the economic recovery, the state and local government budget reductions made in 2010 and 2011 were beginning to take their gendered toll. And these job cuts (cuts made not by the federal government but by state and local officials) in the public sector were cutting disproportionately deeply into women's employment: during the first phase of the recovery, women lost two-thirds (400,000 out of 601,000) of the government jobs lost.[8] Many of those were elementary and preschool teaching jobs: "The school district in Reading, Pa.—the nation's poorest city—laid off 110 teachers last week, along with hundreds of other employees. As elementary students watched in shock, many of their favorite teachers were pulled out of an assembly one by one and given the bad news by district officials, *The Reading Eagle* reported."[9] Women and men, in other words, were experiencing each successive phase of the crisis, and the slow crawl out of the crisis, differently.

Naming themselves the Women's Scholars Forum, Heidi Hartmann and her eleven feminist colleagues spelled out in a 2011 press release their recommendations for further federal government action. They prioritized reducing unemployment and underemployment of "those most in need, including single mothers, women of color and those with less education." Their recommendations included such specific suggestions as providing federal grants to state and local governments to enable them to hire back the public workers they had recently laid off—not just police and firefighters but also teachers, social workers, and nurses. They also recommended expanding federal eligibility criteria so that more of the low-income women who needed affordable child care and wanted to go to school or take paid jobs could qualify for public child care subsidies.[10]

This network of activist feminist scholars also aimed their recovery-phase recommendations at the persistent barriers preventing women from entering jobs in the male-dominated construction, transportation, and green energy industries. These were, they pointed out, precisely the jobs that paid better salaries than jobs in feminized sectors of the economy, noting that "only 5.8% of American women work in traditionally male occupations."[11] Even when women and men had identical education levels, men in male-dominated jobs were earning more than women working in female-dominated jobs. Educational equality matters, but job segregation by gender matters too.[12] This sort of detailed comparative occupational analysis was the basis on which the Women's Scholars Forum urged that federal enforcement of equality regulations for training and hiring in construction, transportation, and green energy be more vigorous, and that child care subsidies be offered women when they entered training programs for these male-dominated occupations.[13]

There are several lessons to be drawn from this Great Recession gender tale. First, to be fair and effective, any public plan in any country intended to assist those who are jobless or who are job-insecure during an economic crisis must be—at its design stage—based at least in part on an explicit gender analysis of its most likely consequences. Lumping together all the people in a country's workforce as the "unemployed" or the "underemployed"—or even in gross categories such as "youth" or "over-50"—is not useful.

Second, men and women of different ethnic and racial groups relate to the workforce differently. So any plan for public intervention in the economy must be based on an analysis of that society's current racialized gendered job segregation. We must ask: Who holds which jobs? Who has lost which jobs? Who is getting paid what for doing each sort of job? Who has a part-time job but needs a full-time job?

Figure 9. Jenellen Gallatin, a construction worker in Minneapolis, is among the small number of women holding skilled jobs in the American construction industry in 2012. Marisa Wojcik/*The Minnesota Daily*.

Developing answers to these questions requires that, long before a crisis hits, when times are rosy, public census takers and labor department officials hone their skills at collecting gender-sensitive and race/ethnicity-sensitive data. On the day after the banks crash, one cannot simply pluck out of the air the percentage of carpenters who are Latino women or the percentage of elementary school teachers who are white men. The collection of reliable, detailed racially/ethnically nuanced gender-disaggregated labor data is not boring; it is not "merely technical." Collecting such gender-disaggregated information is a demanding, serious enterprise that provides a crucial tool for effective policy making in good times and bad.

A third lesson from this U.S. stimulus package story: women's complex realities and diverse interests are more likely to be taken into serious account during an economic recession if there is already in place a broad-based, multiracial, cross-class women's movement (embracing both organized activists and trained policy-aware gender researchers) to do one or both of two things: socialize politicians and officials into doing gender analysis on their own initiative, and/or exert external pressure on those officials when they do not.

Economic crises, just like wars, revolutions, and natural disasters, happen at particular moments in any society's gendered history. It will be much easier for policy makers (and their supporters and advisors) to "forget" to do a gender assessment of their proposed responses to an economic crisis (or an armed conflict or a new constitution or a hurricane) if there has been no mobilized women's movement created beforehand to develop the questions, collect the information, and set in motion the mechanisms for bringing pressure to bear on those policy makers. If the U.S. women's movement and, within it, feminist historians and economists had not existed in 2009, there is a good chance that the roads-and-bridges solution would have been treated as "reasonable," leaving women—and everyone who depends on women earning a decent paycheck—out in the cold.

AUSTERITY IS GENDERED

In the wake of the economic crisis, conservative parties were elected or reelected in a host of countries. Among those was Britain. In its 2010 national election, the Conservative Party replaced the Labor Party as Britain's governing party by winning a plurality, though not a clear majority, of seats in the House of Commons. The Conservatives made an alliance with the smaller Liberal Democratic Party, allowing the Conservatives' leader, David Cameron, to become the country's prime minister.

Ever since the 1980s' Thatcher era, British Conservatives had been pressing for the government to shed more of its services, to dispense with its welfare-state responsibilities, which had their roots in the 1940s. Conservatives' faith was placed, instead, in privatization—turning over the ownership and running of railroads, housing, water, energy, telecommunications, health care, even the post office, to for-profit private enterprise. With the economic crisis of 2008, and their electoral success soon after, came an opportunity for the Conservatives to push ahead even further with their government-shrinking agenda.

In the name of crisis-era belt-tightening, the Cameron government proposed dramatic cuts in public spending and thus in public services.[14] A contentious nationwide debate ensued. What Britons argued over with each other—in Parliament, in pubs, in the streets, in the press, online, and on television talk shows—was not only whether such an austerity package provided the best way out of the country's economic crisis but also over what exactly government was for.

In 2012, in the midst of this fierce national debate, women at a London-based feminist research and campaigning organization, the Fawcett Society, decided to launch a thorough gender analysis of the Conservative government's proposed austerity package. Their question was deceptively simple: Would the consequences of the government's proposed spending cuts be the same for British women as for British men?

The Fawcett Society was named after Millicent Fawcett, one of the most prominent campaigners for British women's voting rights in the late nineteenth and early twentieth centuries. Under its new leadership, the twenty-first-century Fawcett Society's staff decided to forge alliances with other groups, including feminists inside labor unions, which were doing gender analyses. They decided, too, to hone their skills in feminist budgeting and to bring to bear the same sort of gender consciousness on public financing that they and their predecessors had brought to bear on electoral politics and social-policy making.

They did their analysis at a particular moment in Britain's gendered history, when women activists had made headway in gaining influence in the once-male-dominated labor unions, and when none of the three main political parties was led by a woman, though women's influence was greatest inside the Labor Party. It was a time when women's overall proportion of the 2010-elected House of Commons was 22.3 percent (tied with Malawi at fifty-fourth in the 2012 world legislatures' ranking, trailing just behind the Philippines, Senegal, and Pakistan, though ahead of the United States, whose own percentage of women in Congress placed it seventy-third).

It was a time, as well, when Prime Minister David Cameron had appointed a mere four women, of the total twenty-three ministers, to his cabinet (down from five and six women in the previous two Labor cabinets). Of his twenty-three ministers, he appointed only one person, a woman, from the country's Black and Asian minorities. For many British observers, a class analysis of the new government's cabinet was equally telling: 69 percent of those people the prime minister chose for his cabinet were graduates of elite Oxford and Cambridge, what Britons call "Oxbridge."[15]

Still, there was another important point to note about the moment in Britain's gendered history when the Fawcett analysts decided to launch their feminist investigation of the Cameron austerity plan. Two years earlier, in 2010, while the government was still led by the Labor Party and Labor women members of Parliament wielded considerable legislative influence, Parliament had passed the Equality Act of 2010. Under this new law (its Section 149, to be precise), all public authorities were required to pay "due regard" to rolling back discrimination and to advancing equality of opportunity for men and women. The act went further: to comply with this mandated duty, all public authorities, including all government departments, would have to explicitly weigh the impact of any of their policies and practices on woman and men. This was a major legal breakthrough. Nothing like this existed in U.S. law. If it had, perhaps the Obama stimulus designers would not have come so dangerously close to having launched a masculinized stimulus plan. Section 149 of Britain's Equality Act of 2010 instituted the gender equivalent of a requirement that government bodies do environmental impact assessments early in the process of crafting any public policy or public project.

This innovative Equality Act became a strategic instrument in the hands of the Fawcett Society. They could—and did—argue that the Treasury (the powerful government ministry that oversaw all the proposed Conservative spending cuts) had been more than merely unwise or shortsighted in not assessing the specific ways in which the Cameron austerity package would affect the economic relationships between women, men, and the economy. The Treasury had also acted in violation of the law.[16]

What the Fawcett Society's 2012 report, *The Impact of Austerity on Women,* revealed was that, compared to British men's lives, British women's lives would "bear the brunt" of the Conservative government's austerity cuts in public spending.[17] The hardest hit by the Cameron austerity cuts would be Britain's single mothers and their children. This was no small matter. By 2011, 26 percent of all of the country's households with dependent children were single-parent families. And 92 percent of those single parents were women.[18]

The Fawcett Society's budget-focused researchers went about their feminist investigations methodically. First, they examined what the Conservative government's cuts would mean for women's employment. Then they examined what the cutbacks in public services would mean for women's economic opportunities and for their daily burdens, such as child care. They found that British women disproportionately held jobs in the public sector—working for national government departments, but especially working for arms of local governments: "Around 40% of women in work in the UK are employed in public sector jobs, with women accounting for 64% of the public sector workforce overall," the Fawcett Society researchers discovered.[19] Looking deeper, they found that women constituted 75 percent of all local government workers.[20]

One of the reasons that British feminists paid particular attention to women's losses in public-sector employment, in addition to the sheer number of women affected, was that, thanks to the women's movement's successful campaigning since the 1970s, public-sector jobs had become among the fairest jobs in Britain. By 2008, those officials who hired and promoted people for public-sector jobs were far more likely than their private-sector counterparts to be required to follow antidiscrimination procedures. Those same legal requirements called for a greater number of local public officials than private employers to follow antidiscrimination procedures in offering job training opportunities and in providing child care, maternity leave, and pensions.[21]

In the British system, the central government is the chief funder of local governments. So, taken together, these findings meant that every central-government cut in spending that caused local governments to cut their own payrolls would redound more heavily on women than on men. Moreover, 77 percent of all employees working for the country's famed National Health Service are women—doctors, nurses, nurses aides, medical social workers, cleaners, administrators.[22] Thus every step taken by the Conservative-led government to trim or privatize the National Health Service in ways that reduced the latter's personnel would undermine women's job security more than it would men's.

Staying focused on the gendering of jobs and of austerity measures, the Fawcett investigators turned their feminist searchlight on the Cameron government's own stimulus package. This was important, since the Conservatives were arguing that, although people would be losing jobs owing to cuts in public spending, the new jobs created via the government's stimulus plan would significantly compensate for those losses. The Fawcett researchers examined the parallel study then being done by a coalition of British analysts called the Women's Budget Group. Their finding: the Cameron government's National Infrastructure Plan "will be largely spent on physical infrastructure," and thus "women are unlikely to benefit from any new opportunities created, unless specific measures are taken to address under-representation of women in the male-dominated Science, Engineering and Technology (SET) sectors." At that time a mere 5.3 percent of British working-women were in these sectors, as compared with 31.3 percent of all British working men.[23]

Either no one inside the Conservative or Liberal Democratic policy circles had paid attention to the gender rethinking that the Obama administration had done two years earlier, or they had noticed but had decided that such a rethinking was not germane to their own British political economic agenda.

Next, going beyond jobs, the Fawcett analysts investigated what cuts in the public services themselves would mean for women and men. A feminist analysis of any labor market offers a realistic investigation of the mundane burdens that keep women out of decently paid work: lack of affordable child care, carrying the extra responsibilities of elder care, being constrained by a partner's domestic violence, and lack of affordable, reliable public transport. It follows that any austerity measures that forced local governments to reduce public services that help women cope with these burdens—child care centers, elder care centers, domestic violence hotlines and shelters, legal aid services, job training programs, public buses—are measures that would further roll back women's ability to take advantage of paid job opportunities. In so doing, these public service cuts would further widen the economic inequalities between men and women.

Fawcett researchers complemented their statistical analysis with interviews in order to more fully understand the mundane yet complex realities shaping Britain's gendered job market during the economic recession. One woman they interviewed explained how the ending of a local government-funded child care program, Sure Start, would affect her access to full-time paid work:

> I cried when I found out that the fantastic Sure Start nursery that my then 2 year old daughter, Eva, goes to had been earmarked for closure by the Camden Council [one of London's local metropolitan governments]. I was pregnant again and had been comforting myself that at least when it came to returning to my full-time job after maternity leave the one thing I wouldn't have to worry about was childcare, as the certainty was taken away.... We waged a vigorous campaign to save the Center ... but the best we could do was secure an understanding from the Council to seek a community provider.... At best it feels like a hollow victory.[24]

Simultaneously, while they were conducting their own economic analyses of the government's austerity actions, these British feminist-informed researchers sought to spread the skills they had been developing so that women with all levels of education living in Britain's diverse communities could conduct their own austerity studies and use their findings to hold their own local officials and national members of Parliament accountable. One such tool was created and distributed by the Trades Union Congress (TUC), the country's largest labor union federation. Titled the *TUC Women and the Cuts Toolkit,* it offered hands-on, down-to-earth information showing women in economically hard-hit towns such as Coventry, Sheffield, and Leeds how they could do their own investigations of local economic conditions and current policies toward housing, employment, legal aid, violence against women, and transportation—and then use those findings to pressure their own public representatives.[25]

Feminists working as journalists in the British media made use of the information and analyses being developed by feminist organizations to publicly challenge what they saw as the patriarchal assumptions fueling the government's austerity policy-making. As in the United States, so too in Britain: a crisis-era public discourse that painted women and their paid and unpaid labor as trivial, wasteful, or even unnatural could provide a potent rationale for not taking women's economic realities seriously—a rationale for either ignoring women's economic plight or actually punishing women for the lives they were allegedly living. As longtime feminist journalist Polly Toynbee noted in her International Women's Day column on March 8, 2012, each of the myriad cuts that the Conservative/Liberal Democratic government instituted was based on an implicit model of the allegedly natural household: "Intentionally or not, a male breadwinner with a dependent woman carer at home is the model on which the cuts are crafted, removing the supports to independence and sending women home."[26]

No group of British women was more likely to be denigrated or dismissed in the Conservative government's austerity discourse than single mothers. It would be far easier to cut public spending on parental income subsidies, child care, housing, and training if one believed and encouraged voters to believe—without checking one's facts—that most single parents were irresponsible teenage girls, were members of ethnic and racial minorities, were shunning heterosexual marriage, and were deliberately trying to get by without entering the paid workforce.

Tanya Gold, another British, feminist-informed journalist, sought to puncture holes in this public discourse by publishing an article revealing the facts about Britain's single mothers, drawing on the research of the established independent single-parent advocacy organization Gingerbread. She noted that, contrary to what she heard as the ruling Conservative Party discourse, the percentage of British households that were headed by single parents had not increased in recent years. The jump actually had occurred decades earlier, in the late 1960s, the 1970s, and the 1980s, as marriage no longer so fully defined a woman's social status, as divorce became more feasible, and as women gained more access to paid work. Furthermore, Gold pointed out to her readers, a mere 3 percent of British single mothers were teenagers, "a number to make misogynists gawp." The median age of single mothers in fact was thirty-eight. Furthermore, a majority—55 percent—of British single mothers had had their children during a time when they had been married, and only since then had become widowed, divorced, or separated. Overwhelmingly, Tanya Gold informed her readers, British single parents (87 percent of them) were white. And a majority—57 percent—were doing paid work, though their jobs were among the lowest paid and most insecure.[27]

Across the Irish Sea, feminists in Ireland were conducting their own careful feminist analyses of what the Great Recession meant for diverse Irish women. They were in regular communication with British feminists and had read the Fawcett Society's austerity reports. In addition, Irish activist-scholars such as Ailbhe Smyth had for decades been working to improve the conditions of the country's poorest women, as well as its disabled women, lesbians, single mothers, and new immigrant women. So when Ireland's own economic bubble burst, they were ready with the tools and concepts to make visible the gendered dynamics of their country's crash. Irish feminists noted that women were rare in the highest ranks of the country's banks, and that there was only one woman on the twelve-member board of Ireland's Central Bank. Moreover, in the wake of the crash, the male-dominated Irish government appointed no women to the committee to investigate the Irish banking industry.[28]

Irish feminists also did gender analyses of the postcrash economy, finding that Ireland's young women had even higher rates of unemployment (28 percent) than did young men (23 percent), that women of all ages were being hit by unemployment at higher rates than men, and that the wage gap between the women and men who were fortunate enough to have full-time jobs was 15 percent. Having a feminist economic curiosity, the researchers went beyond the narrow definition of *economy* and investigated what the recession meant for women's relationships with their partners and their extended households. They tracked the consequences for Irish women who slid into poverty, as well as the insecurity of living in a country lacking reproductive rights. The lack of access to contraception and safe abortions mattered in prosperous times, those years when the media started calling Ireland the "Emerald Tiger." But that lack matters all the more when jobs are lost and public services are cut. Domestic violence has an economy too. For example, activist women supporting the city of Donegal's shelters and hotlines noted that in the months between the end of 2008 and early 2011, as the whole Irish economy teetered, there had been a 10 percent increase in the town's helpline calls and a 22 percent increase in women reporting domestic violence to the police.[29]

Feminist economic research, feminist budgetary analysis, feminist media analysis, feminist labor activism, feminist public services activism—this was the quintet of efforts and skills that British and Irish women brought to bear on the post-2008 economic crisis. Together, these efforts and the use of these skills were aimed not only at challenging ruling parties' rationales for their austerity choices but also at holding elected representatives publicly accountable for the consequences of their patriarchal responses to the recession. Furthermore, together these feminist investigations and activism were designed to empower women and their male allies, to provide them with the tools and the information they needed to make their own realistic sense of their country's gendered political economy and to act on that realistic assessment. This was feminism at its most serious.

WHAT'S MISOGYNY GOT TO DO WITH IT?

The London journalist Tanya Gold wrote that hearing that a mere 3 percent of Britain's single mothers were teenagers would "make misogynists gawp." She chose her words carefully. She did not say *sexists*. She did not say *patriarchs*. She said *misogynists*. Why? When is misogyny at work? What is there about an economic crisis that emboldens misogynists?

Let's clarify some important terms. *Patriarchy* is any system of beliefs, relationships, and practices (all three reinforcing each other) that privileges masculinity—and most, though not all, men—and that simultaneously subordinates anything and anyone considered feminine, even (especially?) when men place a select group of women on a "pedestal." Banks can be patriarchal. So can political parties. Families, universities, sports teams, and social movements can become patriarchal. So too can entire societies. Any group or country that has been patriarchal can be made, step by conscious step, less patriarchal.

Sexism is the package of beliefs and values that rationalizes patriarchy, that makes patriarchy seem right or natural or both. Sexist ideas can be partial or full-blown. A person with full-blown sexist ideas believes (1) that men and women are fundamentally different, (2) that women and men should play different roles in a society (or in a social movement or in an organization), (3) that what men do is more valuable and more skilled than what women do, and, crucially, (4) that manly men are equipped and obligated to guide, supervise, protect, and control women. No one is born holding sexist beliefs. Sexism has to be learned. Therefore, it can be unlearned.

Misogyny is an attitude of fear and contempt toward women and femininity. A lot of sexist ideas and behaviors stop short of misogyny. When misogyny infuses patriarchy, the system becomes infected with virulence and hatred toward the feminine.

The misogynist holds independent women in contempt, a contempt that often masks deep anxiety. Misogyny can camouflage a masculinized fear of losing control over women, especially control over women's sexuality. The misogynist (male or female) disparages the woman who sees no need to rely on masculine protection, supervision, or guidance. She is castigated as "unnatural"; she is "fallen"; her very existence is an insult; she is unworthy of any respect or of rights; she "gets what's coming to her." Not surprisingly, then, misogynists often brand the independent woman a "whore" and a "lesbian" in the same breath.

To be the object of sexism is impoverishing and marginalizing. To be the target of misogyny is dangerous. Thus the policy-making misogynist who "gawps" at the revelation that, in fact, few British single mothers are teenagers is startled to learn that a cherished basis for his unabashed contempt—the allegedly promiscuous, out-of-control teenage mother—has been snatched away.

Since the 1990s, many of us have learned that misogyny—beyond mere garden-variety sexism—has fueled such gross abuses of girls and women as honor killings, international sex trafficking, physical exploitation of migrant domestic workers, and systematic wartime rapes. We have come to see that tribal chiefs in remote Central Asian villages, members of European crime syndicates, and AK-47-wielding militiamen may be not simply sexists but misogynists. We also have come to recognize that certain outrageously sexist right-wing radio-talk-show hosts in the peacetime affluent world are misogynists. We acknowledge that they have taken their sexism into the zone of misogyny insofar as they infuse their social commentaries with virulent contempt for women as progressive politicians, women as competitive athletes, and women as reproductive rights advocates. They use their access to publicly licensed airwaves to foster hatred among their listeners.

Their misogynist charges are framed as humor. Misogyny, however, is never funny.[30]

What we perhaps have not yet fully comprehended is that misogyny can infect the outlooks and actions of "respectable" civilian policy-makers. For instance, democratically elected members of national and state legislatures can become misogynists. That possibility might be harder to take seriously because these seemingly respectable misogynists do not seem as over-the-top, as openly driven by anger at women as, say, a militiaman engaged in a sexual assault or a bombastic blogger or radio commentator. Sometimes, in fact, in their behavior toward some chosen women, these practitioners of misogyny may appear to be models of politeness, even gallantry. They hoist a very particular, narrow model of femininity up onto a pedestal precisely so they can disparage all other forms of femininity. That is, it is possible that *gallant misogynist* is not an oxymoron.

In the later phase of the recent U.S. economic crisis, when recovery struggled to take hold and partisan passions were fired by upcoming national electoral rivalries, feminists began to talk about the "war on women." Women's advocacy groups such as Feminist Majority, the National Organization for Women, EMILY's List, NARAL (National Abortion and Reproductive Rights Action League), Planned Parenthood, SisterSong (the African American women's reproductive rights organization), and the recently created Women Occupying Wall Street, as well as mixed-gender groups such as MoveOn.org and the American Civil Liberties Union, developed and propagated the phrase "war on women."[31]

This was in early 2012, when the Republican primary contests in state after state included a number of especially conservative candidates vying with each other for their party's presidential nomination. Among them, the strongest and most outspoken on women's issues was Pennsylvania's former senator Rick Santorum. Santorum's campaign ultimately failed to halt Mitt Romney's electoral momentum, but over the months of the primary elections his call for women to return to "traditional," narrowly circumscribed familial roles within heterosexual households elicited considerable support among mainly white voters who identified themselves to pollsters as supporters of the pro-small-government Tea Party movement. Santorum, a Catholic, garnered support not only among Catholics but also among American voters who described themselves as Evangelical Protestant Christians. Moreover, his votes came not only from conservative white men but also from conservative white women. According to a March 2012 *New York Times*/CBS public opinion poll, 73 percent of Republican-identified female voters said that Rick Santorum "understood the needs and problems of people like them."[32] As one Louisiana white woman voter explained to a journalist on the eve of her state's Republican primary, "I can tell you why he does well with me, because he's strong on family values and he's very religious.... I think this country needs to have a renewal of its moral compass, and this is the man to do it."[33]

The women's rights and women's health advocates who coined the phrase *war on women* sought to highlight what they saw as the links between myriad Republican-promoted legislative efforts at both state and federal levels to limit women's rights. In particular, these women's rights and women's health advocates focused on the connections between attempts to (1) cut public spending on women's health care, (2) defund women's health clinics, especially those run by Planned Parenthood, (3) obstruct women's individual opportunities to bring law suits against employers for sex discrimination (represented in 2012 by the proposed Paycheck Fairness Act), (4) create more barriers to women's access to legal abortions, (5) roll back sex education programs in schools, and finally, (6) dilute laws intended to protect women from domestic violence (stipulations in the reauthorization of the Violence Against Women Act of 1994). Women's advocates argued that these attempts were not merely discrete legislative processes occurring in Washington and in a dozen different states. Instead, they contended, these seemingly disparate efforts were all of a piece. That is, they should be understood as a comprehensive, coordinated campaign by conservative activists, their major donors (such as the billionaire brothers Charles and David Koch), and their Republican state and federal legislative allies to restrict women's reproductive autonomy and women's economic independence.

And, these activists further asserted, those two things—women's reproductive autonomy and women's economic independence—were integrally related. This, in fact, was an understanding that gender conservatives and feminists shared: that a woman's economic independence and her physical health, security, and autonomy are mutually interdependent: curtail one, and you curtail the likelihood of the other. Men and women who see patriarchal relationships as imperative for social stability and moral rectitude see such curtailments as a societal and a personal good. Feminists see such curtailments as jeopardizing women's safety, security, integrity, and citizenship and as thereby subverting democracy itself.

Feminists went further. They asserted that, because the backers of these disparate, though interconnected, policy proposals at both the federal and state levels appeared to be motivated by such an intense, collective misogynist determination to push America's allegedly wayward women back into the status of patriarchal dependents, it was appropriate to see them as fomenters of a war.

Since the late twentieth century, "war" has become a favored metaphor in American public discourse: there has been the war on poverty, the war on drugs, and most recently, the war on terror. The image of war conjures up not only the threat of physical assault but also an exceptional degree of coordinated mobilization, together with the image of a common enemy. In a society such as contemporary America, where militarized values and militarized imagery have proved so potent in garnering popular approval, launching a war can attract wide public support. In these earlier American policy-driven "wars," it was the wagers of the war—the antidrug campaigners, the antipoverty activists, the antiterrorism strategists—who embraced the concept of war. If they could persuade their fellow Americans that they were determined to wage a war against drugs, poverty, or terror, they stood a good chance of convincing the public that they were *serious*. After all, war is always serious business.

By contrast, in the case of this recent Great Recession–era war on women, it was the opponents who insisted on calling it a war. Women's advocates were not conjuring up war to mobilize for a worthy common cause. They were conjuring up war to point out that this was a dangerous, coordinated assault. The assaulting enemies, they warned, were their fellow citizens, misogynist American conservatives.

For their part, the wagers of the apparently coordinated campaign to roll back women's independence vehemently denied that they were waging a war. Instead, the backers of new restrictions on contraception availability and on abortion eligibility, of cuts in health care spending, of bans on sex education, of efforts to weaken laws enabling women workers to bring sex discrimination suits, and of efforts to dilute domestic violence enforcement argued that these should be seen by the public as separate legislative processes, each introduced to address what its drafters saw as a discrete problem. That is, the backers of these measures contended that there was no war; there was simply good policy making. Therefore, these conservative lawmakers contended, each proposal, whether introduced in the Alabama, Virginia, Michigan, or Texas legislature, or in the national House of Representatives, deserved to be judged on its own merits. An underlying misogyny, they insisted, had nothing to do with it.[34]

To what extent was this spate of legislative efforts to limit American women's autonomy caused by the Great Recession? The "war on women" discourse began during the early phase of the still-uncertain economic recovery. But by itself, simultaneity is not proof of cause. After all, radio commentator Rush Limbaugh was disparaging women's rights advocates on air as "femi-nazis" well before the banking crash of 2008. Limbaugh might have had an especially powerful microphone, but he was not alone during the years of the banking bubble in enjoying a license to hurl crudely misogynist epithets at outspoken women such as Jane Fonda, Gloria Steinem, Alice Walker, Nancy Pelosi, and Hilary

Clinton. Likewise, conservative antiabortion campaigners had been organizing across the country for the preceding three decades. *Roe v. Wade* was imperiled almost from the day in 1973 when, by a seven-to-two majority, the Supreme Court justices accorded legal protection to women's right to abortion. So too, male U.S. military commanders had not waited until the banking bubble burst to sweep under the Pentagon's bureaucratic rug the thousands of rapes committed by U.S. military men against U.S. military women, as if women soldiers' safety did not matter. Similarly, trying to get lawmakers, police, and judges to take domestic violence seriously certainly was not a new challenge in 2008. And the gender pay gap between American men and women had been documented since the 1970s.

So what was new? What effect did the Great Recession have on the character of sexism in America?

Two changes may have pushed American sexism closer to misogyny. First, the economic crisis heightened many people's sense of insecurity. Many turned anew to the family, especially to the religiously sanctioned family, as their shelter of last resort when the economy collapsed and the government seemed ineffectual. Independent women, long held to flaunt the codes of the conventional family, now could appear even more threatening. Amid housing foreclosures and failing banks, the portrayals of sexually and economically autonomous women—and those who advocated on their behalf—as not only violators of societal norms but also immediate threats to one's own well-being could begin to sound reasonable. Just as militarizing notions of the stranger can turn vague discomfort into outright hatred, so wielding misogynist notions of the unconventional woman can convert anxiety into assault.

Second, the Great Recession welded sexual politics ever more tightly to job politics. Neither job discrimination nor efforts to restrict women's sexual autonomy started in 2008. But escalating unemployment and many people's need to take refuge in a conventionally organized family came together in a way that made women's economic autonomy and women's physical integrity appear to many Americans more symbiotic than ever—not only in the eyes of feminists but also in the eyes of antifeminists. The intense insecurities of the time seemed to enable campaigners to infuse opposition to these mutually dependent gendered rights with hatred.

Misogyny did not have its origins in the economic crisis. But widespread economic anxiety became misogyny's enabler.

CHAPTER SIX

Militarism, Patriarchy, and Peace Movements

In Conversation with Cynthia Cockburn

What follows is a conversation between Cynthia Cockburn and me initiated by Marsha Henry and Paul Kirby, coeditors of a 2012 special issue of the *International Feminist Journal of Politics*, which was devoted to new research on the workings of masculinities during and after armed conflicts. Cynthia is a British feminist scholar-activist known internationally for her investigations of feminists involved in activism against militarism in a score of countries, including Colombia, India, Israel, Japan, Cyprus, and the former Yugoslavia. Among her best-known books are *Brothers, The Space Between Us, From Where We Stand,* and most recently, *Antimilitarism.*[1]

Cynthia is on the faculty of the University of East London. She is a skilled photographer and a committed member of the feminist peace group London Women in Black. Over the years, Cynthia and I have shared hunches and puzzles, as well as many mutual friends. This conversation between us occurred via email between London and Boston over the course of two months, from September to November 2011.

> CYNTHIA E.: I was trying to think when you and I first met. Was it in London? In the early 1990s? But I read you long before I met you. Your book *Brothers,* which came out in 1983, tracked the malleable sustainability of workplace male privilege, observed while you

were part of a community printing press. It's still one of my all-time favorite feminist books! So what led you from charting the genderings of London printers to charting the genderings of militarism?

CYNTHIA C.: It was 1989 when *Bananas, Beaches, and Bases* came over my horizon like a shining star. In that book you lit up the presence of women on the international stage, pushing the fellows back into the shadows a bit. You were someone who helped a lot of women here think more internationally. And for me, at that moment, looking beyond Britain meant looking to continental Europe. From 1985 to 1995 we had a lively European Forum of Socialist Feminists. And I think it was the shock of the outbreak of war in the 1990s in Yugoslavia (war again in *Europe?*) that pulled me out of a long preoccupation with workplaces and trade unions and drew me to war zones where the relation of men to women was not just disadvantaging but often lethal.

CYNTHIA E.: For me, the feminist turning point came after I'd spent seven years digging into the ways that government elites in so many countries (Russia, Iraq, Syria, the United States, Britain and former British colonies, Canada, Malaysia ...) worked hard to manipulate race and ethnicity to build the sorts of militaries and police forces they imagined they could trust. Then, belatedly, in the early 1980s, I was pushed by students to realize that I'd been talking only about men. I'd spent all these years thinking about men of different races and ethnicities as soldiers and as elites without being at all curious about women—or even about men as men! It was one of those moments that was acutely embarrassing and, simultaneously, so energizing.

CYNTHIA C.: 1995 was a turning point for me. By 1995, I'd been researching and writing for fifteen years about men and their continuing grip on advantage in jobs and organizations. But always I'd had in mind a "constituency" who could use my research on men, a constituency of women, women trying to get their fair share of technological and organizational skills and opportunities. In the fifteen years since that turning point, like you, I've been listening carefully to women talking about war in a load of different countries. And what I've learned is that when they're puzzling over the causes of war, asking themselves what keeps war on the boil, what "breaches the peace," one factor they notice is the affinity of dominant and popular forms of masculinity to aggression, to rivalry and fighting.

CYNTHIA E.: Yes, your terrific books have revealed women activists to be such sharp analysts of masculinized militarism. Activists create theory! Women I've talked with—in Chile, Turkey, South Korea, Japan, the former Yugoslavia—also have been quick, I've found, to see how particular cultures of masculinity are causally connected to domestic violence, the prostitution industry, and militarism. That is not a connection that many women, even activists, have made here in the United States. Do you find that, too—that women who've directly experienced the most explicit forms of militarism have crafted this analytical breakthrough— tracing the causal connections between militarism and domestic violence—and offered it to the rest of us? It's been a breakthrough that could be crucial for many feminists in Europe and North America, couldn't it?

CYNTHIA C.: Absolutely. In England women tend to see domestic violence as one problem and war violence as a different one. Women's Aid deals with the first, Women in Black addresses the other. But when I was in Okinawa, I met activist women who are living right alongside the razor wire of the U.S. military bases. They see the armored vehicles trundling about their "peace-time" streets, soldiers drinking in the red light districts, and they find themselves campaigning *both* to get the bases off their islands *and* for an end to exploitation and abuse of women. The women they support are survivors of military prostitution and soldier rape *and also* "ordinary" domestic violence and "ordinary" trafficking. It's these Okinawan feminist activists who've brought home to me a useful way of seeing violence, not just as separate instances but as linked in a "continuum." They're saying the instances are somehow causally connected across different moments (peace—war—postwar), across different places (home—street—battlefield) and across different types of violence (sexual violence—gang fights—bombing raids). So, to answer your question, yes, it seems to me that a valuable new insight into violence shows up from a feminist standpoint in or close to war. And ultimately what their thinking adds up to is a fresh analysis of war—yes, capitalism and nationalism cause war, but the patriarchal system of male dominance too gives rise to war-thinking, the war-habit. In particular, it's the combative, controlling form of masculinity it needs and favors.

CYNTHIA E.: Over the last thirty years, feminists in so many countries have arrived at three important analytical conclusions. First, that governments cannot militarize their policies and operations without making most women complicit. So feminists in countries as different as Chile and Japan have been shining a bright light on the pressures placed on women, pushing them, luring them to lend their emotional and physical labor to militarization. That is, you cannot tackle war waging, many feminists have found, unless you take seriously the efforts to militarize women—and what causes some women to resist those formidable pressures and lures.

Second, I think, feminists have uncovered mounting evidence that wars (and preparations for wars) rely on very particular forms of masculinity—not merely one but several forms—the militarized masculinity of the weapons engineer, of the civilian national security "expert," of the chauvinistic politician, of fathers urging sons to enlist, and of weapons-wielding combatants themselves. So lumping together all sorts of militarized masculinities isn't very helpful when you're trying to loosen the grip of militarism on any society.

Third—and you've emphasized this in your own recent writings—grappling with the ways women are militarized and the ways men are militarized has to be done together. That means monitoring and challenging *patriarchy*. Patriarchy is the system that links militarized femininities to militarized masculinities in a way that sustains the domination of certain brands of masculinity while keeping women in their assigned places. Racism fuels militarism; so does unrestrained capitalism; so does state authoritarianism. Many prominent critics of militarism seem quite comfortable with analyzing these three militarizing dynamics. But they shrink from examining the workings of patriarchy, don't they? Feminists in dozens of countries, however, have been warning us: if we ignore the workings of patriarchy, militarization will rumble destructively on for generations.

CYNTHIA C.: So what do we do with this feminist understanding of war? How do we operationalize it in working for peace?

CYNTHIA E.: Hmmmm. I think taking these activist feminists' insights seriously means we can't lazily imagine that, in the name of urgently resisting warmongering or militarized oppression, we can allow masculinized privilege to go unscrutinized inside peace or prodemocracy movements. Feminists' approach—"Let's engage in internal feminist scrutiny *now, not later*"—certainly can strain a social movement. And has! I remember a young feminist conscientious objector, Idan Halili, standing on stage in a small underground theater in Tel Aviv, telling us that one of the lessons she'd taken away from reading Virginia Woolf's *Three Guineas* was that turning those conscientious objectors (mostly young men, and a few women) willing to go to jail into heroes of the antimilitarism movement could unwittingly perpetuate exactly the sort of masculinized privilege that nurtures militarism. Many of us there that night, of course, were on the verge of turning *her* into a hero because she was willing to do the risky macho thing, go to jail! So feminist analysts make women visible in ways that make men's assumptions about their own manliness visible. That, as you and I have learned, can make a lot of people nervous.

CYNTHIA C.: In the last three or four years, traveling to different countries to do research on antimilitarism, I've met a lot of feminist antiwar activists that have walked away from mixed organizations in order to set up autonomous women's groups where they can develop their own analysis and methods. But I've also met a lot who feel it's important to hang on into the mainstream organizations, in order to work *with* men and convince them of the significance of a feminist analysis of war—which after all is proposing something of vital concern to men as well as women. They're saying if masculinity is part of the problem, men need to be part of the solution. That's a tough thing to do. Because when they try to get that notion, the idea that "gender has something to do with it," accepted in their organization's thinking, they simply aren't heard. They tell me, "mention gender and men take a step backwards." Over and again, they say, "the men just don't get it." And even if the odd man here and there does acknowledge that gender is an issue, and that men in the movement need to change in response to the feminist critique, he thinks it means *anybody* but him personally.

CYNTHIA E.: You're right, we're at a tricky point right now. Patriarchy is slippery. As you showed back there at the London printers, patriarchy is malleable. It's constantly being updated. Patriarchy doesn't always look like gun-wielding contractors or brass-bedecked generals or Murdoch's media warmongers. To be sustained, patriarchy needs men in peace movements who think they know best, men on peacekeeping missions who assume that it's rival men who are the people most needed at the peace-negotiating table; patriarchy relies on even those men in academia

Figure 10. Among the feminist antimilitarist activists
interviewed by Cynthia Cockburn were Women in Black
in Bangalore, India, campaigning here against communal-
ist violence, 2004. Courtesy Cynthia Cockburn.

who imagine they can study masculinity without paying serious
attention to women and the politics of femininities.

CYNTHIA C.: There's something I notice and wonder about. It's the
fact that, on the left, generally speaking, there's an acute awareness of racism and the need to counter it, actively, openly. And I

mean on the *white* left. People don't let being phenotypically white, or ethnically of the dominant group, stop them being actively, committedly antiracist. Indeed, there's real shame felt in being otherwise. Likewise, some of the people most engaged in the left, for whom "class" exploitation is an analysis they deploy, a language they speak, that defines a struggle they commit to, are in fact middle class, property-owning people. But they don't let that stand in the way of their working class activism. Why is it, then, that when it comes to sex/gender, being a man is so very often sufficient to inhibit antipatriarchal thinking and profeminist activism?

CYNTHIA E.: My hunch—and this comes from listening to feminist antimilitarist activists in places like Turkey, South Korea, Sweden, and the United States—is that many men are afraid. They perform their fear with dismissive bluff. But I think it's fear at work. They are afraid that if they take feminist ideas about patriarchy seriously they'll be considered "soft" by those men they most want to take them seriously. A lot of men have learned to be frightened of being "feminized" in the eyes of other men. Perhaps many men in antiwar movements feel as though it already takes "guts" in a patriarchal society, as a man, to challenge militaristic beliefs and values, since accepting those is a common measure of being a "real man." So to go the next step, to actually challenge masculinized privilege itself, may appear a risk they think they can't afford to take. The patriarchal "gaze" of men toward other men can be a potent form of policing. Have you found this?

CYNTHIA C.: When women are facing up to something scary and troubling about our gendered lives, we often collectivize it, don't we? We listen to each other in consciousness-raising groups, we form organizations—and we've built a women's movement addressing very personal things (and politicizing them). Men don't seem to reach out to each other so readily in these ways. I mean, yes, they bond around *doing* and *achieving*, but masculine codes seem to keep them from bonding around the exploration of painful feelings and troubling behaviors. There's one campaign I know of, the White Ribbon Campaign, which started in Canada—a group of men committed to discussing, acting on and ending male violence against women. There's a branch in England. It's great—and so rare to find men talking to each other like this about gender issues and not only just talking but going out and campaigning together, openly supporting women activists. But do you know of any groups of men in the antimilitarist, antiwar and peace movements who get together to analyze and resist the deformation of manhood by militarization? That would be so helpful. They could be great partners of the feminist antimilitarist movement. I've learned from your writing how much the state involves women in militarization, and how we have to resist that. And it's true. But don't you think that for war to end, actually, *men* have to become self-aware and refuse for themselves, as men and with other men, the violence that's expected of them, the association of masculinity with militarism?

CYNTHIA E.: I've seen Turkish men active in the small but important conscientious objectors movement there start to listen seriously to Turkish feminists. And I understand that there is a growing number of South Korean antimilitarist men who are taking on board the ideas developed by Korean feminists. But here's my worry: so long as any male activists are operating within a larger patriarchal social system (call it the EU or Congo or the United States or India), their steps to think and organize on their own— even if for a seeming antisexism goal—can garner privilege for them as men. They give a nod to feminists, but take on the cloak of "the really serious thinkers," of "the most sophisticated strategists." So the challenge, I think, is for men who are genuinely critical of militarism to become personally and collectively reflective about masculine privilege *without* converting their newfound awareness into yet another reason for men to take the activist or the intellectual lead!

CYNTHIA C.: Perhaps it goes back to the duality that's at the root of feminism. We've always been talking about *difference,* a different world, *and* at the same time about *equality* in the actual world. So in the case of militarism we're talking about getting a feminist analysis of violence and war—a "different" perception—understood and accepted in the peace movements. And at the same time we have an "equality" goal, equality between women and men in those movements. A mutually understood analysis and a truly respectful partnership. To get both—that would be so good!

CHAPTER SEVEN

Failing to Secure the Peace

Patriarchal Assumptions and Their Consequences for
UN Operations in Haiti

A Conversation with Nadine Puechguirbal

This public conversation took place on October 26, 2004, during the U.S. war in Iraq and a major UN peacekeeping and humanitarian aid operation in Haiti. The event was organized and hosted by the Consortium on Gender, Security and Human Rights, directed by Carol Cohn. Today, the Consortium is located at the University of Massachusetts Boston. Carol Cohn herself is a widely published feminist scholar in the field of gender and international politics. The venue for the 2004 conversation was the Fletcher School of Law and Diplomacy at Tufts University on the outskirts of Boston. Most of the members of the audience that evening were midcareer women enrolled in graduate programs in preparation for work in international organizations. They had been lobbying the university to infuse the graduate program with more gender analysis.

Nadine Puechguirbal, a French feminist with a PhD in political science from the Sorbonne, has had exceptionally rich hands-on experience in conflict and postconflict societies, working with both the United Nations and the International Committee of the Red Cross. She has served as a gender advisor and a gender analyst in Chad, Congo, Somalia, Rwanda, and the former Yugoslavia. When this conversation initially took place, she was serving as Senior Gender Adviser for the UN Stabilization Mission in Haiti.

Among Nadine's publications are "Peacekeeping, Peacebuilding and Post-conflict Reconstruction," a chapter in *Gender Matters in Global Politics,* edited by Laura Shepherd, and "Discourses on Gender, Patriarchy and Resolution 1325," in the journal *International Peacekeeping* (2010).

In 2012, at the time when Nadine wrote the epilogue that appears at the end of this chapter, she was serving at the UN's New York headquarters as Senior Gender Adviser in the UN's Department of Peacekeeping Operations. None of the opinions she expresses here are official positions of that department.

NADINE PUECHGUIRBAL: First of all, before we start, I would like to say that it's a privilege for me to participate in such an event together with Cynthia Enloe, because her work has really influenced my own work in the field. So, thank you.

What I am going to be talking about is what happens when we don't integrate gender in peacekeeping. Or what happens when we integrate it wrongly, or when we think we've integrated it—like a lot of people in my mission think they're gender sensitive—but we really haven't. I'm going to just use a few concrete examples, and then we'll see at the end if we have more time for questions.

I would like to start by talking about the situation in Haiti. We had a hurricane a few months ago, and one city, the city of Gonaïves, was really badly damaged following the flooding. So the UN community, the international community—everybody— was mobilized to go to Gonaïves and organize the humanitarian assistance. I found it really interesting to realize how gender insensitive the humanitarian community was. You know, I used to work for the Red Cross ten years ago before going to work for the UN. It was amazing to realize that nothing has really changed in the humanitarian mentality. So let me give you a few examples.

I did a few trips to Gonaïves with a Haitian women's organization. I accompanied the [Haitian] Minister for the Status of Women, and I did my own trip to just find out for myself what was going on there. We did an assessment to measure the impact of the flooding on women and girls. You have to know that at the very beginning, when the first trucks with food were trying to reach the distribution point, they were just completely looted by strong young men. And of course, the women who were in charge of families and communities, and really needed the relief items, never got anything.

So the humanitarian community thought, "Oh, we have a problem." They started a distribution system through the women. "We are going to have women as the direct beneficiaries of our assistance." Fair enough. So they organized the distribution points. They made sure that the population was informed about this new system. They asked the women and the young girls to line up and receive the rations.

But then if we think about the security of those women and girls—I think this was never considered, never even thought about, and I'll tell you why. In the organizing committee, there was not a single woman. It was the local community, together with the international community, that thought, "We're going to have a bunch of men who are going to decide for the women." It was the same as during peace processes when men want to represent women. So of course, the distribution points were established according to some rules that were not really what women wanted; and the distribution points were sometimes very far away from the home. The same for the water points: they were far away from home. But it didn't really matter to the humanitarian community—they were really happy with the new plan.

Now, thinking about the security aspect—nobody had thought that those women might be endangering their lives when they leave their homes and go to fetch the water or receive

Figure 11. In the aftermath of tropical storm Jeanne, Haitian women line up in the sun at a UN distribution point in Gonaïves to receive water and food, September 2004. UN Photo/Sophia Paris.

the food. Security was organized around the distribution points by the peacekeepers. So I was told, "You don't need to worry— the security will be organized by the peacekeepers, and the women will be safe." Okay, so the women will be safe while they're at the distribution point, but nobody really cared about what happened when they left the distribution point. I was told, "We can't do anything, because we don't have the human resources, we don't have the equipment, and we don't have enough peacekeepers. So the women just have to organize themselves within their own communities."

We started to receive reports of sexual violence against women at the very same time. No wonder, right? But that's not the end of the story. The other problem we had is that, when I visited the distribution point, we realized that women had been queuing and waiting in line for hours under the sun, since seven in the morning, and now it is midday, and they still haven't received any food. Why? Because there were some coordination problems between the people in charge of the warehouse, the people in charge of the trucks, and the people in charge of the security. They couldn't reach an agreement on when the trucks could be loaded and when they could get out of the warehouse. And if the women are waiting, the attitude was: "Well, there's nothing we can do."

I remember raising this issue with the coordination committee, and they told me, "You should be happy already. You got what you wanted—women are direct beneficiaries of the food." In terms of security, it's interesting: we think of security as meaning immediate security on the spot. What happens afterward isn't thought about.

I remember watching those women wait in the sun and not complaining about anything, just wanting to get their food and leave. You had pregnant women, you had old women; and the young men around, just watching them and waiting. We don't really know what happened after. So we talked to those women, we talked to people in the community; and they started to report a few cases of sexual violence. My office facilitated a trip to the city for a Haitian women's organization so they can do their own assessment. Now we see if we can cross-check information; and if the facts are true we can start proposing a solution for their own protection.

What I found very interesting in this case is, first of all, that none of the women were consulted about the organization of humanitarian assistance. Again, it tells us why we still see women as perceived beneficiaries, as victims: "They don't need to participate in the decision-making process, because we can do this for them." It's now 2004, and I saw this same thing ten years ago. I'm just wondering: Why are we still in that situation in 2004? And why can't the humanitarian community have a gender-sensitive approach? And I was told many times: "It's an emergency. We have no time for gender; we'll add gender later." And I keep responding that "later will be too late."

But that is not the end of the story. Here is another dimension: at the same time, the humanitarian workers decided to organize shelters. You have to know that in Gonaïves people lost everything. They lost their houses, so they found a temporary place in the shelter. But we all know through our experiences with refugee camps or camps for displaced people that the "temporary" will very often last. So the humanitarian community was not really willing to work on those shelters, because they said, "Well, it's temporary—we'll relocate people later." It's been going now for one month, I think. And in those shelters I've found many women, young girls, and children hanging around without anything, in complete destitution, completely abandoned. It was really shocking. I can tell you the great Haitian feminists who were working with me and doing their own assessments—they were really shocked by what they saw. They told me they were really shocked by the lack of dignity. Those women had been stripped of all their dignity. They were just left in the shelter, they were not given anything, and they were certainly not put in charge of the organization of the assistance [at] the shelter.

And then there is the problem of not having gender-disaggregated data. I was handed a piece of paper, and on it was written: "Population of shelter: 200 people," which does not help me a lot, because you don't know how many men, women, boys, and girls. You can't assess their vulnerability. You can't tell who has the most needs if you don't know if there are pregnant women, old women, and teenagers. There were a few cases reported to us of violence against women in those shelters, and fighting [over] who was going to take over the shelter in terms of controlling the territory and the power. The same happened in the medical centers.

I've been thinking about all of this, and how we could improve it. Along with the women's organization, we suggested that the women should be consulted first. How do they want to organize their own communities? What are their needs? Try to again collect gender-disaggregated data so we can do better work and we can better target the vulnerable groups.

I find it most difficult to make the humanitarian community understand that we can't work without gender-disaggregated data. Without it, we won't be able to deliver the same level of assistance to men and women or teenagers or children. I face the same problem over and over again; it seems that it's incredibly difficult for people to break down data collection by gender.

In terms of security, I find it really interesting that, at the United Nations, "security" means that we secure the UN staff, and then we secure the UN assets, and eventually we secure the population. We find in our mandate, in the resolutions adopted by the Security Council, some elements of protection for the population, but it's always very vague. I also find it very interesting when they talk about "protecting women from violence," they don't say how. Very often, as we're seeing in the Congo, we had a lot of cases of sexual violence, and those women were never protected by anyone, not the UN.

So we have all this in our mandate, but it is not really implemented on the ground. In Gonaïves the "security" was mainly securing the food, securing one area for it, but not really thinking about the violence women could be exposed to. And what does this tell us? What is the security concept for the UN? Security is a very broad concept; and in my experience I've seen that, on the ground, the population is expecting more than [what] the UN means by it. I think that when the UN arrives with a mission, we create a lot of expectations. And if "security" is in our resolution and in our mandate, and then the population sees that the UN is going to spend more time protecting its own people and its own assets, I would say it becomes a credibility problem.

So in the case of Gonaïves, it would be very interesting to see also what is going to happen now in those cases of violence. We hope that we won't reach the point of what happened in the refugee camps in western Africa, when a lot of the relief workers were abusing the refugee population, mainly the women and the girls—exchanging food for sex. I hope we won't reach that point in Gonaïves, but you know it's a very poor community now.

Again, I don't think the UN community understands that a lot of women and girls are single heads of households. They have nothing; they lost everything; and somehow they may be obliged to sell themselves if they can't get access to the food. And remember that, after a while, you can be queuing for two or three hours in the sun; and when the truck is empty, you go back home and have nothing. Then you come back the following morning. Some women may change strategy; and some relief workers or peacekeepers may use it as a way to abuse women and girls.

So I think we really have to reconsider the way we approach the humanitarian assistance—and I'm not sure I have a solution. It's just what I've been observing. We made a few recommendations, and we've been trying to think about the security issue, because security is not only the physical protection of the distribution point. To me, it is also people being in a position to secure medical assistance, to secure food, to secure shelter, and not being obliged to fear for their own protection. You will see very often the word *security* is used only in the very physical, material way—especially at the UN. It's just all these dynamics you find on a mission, and it's very hard for us to come to terms with the situation without wondering: Why can't we learn from our mistakes? Why are we facing the same problems in Haiti? The humanitarian assistance workers don't see that their behavior is going to jeopardize the women within their own communities.

So we can do gender training with peacekeepers; we can teach about respecting the local population and the culture. And there again we see the gap between the concepts of security. What does it mean for me? *[For] a peacekeeper* it means that I don't want to be shot, but I can misbehave. There will be no consequences, no one holding me responsible, because I have the power and I can buy everyone and everything within the community, and I can show that I have the power. *Security for a woman* within her own community means: "I may be raped by the peacekeeper." So I think she has a completely different definition of the word. And it's interesting because, in the case studies I've been doing on gender training, we've been trying to put the peacekeepers in a situation where we show them that, by jeopardizing the security of women within their [the women's] own community, the peacekeepers are actually also jeopardizing their [the peacekeepers'] own security, because the perception of the mission will change and the men of the community will be very angry at the peacekeepers. As in the case of the Congo now, where angry people burn UN cars and houses, and staff had to be evacuated—those are the consequences.

I think in the case of Gonaïves that's exactly what's going to happen. We are losing control of the situation. Sooner or later we're going to forget Gonaïves to talk about something else, and those women and young girls are going to stay in the "temporary" shelters. Sooner or later we're going to have protection issues; because if you're the young men in control of the shelter, you're in a gang. You have to know that in Haiti we really have a problem with gangs, and the city of Gonaïves is organized according to gangs that have a certain power in some areas. After a while, I think, if we keep considering women as powerless individuals, not involving them in the reconstruction of the city, we are going to reinforce the gender roles within the community.

CAROL COHN: Could we turn to elections for a moment? Would you take a minute to connect this humanitarian assistance effort that fails to think about gender, and the narrow definition of security, to another part of the work of MINUSTAH [the UN's mission for Haiti], which is to prepare an electoral process? What impact do they have on your ability to prepare an effective electoral process that's going to become the basis for sustainable peace?

NP: It would be the same pattern, I think, in terms of securing the electoral process. What does it mean?

Regarding "security"—for the United Nations, "securing" the electoral process means that on election day all of the polling stations will be secured. So the civilian police are going to organize the security, and the military and everybody will be involved. What I haven't heard yet is how are we going to ensure that men and women are going to vote? And I know, because I've been talking to a lot of people—feminists and nonfeminists alike—and they are very concerned about violence during election day.

In Haiti you find very few women who want to get involved in the electoral process as candidates and as voters. *Why?* Because past elections in Haiti were marred by violence, and they are scared. We've had a lot of cases of really violent elections, so now the women, who have so many responsibilities, fear for their lives. Remember, 60 percent of single heads of households in Haiti are women. They don't want to leave their own families and children behind and take the risk to go and vote. So we have to ensure that on election day those women, and those who live in very remote areas, and those who are scared to walk a long way to the voting station, are going to feel secure enough to go.

I think we haven't considered the protection *of women* in this case of elections, because we keep talking about ensuring the security *of the location*. Again, it is parallel to what I said regarding securing food distribution points: the peacekeepers will be present at the location where you are going to vote. What's happening around that point, whether women can even leave their houses to vote—no one has thought about any of this. Maybe the community itself could tell us how they're going to organize this. Maybe the women, if we consult them, will tell us how to deal with the violence. If we want to have a good process, and elections that are really representative, men and women need to feel safe, and we really need to focus on that. Many men have personal weapons in Haiti. Women don't. And obviously, when we talk about security, I think the UN people think that it will be safe because we'll have enough peacekeepers around the polling stations—so they don't see how the wider security situation can affect the women. I really want to get statistics out of that election day. I really want to see how many women are registered, how many women went to vote. And then we'll see—maybe it will be too late, but at least we'll have a better picture of where the problem was, and can learn from that for next time. Thank you.

CC: We turn now to Cynthia Enloe, who will bring a similar lens to thinking about the gendered failure to secure the peace in Iraq.

CYNTHIA ENLOE: In thinking about Iraq, I tried to imagine: What keeps people—both men and women, in various organizations— from thinking that the security of women is important? I'm interested in how any of us take something and manage to treat it as if it's "not serious." *Serious* is such a loaded word. It's such a strived-for attribute. Just think of how much work all of us do to be taken seriously, and how many of us think we're jeopardizing our status—as a serious person thinking about security, a serious person talking about diplomacy, a serious person talking about international political economy, a serious person talking about politics; just think about how much *you* believe you are jeopardizing your own hard-fought-for, tenuous hold on your status as a "serious person"—when we raise the topic of gender. You have the feeling that if you raise gender, your purchase on the hard-won status of being "serious" is in jeopardy in some circles. Not in this room, right? But outside this room ...

What are the silent assumptions that trivialize security issues for women? Here's my in-progress list:

THE FIRST ASSUMPTION IS: *Well, women are insecure anyway.* Now imagine if that assumption were put on the table for discussion, rather than just being left a comfortable, unspoken assumption. Imagine if it had to be explicitly examined. A lot of things that are assumed, are assumed so that people don't have to think about hard things. A lot of assumptions are made so that you don't have to spend scarce resources. A lot of assumptions are made so that people who are already completely stressed out don't get any more stressed out. That is why we are so devoted to a lot of our assumptions—because we are already stressed out. Who wants to be stressed out more? You think, "I like this assumption. Let's hope no one asks me to defend it. Let's just hope everyone else shares it." So silent assumptions are very comforting, especially to stressed-out people.

THE SECOND ASSUMPTION IS: *Women's experiences of insecurity are no different than men's experiences of insecurity.* This is what Nadine so brilliantly charted out for us as being untrue. But again, the motivation for making the assumption is the same as for not gender-disaggregating data. Every time gender is not used to disaggregate data, it is so that the consequences of revealing what you would reveal if you disaggregated the data don't have to be dealt with.

There's an enormous incentive not to gender-disaggregate data. For instance, what percentage of tenured faculty at Fletcher are women? Why isn't that scrawled in graffiti all over the walls of this university? Why isn't that something that all of us know? Isn't that weird? [Update: Shortly after this event a small group of Fletcher School graduate students came together to launch an investigatory project, the Equity Project, collecting gender-disaggregated data on myriad aspects of the Fletcher School's operations, from course content, to course enrollment, to speakers fees, to types of faculty contracts.]

Gender-disaggregation of data has consequences. It makes inequities visible. Once you make inequities visible, you are also likely to make visible the power dynamics that create those inequities. Who wants to do that? So not having a gender analysis of insecurity is a way to lessen the number of issues on the table. There's a lot of incentive to be incurious. Incuriosity is a political act. Every time one chooses to be incurious about something, one is choosing a political outcome. Incuriosity is politically comforting—and it's politically empowering to some people.

ASSUMPTION NUMBER THREE: *Any intimidation of women will stop once other forms of insecurity are rolled back.* This is the security-thinker's version of trickle-down economics. You think women's security flows directly from security as it is usually defined. Even if you think the kinds of insecurity that women experience are distinctive—particularly vulnerability to sexual assault—you can still imagine that once you deal with the male militias and focus your attention on getting them to hand in their weapons, then everything else can be dealt with. This means you don't have to think about women's forms of insecurity now. You can just think about the thing that you'd rather think about, which is the men with guns. It will trickle down in security planning, just as in economics.

Trickle down, again, is a lazy person's approach to causal analysis. You assume that [the idea that any intimidation of

women will stop once other forms of insecurity are rolled back]
is the most important thing to think about regarding this issue
[men with guns], the issue you've been trained to think about,
that you get some kudos for because you use the skills you
learned in order to address it—and you assume that you don't
have to think about the forms of insecurity that in fact you've
never been trained to deal with.

ASSUMPTION NUMBER FOUR (AND THIS IS A VERY POTENT
ASSUMPTION): *There will always be violence against women. It's just part
of the human condition.* I hate *always*. *Always* is so ahistorical. It is
really a word that makes you stupid. *Always* is a way to turn off your
mind. If something is "always" there, you don't have to explain
it—because it's always been there. It's like saying "prostitution is
the oldest profession" so that you don't have to think about prostitution. Because if it's the oldest profession, that means it's always
been there... And if *there will always be violence against women; it's just
part of the human condition.* That means it's not part of the crisis: it
was here before the crisis; it will be here after the crisis. It's not the
thing we've been trained to analyze, to prevent, to prosecute. It's
not something you can use professional skills to reverse. It's just
always been there, and it will always be there.

So when your operational money is scarce, your time is
scarce, your Land Rovers are scarce, that "always" is very
comforting. Plus, it sounds so cynically sophisticated. As if you
have knowledge of the breadth and depth of the way things have
been and will continue to be. Well, *always* is *not* sophisticated.
What would happen if you took all these assumptions seriously,
all these unexamined assertions that allow women's insecurity to
not be dealt with? You would then have to put them on the table,
where they would have to be analytically and explicitly chewed
over. *That* would be sophisticated.

ASSUMPTION NUMBER FIVE: *Insecurity that is male-on-male (for instance,
armed militias fighting each other) is more detrimental to political stability*

and stable governments than is male-on-female violence. That is, men's violence against women may be awful, it may horrify you, but nobody has ever taught us to calculate the causal relationship between domestic violence, or rape, and governance. That doesn't mean we couldn't learn how to do it. That doesn't mean it doesn't take explicit professional skills that we all should develop. But since nobody's taught us how to do it, and nobody's rewarded us for trying to do it, we can't even imagine how tackling domestic violence and tackling rape would, in fact, have anything to do with enhancing governance. And because we haven't figured it out analytically, we don't know how to argue it when it shows up on the table. So silence prevails. If seriousness is measured in terms of what affects the level of political stability, and no one tries to figure out when and how violence against women affects political stability ... the topic falls off the table— and nobody notices.

Now I'm going to skip from assumption five to assumption ten because I certainly don't yet know the full list. You will have to fill in assumptions six, seven, eight, and nine.

So here's ASSUMPTION NUMBER TEN, which keeps women's distinctive security concerns off the table and not dealt with as a serious issue: *The oppression of women is good for political order.* Questioning that unspoken assumption would be a radical act. Even wondering if that assumption is informing the marginalization of women's security concerns may feel radical, pretty outrageous. But then pause; think about the history of domestic violence. Think about all the efforts made in so many countries, in so many eras, to reduce domestic violence against women: if the physical insecurity of women were seen as a threat to the political order, wouldn't there have been an urgency expressed by local and international political elites to roll it back? It is virtually never the political elites who launch those efforts. Rape crisis centers weren't founded by political elites. Domestic violence wasn't named and addressed through the creation of hotlines and shelters by political elites. In fact, almost all the efforts to tackle the trafficking of women, wartime rape, date rape, marital rape, sexual harassment, domestic violence of all sorts—almost all those efforts have been made initially by activist women outside of governments; they have been resisted by governments with all kinds of economic systems and all kinds of religious and political ideologies.

I'm not saying that all people you're sharing a table or a Land Rover with explicitly believe that violence against women supports political order. But way deep down, individuals with influence, as well as whole institutions and entire political cultures, have operated historically *as if* that were true.

CC: We've just heard two really provocative presentations, and I'm sure that many of you have comments and questions. (Not to mention, we still have assumptions six, seven, eight, and nine to fill in!) Let's get a few questions and then ask our speakers to respond.

QUESTION FROM THE AUDIENCE: My question is for both of you, but specifically for Nadine. When I heard you speak last year, you were talking about the Congo, but now that you're speaking about somewhere as close as Haiti.... I start making parallels between what happened in Massachusetts and in other university communities during the Sandinista period, where thousands of volunteers took themselves down to Nicaragua; people literally went there in delegations and built schools and medical centers. For a while there were volunteers who went there on their own dollar and made life better for people in Nicaragua. After the hurricane I was calling groups here trying to find a way to volunteer. What's your sense? I'm just trying to move up a step from useless.

Q: I also have a question for Nadine. I've worked on refugee and IDP [internally displaced person] issues. You were talking about

the question of security at the UN, and I'm wondering: is the
problem in the defining of "vulnerable groups"? I've found that
we [outside observers] actually organize in parallel frameworks
to the UN and NGOs, which then leads to a gap between what
mandates are set up to do and what happens on the ground,
because there is a resistance that is formed. As someone who
works at the UN, how do you begin to challenge the definition of
who victims are? And does this cause a bigger problem for the
UN in the future—because there's this active resistance against
anything that's being done on the ground?

Q: My question kind of relates to that. How do you approach
changing the peacekeeping officers' definition of security with
regard to the elections—especially because I think that will
affect Iraq and Haiti. How do you encourage them to extend the
boundary of that?

NP: Let's start with the issue of the volunteers who want to go to
Haiti. I think it's great to want to contribute to the reconstruction of a place, but volunteer work can be very counterproduc-
tive if it's not well organized. First of all, volunteers need to be
briefed and well-coordinated, and have to meet the needs on the
ground. And [problems can arise] especially when we don't have
any gender-disaggregated data and we think we are going to
assist "communities." "Communities" are composed of men,
women, girls, and boys, who have different needs. I've seen in
Haiti a lot of volunteers not knowing what to do. It's not sustainable. We can't do volunteer work in an emergency. It can maybe
provide some relief in the very short-term, but it often creates
more problems in the long-term. That's why I think that volunteer work, if it isn't well coordinated and really targeting the
problems, can do more harm than good. We have to be very, very
careful. When we work in the field, we don't have time to take
care of the volunteers. It's going to create a burden for the
operation.

What I've seen are national volunteers who are really reluctant to participate in the relief operation because they were not properly prepared, they had their own families to take care of, and they were not psychologically prepared. No system has been provided to assist them, so I think it was putting a lot of burden on those volunteers. It's just a question of getting organized and getting a proper assessment. Because what is happening now in Gonaïves is that we are not properly meeting the needs of women and girls; and in the mid- and long-term, we will have more problems than we have right now. This may have consequences later. Young people, old people, who were already more vulnerable than other groups and don't have the proper assistance, won't be able to recover.

Also, very often we bring in outside assistance when we already have the human resources in the country itself. But because they're perceived as "beneficiaries," we don't think they would be able to participate in the reconstruction with minimal assistance at the beginning. We need to use the local resources before bringing in any outsiders.

And to answer your question about the vulnerable groups: if you looked at every single definition at the UN, or within the humanitarian community—I think we're talking about perceived beneficiaries who are going to receive the assistance, right? Nowhere have I seen beneficiaries put in a position of power. There have been some attempts in refugee camps to empower women and, in Gonaïves, give the food through the women.

Very often humanitarian people think they have a brilliant idea—to give the food through the women—without thinking about the structure of the community. And this reminds me of a case in a refugee camp in Tanzania when the UN High Commissioner for Refugees organized a system of distribution through the women, empowered the women in all kinds of activities—food delivery, a kind of microproject. And the husbands or the partners of the refugee women were complaining, and saying, "We see that UNHCR is a better husband." They were deprived of their own status as providers. And this created a lot of security problems within the camp and created a lot of pressure for the women.

What I find interesting in the humanitarian community is that you have the "vulnerable group," and women are part of the vulnerable group. And all of a sudden the humanitarian community wants to be seen as doing something for the women. And they put the women in charge of food distribution but isolate them from the community. I think what happened in Tanzania is the men withdrew completely from the organization of care and decided to do a passive resistance until the situation changed. So UNHCR had to revise their own program and occupy the men. They had to give the men some activities so they could feel of some value again.

What I've seen in the humanitarian community is this disparity between the givers and the people who receive. I've seen a lot of people in the humanitarian community who feel good because they are the givers. And you unconsciously put yourself in a position of power over the beneficiaries because they're so powerless in their own situation. Then the humanitarian community, as the givers, will feel that you can't empower those refugees, because you will give away your power. I have a lot of colleagues who disagree with me, but I think they are in denial; I think the very humanitarian mentality is that they feel good about what they are doing, and very few of them would think about empowering the local people they are helping.

It's always striking for me that we can't remove the women out of the "vulnerable group." In all the UN texts, women are part of the "vulnerable group," together with children and the handicapped and the old people. I find this interesting because finally we are using sex as a variable, treating women as a minority group within another minority group. Within "handicapped" we have male and female, right? So why do we put the women with those groups anyway?

I haven't seen a lot of evolution in the humanitarian mentality. Yet each time I've been told, "It's an emergency; we have no time to think in gender terms; we'll do it later." I would like to think of one example of a gender-sensitive operation, where gender has been mainstreamed from the beginning, when we know our target groups and know what our limits are from the very beginning, and we know how vulnerable the people are, and we can use the local resources instead of bringing all the support from the outside.

I think the question about definitions might be better for Cynthia to answer, because I don't think the peacekeepers who are working for peacekeeping operations are really prepared for the peacekeeping task. I think it was Sandra Whitworth who said soldiers are not born, they are made.

So just to finish on that question—the peacekeepers are trained to be soldiers, trained to kill and to go to war. Then you send them to a peacekeeping mission, where they can't use force except in self-defense, and you ask them to do a lot of work being military observers—like in the Congo. So you ask them to secure an environment, to secure an election, but still they can't use force. I think there is a contradiction in the very definition of who is a peacekeeper and what the mandate of the peacekeeper is. And we don't have time to start this discussion, but peace-keepers are mainly men. In my mission we have only 1 percent of women in the military. Brazil, for instance, contributed two thousand troops and not a single woman. The women who are in the military in Haiti are mostly nurses or only in support roles.

CE: Part of it is because a soldier gets extra pay on peacekeeping missions. So the donor government's defense ministry officials often select the most privileged units of their military to do the most privileged operations—and for many governments, sending troops on an international peacekeeping mission is deemed prestigious. And who are those? They're the Special Forces and combat units. The UN's Department of Peacekeeping Operations does not get to choose which units from each donor government's military are sent to serve as UN peacekeeping units. It will often be the most combat-defined units who get the privilege—that is, the extra pay and chances for promotion. These, of course, are typically among any military's most deeply masculinized units. There are lots of reasons to go into a peacekeeping mission; they have very little to do with peace. They often have a lot to do with stripes on your sleeve, and your pension. That's one of the structural problems in the distortion of militarized, masculinized peacekeeping.

NP: And I think you want peacekeepers to really care about the protection of women. They are seen as the protectors, and they are going to protect the population and they see women as really nonexistent. If women are part of the community, that's enough. I remember working with military observers where they couldn't see women as relevant. First of all, I've heard many who are telling me: "Why do you want women to go vote? They have enough to do at home, right?" So we could have this long discussion about the definition of *peacekeeper,* but I don't think they are very well equipped mentally to be part of the peacekeeping mission.

CC: Let's take another group of questions.

Q: I've been reading some of the UN documents pertaining to gender mainstreaming, and I notice that, institutionally, *gender* often is used to mean only *women.* I wonder if it might make a difference if we made men feel like stakeholders in gender mainstreaming? I know this gets into kind of dangerous territory when you talk about the benefits for men, but I wonder if they may be on board a little more if they realize we are talking about masculinity as well, and talking about them as stakeholders?

CE: Often there are two incentives to conflate *gender* with *women*. The first incentive is that conflating *gender* with *women* is often the only way you can get women taken seriously, by slipping them in through this sociological, diffuse notion of gender. So some people who want at least some attention paid to women, in some form, are quite comfortable with conflation because that's the only way you're going to get those concerns on the decision-making table.

The second group that is quite comfortable with *gender* being conflated with *women* has a different incentive—they are the ones who don't want to talk about masculinity. After all, once you're talking about masculinity, you're talking about most of the people at the table—and their superiors. Once you're talking openly about masculinity, you're talking about the kind of bonding that goes on even among rival political party heads in preparing for an election, and that becomes tricky.

NP: You mention men as stakeholders in gender mainstreaming. In different peacekeeping operations, when you give those guys some responsibility and they feel that you take them seriously, they are willing to do something on gender. In the Congo, we created a gender-sensitive checklist for the military observers, because we were sick and tired of having reports by those guys saying they talked to "the community," [when] they talked to the male elders and they had nothing to report. So we asked them: "Can't you give us more information about what men and women do in the community?" So we created this ten-question gender-sensitive list, where we wanted to know: Who has the power at the local level? Is it a man? Is there a woman working with him? What is the local structure? Who has the religious power? Who has the cultural power? What are the needs of the men, the women, the boys, and the girls? Have you witnessed any acts of violence?

And I noticed a couple of guys taking this very seriously, because it was their mission to introduce the checklist among the other guys and go to the field—and maybe they were bored and we provided them entertainment. You know, peacekeeping can be boring sometimes when you're a military observer in a remote area. So I think we try to interest them in the work of gender in a nonthreatening way. And I've realized that if you give them something to do that is, of course, not an additional workload and not threatening to them, they're happy to do it. But you have to try and involve them in your work and improve their relationship with the local community also. But it's not the system that's doing that. It's our initiative as Gender Advisors trying to find strategies for gender mainstreaming. So you see the problem we have—in every single mission we have initiatives, but when the particular people who created them leave, nothing will remain and the next person involved will have to find new ideas to have a gender-friendly approach. Without the gender-friendly approach, you can't really work on strategies for gender mainstreaming.

CAROL COHN: Thank you both and thanks to all of you who came and took part this evening.

EPILOGUE, 2012

Haiti after the Earthquake and the Hurricane:
Lessons Still Not Learned?

Nadine Puechguirbal

Like wars, natural disasters and their aftermaths are gendered. Because women and men play different roles in society, they will occupy different locations, assuming different responsibilities, when a natural disaster strikes, as well as during the days and months when people are trying to pick up the pieces. Haitian women and men have been coping with a decade of violence interspersed with natural disasters.

One possible consequence of the 2010 earthquake in Haiti may be an increase in the number of women who are breadwinners. Although sex- and age-disaggregated data are not available, an assessment of the impact of the earthquake shows that the formal business sector was severely affected by the destruction of infrastructure. As the majority of women continue to work in the informal sector, selling goods in markets, they may be better off economically than the men who worked in the formal economy. Already overburdened with their daily chores, women have had to take on more responsibility in order to care for unemployed men and extended families. Increasing reports of domestic violence may be linked to the postquake situation, with more men becoming dependent on women for their daily subsistence.

At the same time, the most prevalent local Haitian masculinity clashed with the hegemonic masculinity of male international humanitarian workers and the UN peacekeepers who provided security around the food distribution points. To facilitate the distribution, international humanitarian agencies targeted women as the sole recipients of food vouchers. This approach did not really empower women, as they ended up with a heavy workload and were increasingly exposed to violence once they left the secure perimeter of the food distribution point. Given the dichotomy of powerful givers versus powerless receivers, Haitian men may have felt alienated by international peacekeepers who were protecting Haitian women from their men, defined by aid workers and peacekeepers as potential looters and thus as posing a serious threat to the delivery of humanitarian assistance. That is, in the wake of the 2010 earthquake, international humanitarian agencies ignored local gender-power hierarchies, creating artificial gendered spaces for the delivery of humanitarian goods. To adequately meet the needs of women and men, girls and boys, one has to make them visible; one has to uncover the reality of unequal relations. But as Cynthia Enloe writes, "There's a lot of incentive to be incurious." Curiosity brings to the surface a completely new picture of the reality.

The fact that we do not take women seriously prevents us from assessing the real impact of patriarchal power and privileges on society. This was true when I first served as the Senior Gender Adviser for the UN peacekeeping mission in Haiti in 2004. It was still depressingly true when I returned to Haiti with the International Committee of the Red Cross in 2010 in the aftermath of the earthquake.

We who work in international assistance seem never to have learned any lessons from past natural disasters in Haiti. In 2004, a hurricane severely hit the city of Gonaïves on the western coast. As would happen again in 2010, women were asked by humanitarian staff to line up under the scorching sun to receive relief assistance, not with the aim of empowering them, but to ensure that the distribution would go smoothly. The staff perceived these women only in their traditional roles as caregivers within the household. The assumption behind this approach was that women were "naturally" more peaceful than men and would create fewer problems for the humanitarian agencies and for peacekeepers assigned to the distribution points. This approach was adopted after a few young men looted trucks loaded with humanitarian assistance. Violence exerted by local men was considered by international staff members to be a serious enough matter for aid organizations to take explicit steps to deal with it. By contrast, the fact that, under their new "smooth" system, Haitian women were attacked after receiving their food rations was perceived by the staffs of these same organizations to be simply collateral damage in their own invisible realm.

In the aftermath of the 2004 hurricane, I repeatedly witnessed Haitian women's exclusion from the decision-making processes that so directly affected their lives. Women were not represented on local committees in charge of managing humanitarian assistance. For example, they were not consulted about where the international agencies would locate water- and food-distribution points, although these women were put in charge of collecting the water and receiving the food rations. To have learned lessons from past natural disasters would have required staff members to make women visible and, even more radically, to have started considering them as actors, not hopeless victims in need of the international organizations' (male) protection. But these lessons were not learned. It takes a gender perspective to deconstruct hidden power relations.

In 2010, women and girls were at risk of violence, including sexual violence, in the postquake camps set up for the thousands of Haitians who had been left homeless. The pattern was not new. Six years earlier, in Gonaïves, I had heard reports from the Haitian women activists I worked with of teenage Haitian girls being made victims of violence in shelters where they were living in the same space as adult men. Two situations with a common denominator: the ordeals of women and girls remained invisible because these ordeals were not perceived by international officials as a serious threat to the humanitarian order that they and their superiors had established, an order that mirrored the internal order of the patriarchal international humanitarian organizations themselves.

International humanitarian organizations continue to apply the same recipes to the management of earthquakes, floods, and hurricanes, with the aim of maintaining a very conservative approach that does not challenge the traditional sexual division of labor. Women are kept in a subordinate status to preserve the privileges of men in power. Gender transformation is vetoed if it challenges the domination of men and jeopardizes their hold on power. Given the dominant culture of masculinity operating inside international organizations, the senior administrators have few incentives to promote genuine gender change.

How can even patriarchal organizations be so blind to the failures of their own and colleagues' past humanitarian policies? I think one answer is that the masculine norm of reference is used by peacekeepers and aid staff members as the so-called universal norm to which women are compared. International humanitarian organizations promote a "gender-neutral" approach to make us believe that women are not discriminated against in the delivery of assistance. However, this is merely a convenient approach, because it does not challenge the status quo. In practice it reinforces existing gender inequalities by leaving out the differential impact of natural disasters on women and men.

I suspect that the beneficiaries of patriarchy are unwilling to make gender inequalities visible and address them. Just as I have repeatedly heard the claim "We will be dealing with gender later," I have also heard decision makers repeatedly use the following catchphrase: "There is still a long way to go before the voices of women are heard, before the rights of women are protected." The value of this seemingly reasonable official language is that it excuses gender inaction. This is key to understanding how the sustainers of patriarchy are procrastinating rather than taking the effective steps needed for solving problems on the ground. It is such a "reasonable" procrastination that it allows them to remain in control, to not lose power. This is a widespread institutional strategy designed to deceive feminists—Haitian feminists and feminists working inside international agencies—who are striving to address gender inequalities and asking for a redistribution of power.

So often staff and managers of humanitarian assistance and peace-keeping efforts put all local women in the catchall administrative category of "vulnerable groups," together with children and the elderly. This may sound compassionate, but in practice this sort of routine operational categorization makes it extremely difficult to break the vicious cycle of stereotypes and gender bias. One does not invite a mere "victim" to a planning meeting. My years of work in societies that have endured armed conflict and natural disaster have convinced me that we need to take women seriously to uncover hidden power hierarchies. At the same time, we need to pay attention to the official and in-house language that influences the way decision makers think about women, and which allows them to not take women seriously.

CHAPTER EIGHT

Egyptian Women, Feminism, Revolutions

The Dinner Party

Marie-Aimee Helie-Lucas, Alexandra Kollontai, Olympe de Gouges, Abigail Adams, Nizihe Muhittin, Violeta Delgado, Antoinetta Saa, Nguyen Thi Kiem, Xiang Jingyu, and Egypt's own early revolutionary feminist, Huda Sha'rawi. I am picturing all these women coming together for a feminist dinner party. Being a feminist meal, it would be a potluck, of course. Couscous, hummus, molokhia, pita bread, Hunan spicy chicken, ripe tomatoes, tofu, borsht, freshly baked baguettes, followed by bowls of longan berries and blueberries—all washed down with ayran, rice wine, cider, white wine, or vodka, followed by pots of black tea and green tea. The mood would be informal, the dishware would not match. Jokes and gravity would intermingle.

On this special evening, every woman around the table would become fluent in Arabic.

Contemporary Egyptian women's advocates, deeply involved in their country's current revolution, would have invited these women who have engaged in earlier revolutions—in Algeria, Russia, France, the United States, Turkey, Nicaragua, Chile, Vietnam, China, and Egypt. Egyptian women today are going through their country's third revolution in less than a century. They will want to compare feminist lessons.

Figure 12. Huda Sha'rawi, an activist in the Egyptian revolution of 1919 and cofounder of the Egyptian Feminist Union, in a photo taken in Cairo, 1923.

Some of the invitees would be from the eighteenth century, many would be from the early, middle, or late twentieth century. Some, such as Nguyen Thi Kiem, Abigail Adams, and Huda Sha'rawi, lived into old age, seeing changes, adjusting their assessments, and experiencing disappointments over decades. By contrast, Olympe de Gouges was forty-five when she was executed with Dr. Guillotine's machine, and Xiang Jingyu was just thirty-three when she was executed by Chiang Kai-shek's agents. Marie-Aimee Helie-Lucas, Antoinetta Saa, and Violeta Delgado are still alive today. Not all of these women called themselves "feminist," a term that did not gain currency until the early twentieth century. Some of them worked inside larger (often male-led) movements and political parties. Others devoted their energies to women's independent organizing. Yet each of these dinner guests organized women or spoke out forcefully for women's aspirations, needs, and rights while engaging in multi-issue revolutionary causes.[1]

Novelist Virginia Woolf, playwright Caryl Churchill, and artist Judy Chicago have each mined the riches of the dinner party. They have revealed that, even when all stay seated politely at their places around the dinner table, passions, memories, tensions, aspirations, and confusions can swirl. But the gathering I am picturing would not be mainly about personal anxieties, artistry, or literary banter. In my mind's eye, today's Egyptian feminists have brought France's Olympe de Gouges, Algeria's Marie-Aimee Helie-Lucas, Vietnam's Nguyen Thi Kiem, their own Huda Sha'rawi and the other women around this imagined dinner table to talk strategy. While the outward mood would be friendly and casual, there would be a shared sense of urgency, of opportunities about to slip away, of patriarchal history about to repeat itself.

THE CONVERSATION BEGINS

As the meal gets under way, stories start to flow. All these women have important tales to tell about revolutions. They tell stories, for instance, about how much work went into theorizing—that is, into making sense of their own country's diverse women not as mere dependents but as full-fledged citizens, of women's double burden combining unpaid and paid work, of the widespread resistance to accepting women as thinkers. They talk about their own personal intellectual journeys toward making sense of public space, power, families, religions, nations, and modernity. Then these women remind everyone present that there followed years of hard, often dangerous and frustrating work, years spent using those ideas to mobilize women, most of whom had been taught to think of themselves only as mothers, daughters, and wives, as dependents, creatures of domestic life.

Reaching for the couscous and spicy chicken, they share their experiences of trying to get women taken seriously as autonomous actors in public life. This was quite different, they agree, from getting women to be taken seriously by their male revolutionary comrades simply as participants in a popular mobilization, or taken seriously solely as contributors to a modernizing economy. If either (or even both) of these rationales had been the sole basis for male revolutionaries taking women seriously, then when that need had passed—when the mobilization period had ended or when the economy had slowed—women could be pushed back into the domestic sphere without the men feeling a twinge of revolutionary embarrassment.

On the other hand, as the diners start dipping into the molokhia they admit that, in societies in which women were scarcely thought of as public actors, as citizens, these two initial arguments for taking women seriously could indeed be alluring. That is, perhaps some of their male colleagues could not quite accept women as their political equals, but at least they could be persuaded that a national revolution was unlikely to succeed if one-half of the nation were left at home.

Under these political conditions, as the feminists around the table may recall, weighing alliances was a strategic process that could prove to be tricky. For instance, when were middle-class women reliable allies for poorer women? When were male nationalists trustworthy advocates for women's rights? When did even avowedly "modern" men slip into patriarchal assumptions about women?

Sometimes, the dinner guests report, the forces of the oppressive status quo appeared so strong that one had to go ahead and forge uneasy alliances, even though one remained unsure of the answers to these strategic questions. Alliances between different generations and classes of women would sometimes founder as each group drew on their different skills, different experiences, different political lessons. One's new male allies, for their part, might insist that you merge your still-fragile women's groups into the larger, male-run movement or party for the sake of "better coordination" or for the "greater cause." Several of the dinner guests, putting down their forks and chopsticks in order to underscore their caveats with gestures, warn against dissolving autonomous revolutionary women's groups before women's rights and women's political influence were fully secured.

Pouring another glass of ayran or rice wine, the feminist revolutionary guests candidly tell each other and their Egyptian feminist hosts about when they clearly saw the risks of women's advocacy being co-opted—and when they did not see the risks until it was too late. They recall that often they had accepted their male revolutionary colleagues' seemingly heartfelt promises that women's concerns, women's genuine empowerment, and women rights would be embedded in laws and constitutional articles "later." After the old regime had been thoroughly dismantled. After the new constitution had been hammered out. After the social chaos of the tumultuous years had quieted. After all the foreign threats had been overcome.

But "later" never came. And the new present had suddenly become too late.

- "Too late" was when the new system had begun to harden, with new circles of senior officials being formed among men, with an occasional token woman, suggests Nguyen Thi Kiem, thinking of her Vietnam experience.
- "Too late" was when their women's groups had been banned, marginalized, or co-opted, Huda Sha'rawi offers as she remembers Egypt's first revolution. Xiang Jingyu scowls slightly at this, recalling her own efforts in 1920s China, while Violeta Delgado, considering her Nicaraguan experience, nods her head in vigorous agreement.
- "Too late" was when, in the name of "restoring order" after the admittedly disruptive years of conflict, the new revolutionary government had passed laws to strengthen the family at the

cost of women's autonomy, adds the Algerian, Marie-Aimee Helie-Lucas, adamantly. Antoinetta Saa raises her glass of Chilean wine in affirmation.

· "Too late" was when, in the name of the postrevolutionary nation's security, a remasculinized military and security forces had been accorded extraordinary political privileges and influence, warn five of the women simultaneously.

· "Too late" was when the new regime was portraying itself in schoolbooks and holiday rituals as having beneficently "granted" women their rights as citizens, Turkey's Nizihe Muhittin and Russia's Alexandra Kollontai say with one voice.

THE HISTORICAL MOMENT

As the tea is steeping, the guests turn to their Egyptian hosts and ask them for their own stories and their own analyses. This imagined dinner party is happening, the Egyptian women explain, at a critical, and violent, moment in Egypt's still-unfolding aftermath of the "January 25th Revolution" of 2011.

No revolution occurs on a blank slate. The Egyptian revolution did not just burst forth at a particular moment in the trajectory of President Hosni Mubarak's regime, they explain to their attentive guests. It happened at a distinctive moment in Egyptians' gendered history and in the ongoing history of transnational feminism. The dinner guests nod knowingly. Each is all too conscious of how significant were the particular gendered conditions preceding her own country's revolution—at what point that revolutionary upheaval came in her country's history of girls' schooling, at what point the revolution came in the history of women's unpaid and paid work, in the history of local standards of "true masculinity," in the history of international exchanges of ideas about women's rights. So they lean forward and ask their Egyptian hosts to elaborate.

They might begin by explaining that the January 25th Revolution was Egyptians' third, coming after the 1919 revolution, which ended

British rule, and the 1952 revolution, which ushered in an era of populist transformation. The latter uprising was led by nationalist army officer Gamal Abdel Nasser. It ended the last vestiges of British power, brought down a corrupt local monarchy, and introduced a sweeping authoritarian welfare state. In 1956, Nasser "gave" women the right to vote. Huda Sha'rawi interjects at this point that voting was a right that earlier had been denied women by her own male nationalist colleagues and friends, even though those same men had relied on women's activism to win the 1919 revolution against British rule.[2] During the 1950s, 1960s, and 1970s, Nasserism welded militarism, a populist nationalism, and welfare subsidies for the country's poor to an authoritarian rule administered by a sprawling state bureaucracy that severely shrank the space for civil society activism.

This Nasserist formula won the support of many Egyptian women, though Huda Sha'rawi's own Egyptian Feminist Union, created in 1923 to challenge their former revolutionary male colleagues' creation of a male-only enfranchisement, was banned by Nasser. Making the history of Huda Sha'rawi and the EFU invisible during subsequent years served to entrench the popular notion that it was Nasser and the 1952 military-led revolution that brought Egyptian women their emancipation.

Hoda Badran, one of the current Egyptian feminists and a cohost of the dinner party, explains to the guests that it was, thus, doubly significant when, in October 2011, on the eve of the first post-Mubarak elections and sixty years after it had been banned, the EFU was revived by Egyptian women revolutionary activists. The relaunched EFU this time was organized by an association of one thousand current independent Egyptian women's groups. Hoda Badran, herself a leader of the Alliance for Arab Women, was chosen by the members to head the reactivated EFU. Michelle Bachelet, an important player in Chile's own recent transition from dictatorship to democracy and now the director of the newly created international agency UN Women, had traveled from New York to Cairo to lend her visible support to the relaunch. Bachelet and the EFU revivers were continuing the sort of transnational feminist links that Huda Sha'rawi herself had cultivated in the 1920s.[3]

Today, as then, transnational feminist alliances have proved at times to be acutely uneasy. The feminists who revived the EFU were not only signaling their commitment to women's influence in the current, ongoing post-Mubarak revolutionary process. As several of the dinner guests note, they also were challenging the gendered history of silence. Reviving lost memories—of earlier women's autonomous organizing, of earlier male colleagues' broken promises—can be crucial to women's success in any current revolutionary process.

This most recent Egyptian revolution was a many-stranded popular uprising, explain the Egyptian hosts. It was fueled by widespread economic distress and political anger at the Mubarak regime's selling off of the Nasserist state enterprises (on which thousands of Egyptians relied for employment). And, despite unemployment spiraling upward, the Mubarak regime dismantled the Nasserist welfare state. Both policies were enacted during the 1990s and early 2000s in the name of promoting the capitalist economic development formula fostered by the International Monetary Fund. The two moves enriched a circle of Egyptian businessmen close to the regime while it spread misery among millions of ordinary Egyptians. Because, as in so many countries, women were more likely than men to rely on public-sector jobs, the Mubarak formula put women at especially high risk of unemployment. Women who lost their state jobs were forced to rely on the informal economic sector, where income was lower and job security nil.[4] By mid-2010, young women between fifteen and twenty-nine years of age had an alarming unemployment rate of 32 percent, compared to 12 percent among men the same age.[5]

One of the Egyptian dinner hosts recalls that a leader of the independent organization Forum for Women in Development in Egypt noted in 2010 that, as the economy deteriorated and more and more Egyptian men sought jobs abroad, the number of female-headed Egyptian households rose. Many of these women were too overwhelmed by their efforts to make ends meet for their families to participate in any aspect of political life.[6] For all women outside the country's small elite, Mubarak's shrinking of the state's welfare programs exacerbated their daily stress as they cared for their families with fewer and fewer resources. By that same year, eight months before the start of the revolution, there had been a rolling wave of dramatic workers' strikes. Several of the strikes and factory occupations had been led by women textile workers in industrial cities such as Mahalla—by working-class women who had reached the end of their endurance of low pay rates and untenable working conditions.[7]

It was at this juncture that the Pew Research Center, a respected social research organization, conducted an opinion survey in Egypt and twenty-one other countries to discover what men and women in each country thought about current gender relations. When asked whether "women should be able to work outside the home," only 61 percent of Egyptians (men and women) polled said that, yes, women should be able to work outside the home. This proportion in agreement was significantly lower than the percentage of Turks (91 percent) and Indonesians (88 percent) who agreed, and somewhat lower than the percentage of Pakistanis who agreed (69 percent).[8] The Pew surveyors then asked an even more heavily loaded follow-up question, a question especially relevant to Egyptians today: "Do you agree with this statement: 'When jobs are scarce, men should have more right to a job'"? Among Egyptian men, 92 percent said they agreed. In stark contrast, only 58 percent of Egyptian women said they agreed.[9]

At this point, one of the Egyptian feminists asks her guests to turn their attention in a new direction in order to briefly consider a state institution that each had had to consider in her own unfolding revolution. As most ordinary Egyptians struggled with unemployment, low incomes, and economic uncertainty, one institution in particular thrived commercially: the military. A distinctive feature of the Mubarak-era system was the military's withdrawal from war waging and its entrance (one might say gallop) into commerce. Senior military officers took over land, made real estate deals, and profited from military-owned resorts and factories. Generals became businessmen who opposed both opening the country's economy to additional international competition and allowing any Egyptian public oversight or public accountability of the military's sprawling business empire. Underneath the commercialized generals was a rank and file made up of both urban college-educated men and rural undereducated young men. In Egypt's system of male conscription, college-educated men who could not avoid service by going overseas to study did their tours and then left the military. By contrast, poor, rural young men were more likely to stay in the military because they lacked the educational credentials to gain civil service employment. Many became members of the dreaded riot police.[10]

Consequently, during the Mubarak years an Egyptian gendered political economy developed that was propped up by a noncompetitive electoral system, a rubber-stamp masculinized parliament, a passive masculinized judiciary, a culture of masculinized elite business cronyism, masculinized policing, and the infusion of billions of dollars of U.S. government aid into the country's masculinized military. That is, it took several distinct but complementary masculinities to sustain the Mubarak regime: suave elite men with London university degrees, sharp businessmen maximizing profits while nurturing political connections, legally trained judges comfortable with doing the regime's bidding, commercially minded generals, rural male rank-and-file army recruits, senior uniformed professional policemen overseeing several different security forces, and nonuniformed poor men who were recruited by the police to act as thugs who could be deployed when the regime sought to suppress strikes or popular demonstrations.[11]

Achieving a revolution in early-twenty-first-century Egypt, then, would require revolutionary women not only to oust Mubarak and his sons but also to successfully challenge this interlocking array of oppressive self-serving masculinities. And it would require women to challenge the array of complementary femininities that daily reinforced each of those masculinities, but to do the latter without feeding a generalized misogyny.

In the latter years of the Mubarak regime, Egyptians pushed the narrow limits of regime-allowed civil society. More and more young people, women and men, had attended secondary school and university. More of them were using the Internet to exchange their own ideas and to track cultural and political trends in other societies. Nongovernmental organizations proliferated, despite being constantly subjected to state intimidation. Among these were scores of groups led by, and focusing on, women. In order to avoid setting off alarm bells among the ever-vigilant Mubarak agents, these activist women carefully framed their activities with other women as being concerned with "law," "development," and "education." Their organizations, independent from the regime, became sites in which women could investigate the actual conditions of Egyptian women's lives, craft concepts to explain those conditions, and hone their organizing skills. Furthermore, through these organizations women could forge alliances with other local independent organizations. When January 2011 arrived, as the Egyptian dinner hosts explain, hundreds of women would be ready with networks, skills, and gender analyses.

During the Mubarak-regime years, the Muslim Brotherhood played a specifically gendered role in Egyptian political life. It was (and remains) an explicitly patriarchal organization made up of middle-class, religiously observant professional men—engineers, doctors, lawyers. Its members espoused the notion that good Muslim women devoted their energies to caring for their families. According to the Brotherhood's model of social order, women leave public affairs to their protectors—that is, to their brothers, husbands, fathers, and uncles. With both its nationwide organization and its alternative ideology, the Brotherhood was seen as a threat by the self-anointed guardian of secularism, the Mubarak regime, which routinely imprisoned the Brotherhood's leaders.

Many feminists in diverse countries (for instance, in Algeria, Turkey, Palestine, the United Kingdom, the United States, Poland,

Serbia, Chile, Mexico, Iran, Ireland, India, Japan, and Iraq) have come to the conclusion that only a form of state that does not support any particular religion can (1) ensure that all sectors of a culturally diverse society have equal access to the state and are fairly represented in that state, (2) guarantee that women are free to choose for themselves how they individually will engage with matters of faith, and (3) ensure that state interpretations of religious doctrine are not written into the constitution and are not used by authorities to restrict women's roles and rights in society. However, the former suppression of the Muslim Brotherhood by the Mubarak state in the name of defending a secular nationalist state now makes it extremely difficult for Egyptian revolutionary feminists to call for a revolutionary secular state during the present debates over a new constitution. When they do, they risk being tarred with the Mubarak brush.

But the Muslim Brotherhood's gendered impacts on Egyptian politics have been even broader. As the Mubarak regime, in pursuit of a crony capitalist economy, rolled back the Nasserist welfare state, the Muslim Brotherhood moved into the resultant vacuum. In villages and modest urban neighborhoods, where most Egyptian women live their everyday lives, it was to the Muslim Brotherhood's local branches that poor women began to turn for needed food and health care. When the first free parliamentary elections came, in late autumn 2011, followed soon after by presidential elections, in June 2012, many women voted for the Muslim Brotherhood's candidates, not only because they had stood up to the Mubarak regime for decades, and not only because their seeming piety offered a sharp contrast to the Mubarak elite's corruption, but also because the men of the Brotherhood had supplied crucial services to many women in their times of need.

Those relatively few women who reaped the benefits of the Mubarak regime were chiefly the wives and daughters of businessmen, senior administrators, and generals. The most prominent was Suzanne Mubarak, the president's wife. An urbane woman, she saw herself—and was seen by many insiders and outsiders—as representing Egypt's "modernity." Part of her modernity was her role as a public advocate for Egyptian women's empowerment, or more accurately, the regime's narrow version of empowerment. Suzanne led the state's National Council for Women. It was this Suzanne Mubarak–led council that, for instance, submitted a periodic report to the international committee that monitors each government's compliance with the UN's Convention on the Elimination of All Forms of Discrimination against Women.

But Suzanne Mubarak's very advocacy—for instance, for quotas for women in the parliament—would have a devastating effect on activist women's efforts in the soon-to-emerge revolutionary period. While electoral quotas for women have proved successful in India and Scandinavia, for most Egyptian revolutionary women and men the very idea of quotas has been irrevocably tainted by its association with the manipulative Mubarak regime. On the other hand, although the regime's grip on power seemed unmovable, local independent women's rights advocates often did what they could to gain Suzanne's support for legal reforms related to gender—for instance, concerning the legal age of girls' marriage, the grounds for divorce, and the basis of child custody. These reforms too, even though they were designed by local women activists, would afterward be treated as suspect because of their association with Mubarak's top-down authoritarianism.

Some of the dinner guests smile ruefully as they listen to this part of the Egyptian feminists' story. As Algeria's Marie-Aimee Helie-Lucas and Turkey's Nizihe Muhittin quickly recognize, a self-serving manipulative oppressive regime can taint an otherwise progressive concept, such as the concept of a secular state or raising the age of consent. That leaves feminists hobbled when the oppressive regime falls.

Several of the other dinner guests, too, had seen firsthand how an authoritarian regime could hijack the women's cause—in order to garner international acceptance for itself, to wrap itself in the cloak of "modernity." Such authoritarian regimes had wielded language, symbols, patronage, and tokenism to ritualistically embrace "women's emancipation." All the while, the principal pillars of the regimes' patriarchal systems had remained intact. The long-term gendered legacy of this authoritarian-regime tactic was a profound distrust—among many of the most dedicated opponents of these regimes—of anything that smacked of women's rights. This association also handed gender conservatives within revolutionary coalitions an instrument with which to sweep women's rights off the table and under the rug.

The Egyptian hosts, however, did not want their feminist guests to imagine that prerevolutionary women's groups were all either co-opted or passive. During these oppressive years, independent Egyptian women's groups kept honing their feminist investigatory skills. For instance, the Alliance for Arab Women issued a report in 2009 daring to chastise the government and Suzanne Mubarak's National Council for Women for claiming that there was little information available about the majority of Egyptian women who lived in rural areas. In fact, members of the Alliance for Arab Women had been working for years in rural villages and had collected their own information about rural women's lives. They found that rural women were enduring even more discrimination than their urban sisters. The causes were geographic remoteness, poorer health facilities (especially in the fields of family planning and occupational health), and a lack of inheritance rights (particularly crucial given that land is the basis for economic security among Egypt's rural residents), as well as a lack of economic opportunities due to the government's neglect of rural services and infrastructure.[12]

Consequently, on the eve of the January 25th uprising, the skills for economic and political participation were unequally distributed not only between Egyptian women and men but also between urban women and rural women. Among the country's fast-growing younger population, education and literacy gaps were narrowing, but in the country's population as a whole the gender gap in literacy was a chasm: Egyptian women were twice as likely as Egyptian men to have been deprived of the chance to learn how to read and write.[13] Furthermore, if democracy begins at home, many Egyptian women would face formidable challenges to being taken seriously in decision making: when asked about the power dynamics in their own households, 50 percent of Egyptian women reported that they had *no* say in household decisions.[14]

A gender gap in particular skills does not have to be decisive, the feminists around the dinner table agree. What is required to offset and then close the gender skills gap is a genuine commitment to including women from all backgrounds in public life, ensuring that women of all classes and regions have access to public life on an equal footing with men. Listening attentively, some of the Egyptian feminists at the table respond that today they are worried about the existence of such a commitment, especially among their male anti-Mubarak compatriots. Just months before the historic protest gathering in Tahrir Square that so many male and female protestors heralded as a new democratic community, only 45 percent of Egyptian men had answered "yes" when the Pew surveyors asked them: "Should women have equal rights with men?" Among Egyptian women, however, 76 percent had answered "yes."[15]

THE VOTING BOOTH, THE PARLIAMENT, AND THE MILITARY COUNCIL

The popular uprising of January 2011, which caught the world's attention and made Tahrir Square a globally celebrated space, had included defiant women and men. The leaders were Internet-savvy young people, male and female, some of whom had been active since 2006 in movements to support strikes by women textile workers and underpaid male workers. Many of the women who camped out in Tahrir Square that January were already active in women's organizations. Within days, the anti-Mubarak demonstrations were attracting Egyptians across several generations. The middle-aged, middle-class men of the Muslim Brotherhood, the best-organized national organization outside the regime, initially hesitated, but they belatedly threw the Brotherhood's considerable support behind the demonstrators.

The protestors in Cairo, Alexandria, Port Said, and Suez endured repeated arrests and physical attacks by the regime's police and their paid thugs, while the army's generals, weighing their own long-term interests, initially ordered their soldiers to be restrained. The guests around the table nod and smile as they recall their own sense of exhilaration at the height of their countries' popular mobilizations. Nothing then had seemed impossible.

In early February 2011, the protestors succeeded in forcing Egypt's authoritarian president Hosni Mubarak to resign. Mubarak and his sons, known for their arrogance, urbanity, and corruption, were subsequently imprisoned and put on trial. *Aljazeera*, CNN, and the BBC provided the world's viewers with hour-by-hour coverage. The local mood was jubilant. So many possibilities seemed to be opening up for the first time, opportunities for building a new kind of Egyptian society, one that could mirror the sense of shared community, shared responsibility, and shared respect that the thousands of activists had experienced firsthand at Tahrir Square during those intense eighteen days.

Revolutions, however, do not happen in one fell swoop, as every woman at the table knows. A revolution takes not only years of preparation but also years of struggle after the initial mobilization. The ongoing efforts to fulfill the revolutionary goals of inclusion and social justice in all their complex forms usually continue for months, even years, after the fall of the most prominent of the regime's figures. When most of the foreign journalists have left and the restless cameras have turned elsewhere, crucial decisions and risky choices still will have to be made by revolutionary feminists.

The dinner guests have been listening carefully to their Egyptian hosts. They nod together at this point with shared understanding. It is often, they agree, during the prolonged transition from the old regime to the new government (or more likely, to a succession of new governments) that women's issues and women's participation get pushed aside. Their own male compatriots tell them: "Now we have to get down to the serious business of constructing a new political system." In this transitional setting, "serious" can translate into men-only street battles. "Serious" simultaneously can turn into men-only negotiations, even if the men doing the fighting and the bargaining are each other's rivals. During the transition, many negotiations between key male players take place behind closed doors in masculinized spaces—for instance, the contemporary Egyptian women chime in to say, between the male leaders of the Muslim Brotherhood, the male leaders of the rival civilian political parties, the male leaders of the state's police forces, and the male generals of the military council.

At the same time, during the months and years of revolutionary transition, feminists face the challenge of keeping even the committed women activists mobilized. Mundane responsibilities can take over. The laundry still has to get washed, children still have to be fed. Elderly relatives still need hourly care that women are expected to provide. Not every male partner understands when a woman informs him that he is going to have to cook his own supper because she has an evening meeting to attend. On top of all this, women students still have to complete their degrees when universities reopen, and women workers still have to hang on to their precious paid jobs as the economy skids.

Following the February 2011 fall of Mubarak, the senior military officers stepped into the political breach. Within days it was clear both to the young secular revolutionaries and to the Muslim Brotherhood that Egypt's generals had no intention of handing over state power and authority soon. Acting through their Supreme Council for the Armed Forces (SCAF), the generals positioned themselves as the preventers of social chaos and as the last bastion of defense against an Islamicized state. They did not talk publicly about their own commercial stake in refusing to move aside for a new civilian-controlled governing system.

With the military's assertion of political power, low-ranking soldiers and police became the masculinized enforcers of order on the street. Demonstrators, who during late January and early February had hurled epithets at the brutal police, had appreciated the military's passivity and interpreted it as support for their cause. Now they had to recalculate. Women who went out to protest the military's rule and the lack of serious reform encountered an escalating sexualized form of suppression.

Women were groped or directly assaulted by police and the nonuniformed thugs in their hire. Once arrested, women reported being subjected to what the prison authorities euphemistically called "virginity
tests." The authorities claimed that such tests were to prevent women
prisoners from making false claims later that they had been raped by
prison guards.[16]

For years before the revolution, Egyptian women had complained—
though rarely to authorities, since that avenue was considered either
shameful or fruitless—about constant casual sexual harassment by
civilian men in public places such as markets, buses, and streets. Having an advantage that earlier women activists lacked—that is, knowledge of the feminist analytical concept "sexual harassment"—Egyptian
revolutionary women could name, investigate, and challenge this sort
of masculinized behavior directed at women, a set of actions and attitudes intended to objectify women and to severely constrain their public mobility. In the years leading up to the revolution, for instance,
women activists had started several projects to take experiences of sexual harassment out of the private sphere—where men had impunity
and women were burdened by guilt and shame. Several young women
cofounded a safe-streets online organization for women, which they
called HarassMap. From their cell phones, Cairo's women could send
HarassMap reports of sexual harassment. Rebecca Ciao, a HarassMap
cofounder, and her small group of volunteers tallied these reports and
produced an urban map of male harassment, available to local women
who had to navigate the city.[17]

In 2008 the Egyptian Center for Women's Rights published an in-
depth study of sexual harassment. The Egyptian women who conducted the study explained that their aim was "to break the silence of
women on the issue, emphasizing that women are neither alone nor
guilty and that they can speak freely about their experiences."[18] The
center's researchers systematically interviewed both women and men
in small and large cities. They talked to married women and unmarried
women. They talked to women who dressed very conservatively,

wearing long skirts and head scarves, and to women who dressed in more revealing attire. They found that most of the men who engaged in harassment were between the ages of nineteen and twenty-four. Many of the male interviewees said they harassed women as a sort of casual entertainment. Some of the male interviewees added that they harassed women in order to boost their own sense of manly self-confidence.

In the end, the researchers came to conclusions that they admitted shocked even themselves and that challenged most Egyptians' presumptions about sexual harassment. First, they found that dressing conservatively did not protect a woman from being harassed by men. The researchers had offered the women interviewees a chart showing six generic modes of female attire in contemporary Egypt and had asked each woman to say which most resembled her own way of dressing every day when in public. Then they had asked each about her experiences with sexual harassment. Their finding: "31.9% of women who reported sexual harassment were ... wearing a blouse, long skirt and veil [that is, a head scarf, not a full facial veil]. 21.0% of women [harassed] were wearing a longer blouse, pants, and veil [again, a head scarf]." This finding, the researchers at the Egyptian Center for Women's Rights argued, undercut the common belief that only the women who dressed in scanty, "unrespectable" clothing were harassed. It also dented that belief's popular corollaries: (1) that women who are harassed "are asking for it," and (2) that women are responsible for their own bodily integrity.[19] Second, "having been taught to stay in crowded places whenever possible and to be careful whenever alone in public, [to consider] crowds as protective, the study taught us the contrary: most forms of sexual harassment occur in very crowded places—in front of schools or universities, in the workplace, at bus stations or on public transport."[20]

Their third finding: "We were also brought up being taught to avoid delays and to return home before dark. However the results of the study show that sexual harassment occurs increasingly during daytime, reaching its peaks at seven o'clock A.M. and two o'clock P.M. in front of schools and when going [to] or returning home from work."[21] And their fourth finding: Women who had paid jobs outside the home were the most likely to be harassed, whether married or not.[22] Sexual harassment, these Egyptian activists contended, was not just an "imported" concept. They were not, as so many earlier revolutionary feminists had been branded by some of their revolutionary allies, merely naive pawns of imperialism. Rather, sexual harassment was a local practice rooted in local gender presumptions that limited girls' access to education, limited women's access to paid work, and shrank young and older women's capacity for full political participation.

It was the prevalence of sexual harassment in Egyptian women's lives that made the absence of sexual harassment inside jam-packed Tahrir Square from January 25 to February 2, 2011, so salient. That historic gathering came at a particular moment. Through Internet networking and labor strikes, young women and men had been building a movement for months. But they had been met with state surveillance and physical brutality. Margot Badran, the feminist historian who wrote the landmark biography of Huda Sha'rawi, and who was in Cairo in early January, before the Tahrir Square mobilization, recalls, "It was the most oppressive, most depressing time. I cannot tell you how heavy the atmosphere was."[23] Thus the radically different atmosphere created by the hundreds of thousands of people who answered the Internet call by the young woman activist Asmaa Mahfouz, to "not be afraid" and to come to Tahrir Square on January 25th, was electrifying.[24] Women demonstrators reported that, while they were in the square in close proximity to thousands of men, many of them young, they not only did not experience sexual harassment, but they also felt safe, gaining a sense of security from the shared sense of common purpose and mutual respect. This was what a nonpatriarchal democracy could feel like.

One of the Egyptian feminists hosting the imagined dinner was Moz'n Hassan, director of the Nazra ("vision" in Arabic) Center for Feminist Studies. Looking back to what she thought during those heartening days of late January and early February 2011, Moz'n Hassan explained: "Women have been able to protest freely without men to protect them and without confronting the usual harassment rampant on Cairo's streets."[25] Activist Marianne Nagui Hanna Ibrahim, another woman who had been there in the square and now was among the feminist dinner party's Egyptian hosts, agreed: "During the 18 days against Mubarak there were no women and men. It was just Egyptians in danger. I was in the square almost daily and I didn't witness a single case of sexual harassment." Then she paused, considering what women's lives had become like during the transition a year later. "But that changed after Mubarak stepped down. We were back to face the reality of where we are as Egyptian women.... We're not a priority even with fellow revolutionaries."[26]

Thus the sexual assaults ordered by the military-headed regime against women protestors in the weeks and months after Mubarak's fall took on extra significance: the culprits now were not individual men and not merely lower-ranking police and thugs; the assaults appeared to be orchestrated from above, by "respectable" elite men. As during the Mubarak regime's heyday, it was a set of unequal relationships between particular men, each wielding a distinctive form of patriarchal masculinity, that was at work. To local feminists, the intention was obvious: to drive women activists out of the political arena and thereby to sap the vitality of the political culture of popular democracy that had found such intense expression during the revolutionary takeover of Tahrir Square.

As the attacks on women protestors persisted through 2011, 2012, and into early 2013, however, they seemed to reenergize many women. More women came out in public to demonstrate specifically against all forms of violence against women, especially those perpetrated by agents of the military-run regime. One activist, Leil Zahra Mortada, concluded her report on a June 2012 women's march with this Facebook assertion: "No matter how deep the wounds are, no matter how many times we get attacked or will be attacked, this will not stop or silence us.... We will see the end of sexual harassment and assault, both state-organized and individual! We will take down patriarchy, sexism and every form of violence based on gender and sexuality."[27]

Simultaneously, the generals of the Supreme Council for the Armed Forces and their appointed civilian cabinet, along with the Mubarak-era judges, were strewing legal boulders along the political transition's path. Women's groups had to be constantly alert and ready to respond to each move that threatened to reconfirm the country's patriarchal system. Thus in March 2011, feminist activists crafted a public letter to the military-appointed prime minister, calling on him to bring women into his transitional government—not mere token or co-opted women but genuinely independent, activist women: "The forthcoming cabinet should include an adequate number of women whose efficiency and integrity have been proven, especially among those who courageously fought against the oppression and corruption of the former regime."[28] The letter was signed by the Nazra Center for Feminist Studies, the Women's Forum for Development, the Center of Egyptian Women Legal Aid, the Alliance for Arab Women, the New Women Foundation, and ten other groups, which together functioned as the Coalition of Egyptian Feminist Organizations.

Soon after, the generals appointed an all-male committee to draft an interim constitution. One provision of its draft interim constitution stipulated that a candidate for president "cannot be married to a non-Egyptian woman," strongly implying that only men could be presidential candidates. Once again, women's advocates had to be ready to shine a critical spotlight on this worrisome provision. The interim constitution's sexist stipulation remained.[29]

During this same confusing period, calls came from various newly confident conservative groups for the repeal of family law reforms that provided more rights for women in marriage, divorce, and child custody, reforms that had been instituted during the Mubarak era. Activists at the Egyptian Center for Women's Rights put together an expansive alliance of 226 local nongovernmental groups to sign their public letter urging those in power not to abandon these reforms on "the pretext" that those laws were merely the handiwork of Suzanne Mubarak. "A lot of intellectual people in the Egyptian society," they stated, "whether men or women, fought for decades for these social gains. Such a pretext is an insult to all the free organizations that worked for social reform in Egypt." Some of the groups joining this alliance were all-women's groups, some were mixed groups. Among the 226 signatories were the Egyptian Media Professionals, the National Center for Human Rights, the Youth Without Borders Community, the Young Christians Association, and the Future Businesswomen Association.[30]

Egypt's first free and genuinely multiparty parliamentary elections would pose a special challenge to Egyptian feminists. Egyptians would cast their ballots by region between November 2011 and January 2012. During this time, women activists would have to strategize together about how to engage with voters and with political parties while continuing to mobilize against sexual harassment and assaults in order to ensure that women could remain in the public arena. At the same time, they would also have to continue monitoring transition-era constitutional and legal maneuvers.

As many of the feminist dinner guests had witnessed firsthand, when revolutionary activism turns into political party consolidation and to electoral competition, remasculinization can accelerate. In both revolutionary and nonrevolutionary societies, political parties frequently have acted as men's clubs. Cracking open political parties has been doubly hard for women because so much happens behind closed doors. Furthermore, political party strategizing—that is, figuring out how to mobilize a sufficient number and distribution of votes to gain state power—is deemed "serious" political business by many men active in political party and electoral politics. Their conventional wisdom: women are good for filling the square, are good at caring for the revolutionary wounded, and may even inspire the masses, but women are not seasoned enough, not hardheaded enough, to hammer out a formula for winning an electoral majority.

In Egypt, Mubarak's long-dominant party was not permitted to run in the parliamentary elections, but myriad new parties emerged during the latter months of 2011. Only one of those, the Union of Egypt's Women, was women-led. Founded by the Arab Women's Association with the support of several hundred nongovernmental organizations, its purpose was to encourage women to vote, and to vote for independent female candidates, as well as to pressure other parties to include women's issues in their platforms.[31] The task, shared by the partners in the revived Egyptian Feminist Union, was daunting. They faced the reality that many more Egyptian women than men were still illiterate and were expected to follow the political leads of their fathers, husbands, and local male clergy. Laila Iskander, a Cairo-based feminist who had devoted two decades to successfully organizing the city's garbage collectors, sounded a warning note before the elections: women in the cities who sought the creation of a secular post-Mubarak state would have to travel out into the rural villages and engage with rural women, explaining to them in those women's own terms what they would lose if the more conservative parties' candidates got their votes.[32]

The electoral system adopted for this first post-Mubarak parliamentary election was the proportional representation party-list system. This choice would have immediate gender implications. All but one of the post-Mubarak political parties were led by men. Each party's leaders would select as many candidates as their party was capable of running. Then, in a crucial next step, party leaders would order their candidates on a single party list, from, say, number 1 to number 200, deciding which candidates would be put in slot numbers 1, 2, 3, 4, and which candidates would be buried down at the bottom in candidate slot numbers 198, 199, 200. When all the popular votes eventually were counted, each party would be allocated the number of parliamentary seats that matched its proportion of the final popular vote. Those candidates whom party leaders had placed near the top of their list would be the most likely to actually take parliamentary seats. The parliamentary candidates with the greatest advantages were those running on the tickets of the best nationally organized parties and those placed near the top of their party's total candidate list.

The Muslim Brotherhood's party—the Freedom and Justice Party—was by far the best organized and had the most comprehensive geographic reach. Also effectively organized was the Al-Nour Party, the party of the Salafis, those men who had adopted the most deeply patriarchal interpretations of Islam. Although electoral rules required every party to run at least one female candidate (though no rule specified where a party's women candidates would be placed on their list), Al-Nour refused to run any women candidates. About 30 percent of all the 2011 parliamentary candidates were women, but most of them ran as independents, with limited resources and without the backing of a political party organization.[33]

When the parliamentary election results were tallied in mid-January 2012, they were not heartening for Egypt's women activists. The Muslim Brotherhood's Freedom and Justice Party won a decisive 47 percent of parliamentary seats. The next most successful party, Al-Nour, won 25 percent of the seats. The liberal parties, more inclined to support laws reforming family law and the personal status code, as well as to support a secular state, were left in the minority, divided and marginalized. Altogether, they held a mere 28 percent of the seats. Women of all parties won slightly less than 2 percent of all the seats in the new postrevolutionary Egyptian parliament. The new parliament would be made up of 9 women and 489 men. The results by party were:

- Freedom and Justice Party—3 women
- Al Nour Party—0 women
- Al Wafd Party (the century-old nationalist party)—2 women
- Egyptian Social Democratic Party—1 woman
- Other parties combined—3 women[34]

More disheartening for Egyptian revolutionary feminists, though not unexpected, were the sentiments expressed by the newly elected women parliamentarians of the Freedom and Justice Party. For instance, Dr. Aza Al Garf promised that she would "work with the rest of the

Figure 13. Women and men voting at a local electoral precinct in Cairo during the first free Egyptian presidential election, May 23, 2012. UN Women/Fatima El Zahraa Yassin.

members of parliament to change all the laws that have destroyed the Egyptian family in the past years such as the divorce laws, the marriage laws, and the vision and mandate of education." She went on to explain, "It is imperative that the structure of these laws be redone to be in accordance with Islamic sharia."[35]

There were more elections to come. The presidential elections, held in May 2012, offered women only male candidates to choose from in both balloting rounds. In the final runoff, their choice was between a civilian elite official from the Mubarak regime and a senior member of the Muslim Brotherhood. The clear winner was Mohamed Morsi, who ran on the Muslim Brotherhood's Freedom and Justice Party ticket.

The generals on the Supreme Council for the Armed Forces begrudgingly accepted the electoral results. The early postelection photographs showed the generals and President Morsi together. No woman appeared in these scenes. The only woman to make a photographic appearance was a foreigner: Hillary Clinton, American secretary of state, was shown meeting separately with the leading general and with President Morsi. Although Clinton also held meetings with women activists, no Egyptian women activists were present in these scenes of high-level negotiation.[36]

The relationships between these competing party, bureaucratic, and army men were neither cordial nor easy. On the eve of the June 2012 presidential balloting, claiming simply to be following a ruling by the senior judges, the generals had dissolved the newly elected parliament. Within a week after taking office, Mohamed Morsi defiantly insisted that the popularly elected parliament meet and that the male-dominated Constitutional assembly (with ninety-two men and a mere eight women) proceed with its work writing a permanent constitution. Meanwhile, the military continued to control the civilian bureaucracy and the security forces, as well as the government's budget. Egyptian feminists took to the streets in January 2013 to protest what they saw as a new constitution written by the male-dominated constitutional assembly and rushed though a popular referendum by President Morsi, a constitution whose articles enabled the military to maintain its unaccountability and which made all too possible a future assertion of the Muslim clergy's authority over women's lives. As both the dinner party guests and their Egyptian hosts agree, budgets and constitutions are serious feminist matters.

Mainstream news coverage portrayed the next stage in Egypt's ongoing revolution as an all-male contest: on one side were Mohamed Morsi and his Muslim Brotherhood supporters; on another, the generals, the police, and the judges; on a third side, the male leaders of the opposition parties; and on yet a fourth side, the opposition street fighters, who were willing to confront the security forces' violence. Despite their continued activism, revolutionary women became almost invisible to most journalists and thus to most news readers and viewers. The unspoken conventional assumption was one that all the feminist dinner party attendees instantly recognize: that the rivalry among men was what was serious; women and their concerns would have to wait until later.

THE TOAST

By this time it is well past midnight. The dinner guests have poured their third cups of tea and finished all of Nguyen Thi Kiem's ripe longan berries and Abigail Adams's juicy blueberries. They have spoken openly for hours about what it was like, in the midst of violence, economic distress, intense personal relationships, and a fluctuating political landscape, to stay attentive and mobilized while constantly recalibrating their feminist priorities in order to match each new circumstance. They have talked candidly, too, about doing all this while still pushing back efforts to turn women into mere national symbols or passive voters or deployable labor resources as the forces of masculinization tightened their grip on postrevolution political life.

Everyone around the dish-cluttered table at this point becomes quiet. Then, spontaneously, all the feminist invitees turn to focus on their Egyptian hosts. Simultaneously, the past revolutionary feminists stand up, face the current Egyptian revolutionary feminists, raise their teacups, and in a chorus, offer a toast: "Here's to NOW, not later!"

CHAPTER NINE

Conclusion

In the Eye of the Beholder

It can be daunting to realize that you have little control over who takes you seriously. In an effort to be taken seriously—or to have a topic you care about taken seriously—by the people you think wield influence, you can do some pretty risky things. You can devote a lot of time to trying to comprehend the priorities, worries, tastes, and even mere quirks of those influential people. They—the policy makers, the donors, the media editors, the prosecutors, the party leaders, the militia commanders, the international peacekeepers, the people with insider connections—gradually can become the most important people in your universe.

They are the beholders. They are the people, usually men, but sometimes women, who can decide to take you and your cause seriously or to relegate you and your cause to obscurity—to a far-off "later." The beholders might even start to loom larger in your daily concerns than your own constituents, the people whose rights and needs originally propelled you into action. If you begin to fixate on the beholders, you are likely to become preoccupied with questions such as:

· What kind of activism does this beholder deem respectable?

· What sort of language does that beholder find reasonable?

· What kind of insecurity are these beholders most anxious about?

When you and your colleagues are feminists, and the significant beholders—those who can decide what is worth taking seriously—are nonfeminists (perhaps even antifeminists), then traversing the landscape of seriousness can become especially treacherous. For instance, you might think that what is driving bankers' risk taking, budgetary officials' choice of cuts, or military peacekeepers' strategic decisions is, in large part, the modernized version of patriarchy. That is, after close observation and months of failing to get their attention, you might come to the conclusion that these beholders are not merely stressed out, they are not merely self-promoters, they are not simply wedded to a certain economic model. They also, you might come to realize, have a stake in perpetuating an elaborate system of structures and cultural beliefs that privilege certain modes of masculinity while pushing to the margins anything tainted with femininity. Nonetheless, outside your circles of feminist allies, you hesitate to say *patriarchy* out loud for fear of triggering dismissal by your significant beholders, the ones who can bestow or withhold the mantle of seriousness on your concerns.

Or you might have a strong hunch that misogyny—contempt for women and for whatever is deemed feminine—is at work when diplomats, local politicians, or even male prodemocracy colleagues shrug off your feminist alarm at women's rising impoverishment or at escalations of violence against women. Similarly, you also know full well that "gender" is not just about women. Doing serious feminist-informed gender analysis, you have learned, requires digging deep into the workings of masculinity. Still, you decide not to use either of these two *m*-words in public, to guard against being written off by the beholders as "too radical."

A third example of feminist strategic self-censorship: you have found in your research that learning who does the laundry, who collects the water, who cares for the children, and who does the unpaid housework after a long day of low-paid work is crucial information if power dynamics are to be fully charted during a war, an economic crisis, or the transition from authoritarian rule to democracy. Yet you downplay your rigorous feminist analysis when, on rare occasions, you are invited to sit at the decision-making table. You are motivated by an awareness that to the ears of the allegedly "sophisticated" beholders you will sound as if you are not a serious player if you start discussing laundry. Being dismissed by the beholders as naive usually translates into being ignored during that rare meeting and never being invited back to future meetings.

These are instances of feminists choosing to round the edges of their realistic, clear-eyed causal analysis for the sake of being awarded seriousness by those who can grant or withhold that crucial political accolade. Such roundings are not unreasonable. One often has to talk in terms that editors, prosecutors, legislators, generals, party leaders, movement leaders, policy makers, or donors readily understand. One might be able to educate the beholders, of course. But that can take precious time, energy, and access. Often the cause—stopping sexual assault, halting the job losses, preventing the generals from reasserting control—feels so pressing that devoting time to teaching the beholders that "patriarchy," "misogyny," and "masculinity" are useful, not scary, concepts seems an unaffordable luxury. At that intense moment, it can appear wisest to keep exerting pressure by using concepts that already are familiar to the nonfeminist beholders: "recovery," "families," "job markets," "stability," "social order," "national security."

The question is: what is lost in translation? That is, by hesitating to call patriarchy by its proper name, or by referring to misogyny as mere sex discrimination, or by skimming over the daily workings of certain masculinities, do we ensure that the depths of the problems are grossly underestimated—and thus the proposed solutions are inadequate from the start?[1]

As we have seen, it takes persistent, undaunted, collective work to get a trivialized phenomenon converted into a serious public issue. One need only look at the combined energy and stubborn activism it has required—since the late 1970s, by thousands of women activists, students, employees, lawyers, and researchers in dozens of countries—to turn sexual harassment into a popularly and legally recognized issue. Yet as French and Egyptian feminists have shown us, despite this substantial achievement no woman today in any workplace or public space—a factory, an office, a school, a military platoon, a parliament, a public bus or street—who files a charge of sexual harassment against a police officer, coworker, or supervisor does so lightly. To bring charges of sexual harassment today, thirty-five years after feminists first crafted the concept, is an action fraught with personal and political risk. The company's "bottom line," the institution's public reputation, officials' prioritization of "national security," supervisor's determination to be seen as running a trouble-free shop, coupled with the free-floating presumption that a woman "must have asked for it," can trump any woman's valid, documented experience of sexualized abuse in a workplace and public space.

To estimate the costs of seriousness, we also could calculate what it has taken to pass the groundbreaking UN Security Council Resolution 1325. That is, what did it require finally, in October 2000, to win Security Council delegates' official acknowledgment that women activists and women's experiences must be taken seriously during and after armed conflicts? To answer this question realistically we would have to add up all the hard work invested by local and transnational feminists to persuade the UN Security Council's member states to pass Resolution 1325 on Women, Peace and Security. The passage of 1325 marked the first time in the UN's history that the Security Council obligated all UN agencies and all UN member governments to take women seriously—not only as victims but also as knowledgeable actors—at every step on the long road from peace negotiations to peacekeeping to postwar reconstruction.

As Nadine Puechguirbal, Cynthia Cockburn, and other feminists with years of gritty experience in war-torn countries, in feminist peace groups, and inside the UN's peacekeeping machinery and UN Women have warned us, however, effective implementation of the resolution's far-reaching requirements remains elusive. It still is not a priority for most of the beholders.

Every day 1325 is subverted by civilian and military officials' dismissive attitudes toward women's experiences of insecurity and toward women's value as decision makers. Twelve years after its passage, in April 2012, Michelle Bachelet, the UN's Under-Secretary-General who heads UN Women, surveyed the implementation of 1325 in Yemen, Liberia, Somalia, Afghanistan, Haiti, and Libya. In conclusion, she offered these two blunt reminders to members of the Security Council: "Women's participation in these processes [of postconflict transition] should not be dependent on the willingness of conference organizers to extend invitations to them," and "women's rights must never be used as negotiating instruments, as a soft bargaining chip to placate certain social groups."[2]

To persuade elites and practitioners on the ground to take seriously all their obligations under 1325 has necessitated coordinated activism inside and outside of the United Nations by widely dispersed feminists—in New York, Oslo, Geneva, Haifa, Belgrade, Kinshasa, Monrovia, Kabul, Dili, Tripoli, Boston, and Prishtina. They have contributed to groups such as the NGO Working Group on Women, Peace and Security; the international and national branches of the Women's International League for Peace and Freedom; Women in Black Belgrade; the Kosovo Women's Network; Isha L'Isha Feminist Center; the Women in Conflict Zones Network; and the Consortium for Gender, Security and Human Rights.[3]

What has become clear in all these peace-building, economic-reform, and revolutionary efforts is that gender analysis is serious. It matters. It has consequences. Refusing to do gender analysis also matters: in its absence, policy will be based on a shaky foundation and be unlikely to achieve its goals. As we have seen, for feminist-informed gender analysis to be taken seriously, feminists engaged in institutional politics and feminists engaged in social movement campaigns must be in constant communication with each other. This can involve overcoming mutual distrust and learning about the obstacles that each faces. It can mean taking each other's work seriously, despite different styles of working, different trip wires of anxiety, different measures of success.

Feminist-informed gender analysis is not merely a technical specialty that one can choose to learn or not. This point has been made clear by the experiences of Egyptian feminist activists challenging the myths perpetuating sexual harassment; by the experiences of Icelandic, Irish, American, and British feminists during the recent economic crash; and by feminist antimilitarists and feminist peace-mission officers. Developing the skills to do a thorough gender analysis takes time and commitment. One has to learn to demand that all data be gender disaggregated. One has to remember to shine a bright light on the gendered behaviors and assumptions of people in elite positions. One has to ask diverse "ordinary" women to elaborate about their mundane (paid and unpaid) economic realities. One has to learn to chart the gendered dynamics within a wide array of institutions and organizations: banks; universities; militias; constitutional assemblies; political parties; humanitarian aid organizations; government committees, departments, and legislatures; and of course, social movements. And then one has to stay analytically attentive over months, even years. To learn these gender analytical skills and put them into action is to develop the capacity to be realistic about not only the impacts but also, even more crucially, the causes of public and private policy.

Doing gender analysis also requires that we investigate both structural and cultural gendered dynamics and then track the causal dynamics between them. The experiences of Haitian, British, Irish, American, Icelandic, French, and Egyptian women have made this necessity clear. That is, jokes in the workplace can turn out to be serious; so can systems of reward. Who is admired for which characteristics can be a serious matter. What men think about women's office or street attire matters, and so does the structure of policing. Together, structures and cultures can promote a certain sort of masculinity at the expense of other, perhaps less damaging, forms of masculinity while marginalizing virtually all but the most subservient sorts of femininity. Reforming structures without deliberately exposing and altering cultures produces only half-baked change at best. Patriarchy is sustainable, adaptable. If masculine-privileging beliefs and values are left relatively untouched, patriarchy can adapt to new structures.

It is comfortable to imagine that the beholders, those who dictate what will be trivialized and what will be taken seriously, are an uncomprehending or arrogant "them." In reality, we are often the "them." To become a beholder, one does not have to be at the top of a pyramid. One can wield relatively modest influence yet still be dismissive of crucial feminist analyses. Becoming a patriarchal beholder involves our making certain decisions, such as these:

- We choose to trust the coverage of CNN and Reuters more than the reportage of Women's eNews and the *Newsletter of Women Living Under Muslim Laws.*
- We take seriously the commentaries of well-known male intellectuals rather than absorb the explanations of feminist activists whose names are new to us.
- We bestow our own mantles of seriousness on ungendered data—data on unemployment, gun ownership, corruption, electoral preferences, foreclosures—without pressing for gender-disaggregated information.
- We treat political party rivalries as if they were more serious than domestic violence against women.
- We find massive rallies in the capital's central square riveting but switch the figurative channel when talk moves on to constitutional reform.

The politics of seriousness are everyday politics. Sometimes they occur on a big stage under the klieg lights. But more often they occur around a table cluttered with coffee cups, or in a pub, or on a crowded bus stuck in traffic. The politics of seriousness go on wherever femininities and masculinities are in action. No place is too mundane for the alert feminist gender investigator.

NOTES

CHAPTER ONE. WHO IS "TAKEN SERIOUSLY"?

1. Han Suyin, *And the Rain My Drink* (London: Penguin, 1961).

2. See, for instance, Cecilia Ng, Maznah Mohamad, and Tan Beng Hui, *Feminism and the Women's Movement in Malaysia* (New York: Routledge, 2006).

3. Cynthia Enloe and Joni Seager, *The Real State of America: Mapping the Myths and Truths of the United States* (New York: Penguin; London: University of California Press, 2011), p. 41; Jane Martinson, *Seen But Not Heard: How Women Make Front Page News* (London: Women in Journalism, October 2012); Amelia Hill, "Front Pages Still Male-Dominated and Sexist—Report," *The Guardian,* October 15, 2012. See also Robin H. Pugh Yi and Craig T. Dearfield, *The Status of Women in the U.S. Media, 2012,* Women's Media Center, February 2012, http://wmc.3cdn.net/a6b2dc282c824e903a_arm6boK8.pdf, accessed February 14, 2012.

4. Rick Gladstone, "Waiting in the Wings, a Survivor of Three Decades of Syrian Politics," *New York Times,* February 4, 2012.

5. See EMILY's List, www.emilyslist.org.

6. For examples of this gendered process at work in international nuclear weapons politics, see Carol Cohn, Felicity Hill, and Sara Ruddick, *The Relevance of Gender for Eliminating Weapons of Mass Destruction* (Stockholm: Weapons of Mass Destruction Commission, 2005).

7. Sheri Lynn Gibbings, "No Angry Women at the United Nations: Political Dreams and the Cultural Politics of United Nations Security Council Resolution 1325," *International Feminist Journal of Politics* 13, no. 4 (December 2011): 522–38.

8. Carol Cohn, Helen Kinsella, and Sheri Lynn Gibbings, "Women, Peace and Security: Resolution 1325," *International Feminist Journal of Politics* 6, no. 1 (2004): 130–42; Carol Cohn, "Mainstreaming Gender in UN Security Policy," in *Global Governance: Feminist Perspectives*, ed. Shrin Rai and Georgina Waylen (Basingstoke, UK: Palgrave Macmillan, 2008), pp. 185–206.

9. Sarah Taylor and Kristina Mader, *Mapping Women, Peace and Security in the UN Security Council: Report of the NGOWG Monthly Action Points, 2009–2010*, NGO Working Group on Women, Peace and Security, October 2010, http://womenpeacesecurity.org/media/pdf-NGOWG_MAPReport_2009–2010.pdf.

10. For more scholarly assessments of the implementation of UNSCR 1325, see Nicola Pratt and Sophie Richter-Devroe, eds., "Critically Examining UNSCR 1325," special issue, *International Feminist Journal of Politics* 13, no. 4 (December 2011).

11. On antisuffragism, see, for instance, Jane Lewis, ed., *Before the Vote Was Won: Arguments for and Against Women's Suffrage, 1864–1896* (London: Routledge and Kegan Paul, 1987); Elna C. Green, *Southern Strategies: Southern Women and the Suffrage Question* (Chapel Hill: University of North Carolina Press, 1997); Julia Bush, *Women Against the Vote: Female Anti-Suffragism in Britain* (Oxford: Oxford University Press, 2007); Louise Edwards, *Gender, Politics and Democracy: Women's Suffrage in China* (Stanford, CA: Stanford University Press, 2008).

12. I first tried to examine this in *Does Khaki Become You? The Militarization of Women's Lives* (London: Pluto Press; Boston: South End Press), and in *Maneuvers: the International Politics of Militarizing Women's Lives* (Berkeley: University of California Press, 2000). See also Enloe, *Globalization and Militarism: Feminists Make the Link* (Lanham, MD: Rowman and Littlefield, 2007), and *Nimo's War, Emma's War: Making Feminist Sense of the Iraq War* (Berkeley: University of California Press, 2010).

13. See, for instance, Karen Turner, with Thanh Hao Phan, *Even the Women Must Fight: Memories of War from North Vietnam* (New York: John Wiley and Sons, 1998); U.S. Government Accountability Office, *Homeless Women Veterans: Actions Needed to Ensure Safe and Appropriate Housing* (Washington, DC: U.S. Government Accountability Office, December 2011).

14. For efforts by U.S. women veterans to get their postwar health issues taken seriously by members of Congress and by Defense Department and Department of Veterans Affair officials, see Brittany L. Stalsburg, "Rape, Sexual Assault and Sexual Harassment in the Military: Quick Facts," Service Women's Action Network, April 2011, http://servicewomen.org, accessed February 2, 2012; Erin Mulhall, "Women Warriors: Supporting She 'Who Has

Borne the Battle,'" Iraq and Afghanistan Veterans of America, October 2009, www.IAVA.org, accessed February 2, 2012.

CHAPTER TWO. LAUNCHING AND NAMING

1. A somewhat different version of this essay, titled "From the Ground Up," appears in a lively collection of personal accounts of becoming feminist and launching women's studies in diverse settings, including India, Australia, South Korea, Canada, Bangladesh, and Vietnam: Rekha Pande, ed., *Women's Studies Narratives* (Cambridge: Cambridge Scholars Publishers, forthcoming).

2. Gertrude E. Noyes, *A History of Connecticut College* (New London, CT: Connecticut College, 1982).

3. Cynthia Enloe, *Ethnic Politics and Political Development* (Boston: Little, Brown, 1973).

4. I have pursued these questions in Cynthia Enloe, *Nimo's War, Emma's War: Making Feminist Sense of the Iraq War* (Berkeley: University of California Press, 2010).

5. *Ms. Magazine's* founding editors celebrated their creation's fortieth anniversary in June 2012 with a party hosted at New York's City Hall: James Barron, "After 40 Years, It's Still Ms. to Readers," *New York Times,* June 14, 2012.

6. Cynthia Enloe, *Ethnic Soldiers: State Security in Divided Societies* (London: Penguin, 1980).

7. Cynthia Enloe, *Does Khaki Become You? The Militarization of Women's Lives* (London: Pluto Press; Boston: South End Press, 1983).

8. Cynthia Enloe, *Bananas, Beaches, and Bases: Making Feminist Sense of International Politics* (London: Pandora Press, 1989; Berkeley: University of California Press, 1990).

9. All the papers accumulated by Gilda Bruckman and me during the 1980–1983 Clark University sexual harassment case—petitions, court transcripts, posters, ledgers of fund-raising donors, university statements, news articles—are publicly available for any researcher to use at the wonderful Schlesinger Library of American Women's History, Harvard University, Cambridge, Massachusetts, under the references "Sexual harassment," "Ximena Bunster," or "Cynthia Enloe."

10. Works written by Ximena Bunster during this period include: "Surviving Beyond Fear: Women and Torture in Latin America," in *Women and Change in Latin America,* ed. June Nash and Helen Safa (South Hadley, MA: Bergin and Garvey, 1986), pp. 297–326; "'Watch for the Little Nazi Man That All of Us

Have Inside': The Mobilization and Demobilization of Women in Militarized Chile," *Women's Studies International Forum* 11, no. 5 (1988): 228–35.

CHAPTER THREE. THE MUNDANE MATTERS

1. This essay first appeared in a slightly different form in *International Political Sociology* 5, no. 4 (2011): 447–450. I am grateful to the *IPS* editors. This connection first became obvious to me when I included chapters on military wives and on women as defense industry workers in the same book: *Does Khaki Become You? The Militarization of Women's Lives* (London: Pluto Press; Boston: South End Press, 1983). Military wives and women defense industry workers come together again in *Globalization and Militarism: Feminists Make the Link* (Lanham, MD: Rowman and Littlefield, 2007).

2. See, for instance, the organizing strategies employed by women in Central and Latin America's globalized banana industry: Dana Frank, *Bananeras: Women Transforming the Banana Unions of Latin America* (Boston: South End Press, 2005). See also Ethel Brooks, *Unraveling the Garment Industry* (Minneapolis: University of Minnesota Press, 2007).

3. See, for instance, Mary Beth Mills, *Thai Women in the Global Labor Force* (New Brunswick, NJ: Rutgers University Press, 1999); Carla Freeman, *High Tech and High Heels in the Global Economy* (Durham, NC: Duke University Press, 2000).

4. Leslie T. Chang, *Factory Girls: From Village to City in a Changing China* (New York: Spiegel and Grau, 2009).

CHAPTER FOUR. DSK, VIKINGS, AND THE SMARTEST GUYS

1. The transnational feminist group of analysts whose members have pioneered this gendered economic critique of the IMF is DAWN: Development Alternatives with Women for a New Era, www.dawnnet.org. Also useful are the studies produced by an international network of feminist economists who conduct research on women's roles in, and the impact on women of, international economics: International Working Group on Gender, Macroeconomics and International Economics, www.genderandmacro.org. A groundbreaking book about asking feminist questions of national and international economic importance is: Marilyn Waring, *If Women Counted: A New Feminist Economics* (San Francisco: Harper and Row, 1988). For further feminist

analyses of the global political economy in which the IMF has played such a central role, see also V. Spike Peterson and Anne Sisson Runyan, *Global Gender Issues in the New Millennium,* 3rd ed. (Boulder, CO: Westview Press, 2010); Shirin Rai, *Gender and the Political Economy of Development* (Cambridge, U.K.: Polity, 2002).

2. Christine Ahn, "The IMF: Violating Women since 1945," Foreign Policy in Focus, May 19, 2011, www.fpif.org/articles/the_imf_violating_since_1945, accessed May 24, 2011.

3. Binyamin Appelbaum and Sheryl Gay Stolberg, "At I.M.F., Men on Prowl and Women on Guard," *New York Times,* May 20, 2011.

4. Ibid.

5. Craig Murphy, professor of political science at Wellesley College, a specialist in the politics of international development, and a longtime observer of the World Bank, spoke about the World Bank's senior leadership, during the International Studies Association meeting in San Diego in April 2011. He speculated that even though senior officials in Washington worked in offices right across the street from the IMF, they may have begun to adopt a new, less masculinist internal culture as a consequence of having begun to give much more serious attention to the alleviation of women's global poverty through their external policies. This hypothesis could be tested by systematically charting the gendered culture dominant inside the World Bank over several decades, from, say, 1980 to 2012.

6. Appelbaum and Stolberg, "At I.M.F., Men on Prowl and Women on Guard."

7. Christine Lagarde, "the glamorous, Chanel-clad French extrovert," and Angela Merkel, the "grounded German introvert," have differed in their external styles and occasionally have differed on questions of economic policy as well. Nonetheless, they built a relationship of trust during the years when Lagarde was the French finance minister and Merkel was the German chancellor. As Lagarde has explained, "There are many circles and many forums where it's only the two of us who are women." Nicholas Kulish and Annie Lowrey, "German Leader and I.M.F. Chief Split Over Debt," *New York Times,* March 10, 2012.

8. Liz Alderman, "I.M.F. Chief to Face French Inquiry on '07 Dispute," *New York Times,* August 5, 2011.

9. "Christine Lagarde to 'Lower Testosterone at International Monetary Fund,'" News.com.au, June 8, 2011, www.news.com.au/business/breaking-news/christine-lagarde-to-lower-testosterone-at-international-monetary-fund/story-e6frfkur-1226071440139, accessed May 9, 2012; Ian Traynor, "EU-wide

Quotas for Women in Boardrooms Rejected," *The Guardian,* October 24, 2012. Five years earlier, in 2006, at the height of the global banking boom, Lagarde had said, "I don't want to go into the war of testosterone versus estrogen.... But there is a little bit of that, where males have to sort of show off and do a bit of posturing and do all this sort of hairy-chested type of stuff that is not strong in women." Quoted in Tracy McNicoll, "Christine Lagarde Named New IMF Chief," *The Daily Beast,* June 28, 2011, www.thedailybeast.com/articles/2011/06/28/christine-lagarde-is-new-imf-chief.html, accessed May 9, 2011.

10. National Council for Research on Women, *Women in Fund Management* (New York: National Council for Research on Women, 2009).

11. Linda Basch, director of the National Council for Research on Women, interview by the author, New York City, April 11, 2012.

12. "Women and Money," *Action Brief,* National Council for Research on Women, 2010, p. 3, www.ncrw.org.

13. U.S. Government Accountability Office, *Financial Services Industry: Overall Trends in Management-Level Diversity and Diversity Initiatives, 1993–2008* (Washington, DC: U.S. Government Accountability Office, May 12, 2012), p. 2, https://docs.google.com/viewer?a=v&q=cache:s6xsUqGYw_U, accessed April 19, 2012.

14. Ibid.

15. Basch, interview.

16. The prevalence of this contemptuous attitude toward their clients—seeing them as "suckers" worthy of being sold questionable investments—was spelled out by a Goldman Sachs executive, Greg Smith, who in the wake of the crash came to see this widespread industry attitude as immoral and decided to resign from the firm. "Why I Am Leaving Goldman Sachs," *New York Times,* March 14, 2012.

17. Gretchen Morgenson and Joshua Rosner, *Reckless Endangerment* (New York: Times Books and Henry Holt, 2011).

18. Sheila Bair, *Bull by the Horns: Fighting to Save Main Street from Wall Street and Wall Street from Itself* (New York: Free Press, 2012); Morgenson and Rosner, *Reckless Endangerment.* For maps showing the national gendered and racialized patterns of American homeownership, subprime mortgage sales, and home foreclosures in the wake of the 2008 crash, see Cynthia Enloe and Joni Seager, *The Real State of America: Mapping the Myths and Truths of the United States* (New York: Penguin; London: University of California Press, 2011), pp. 24–27.

19. Edward Wyatt, "Bank's Lobbyists Sought Loophole on Risky Trading," *New York Times,* May 12, 2012; Nelson D. Schwartz and Jessica Silver-Greenberg,

"JPMorgan Chief of Investments Is Set to Depart," *New York Times,* May 14, 2012; Jessica Silver-Greenberg and Nelson D. Schwartz, "Red Flags Said to Go Unheeded by Chase Bosses," *New York Times,* May 15, 2012; Susan Dominus, "Exile on Park Avenue: How the JPMorgan Chase Trading Fiasco Took Down the Most Powerful Woman on Wall Street," *New York Times Magazine,* October 7, 2012, 32–39, 54–55.

20. Amy Schrager Lang and Daniel Lang/Levitsky, eds., *Dreaming in Public: Building the Occupy Movement* (Oxford: New Internationalist Press, 2012).

21. Tim Adams, "Testosterone and High Finance Do Not Mix: So Bring on the Women," *The Observer,* June 18, 2011, www.guardian.co.uk/world/2011 /jun/19/neuoeconomics-women-city-financial-crash, accessed May 14, 2012. The report itself is: National Commission on the Causes of the Financial Economic Crisis in the United States, *The Financial Crisis Inquiry Report* (Washington, DC: Government Printing Office, February 25, 2011).

22. Gillian Tett, *Fool's Gold* (Boston: Little, Brown, 2009).

23. Gillian Tett, quoted in: Laura Barton, "On the Money," *The Guardian,* October 30, 2008, www.guardian.co.uk/business/2008/oct/31/credit-crunch-gillian-tett-financialtimes, accessed May 14, 2002.

24. Karen Ho, *Liquidated: An Ethnography of Wall Street* (Durham, NC: Duke University Press, 2009).

25. Ibid., 107–8.

26. Ibid., 11–12.

27. Ibid., 106.

28. Ibid., 15.

29. For more on the masculinization of risk taking within banks, see Katja Meier-Pesti and Elfriede Penz, "Sex or Gender? Expanding the Sex-Based View by Introducing Masculinity and Femininity as Predictors of Financial Risk Taking," *Journal of Economic Psychology,* no. 29 (2008): 180–96.

30. "Booklist Interviews Erin Duffy," Library Love Fest, January 1, 2012, http://harperlibrary.typepad.com/my_weblog/2012/01/booklist-interviews-erin-duffy.html, accessed April 23, 2012.

31. Erin Duffy, *Bond Girl* (New York: William Morrow, 2012), p. 21.

32. "'Bond Girl': Erin Duffy on Her Wall Street Roman a Clef," *Shelf Life,* February 10, 2012, http://shelf-life.ew.com/2012/02/10/eron-duffy-on-her-wall-street-roman-a-clef, accessed April 23, 2012. Another recent novel set inside a Wall Street investment firm and based on interviews with women and men working in the financial industry is: Sohaila Abdulali, *Year of the Tiger* (New Delhi: Penguin, 2010).

33. Kevin Roose, "A Hazing at a Wall Street Fraternity," *New York Times,* January 21, 2012.

34. Louise Story, "A Secretive Banking Elite Rules Derivatives Trading," *New York Times,* December 12, 2010.

35. National Council for Research on Women, *Women in Fund Management,* p. 11.

36. Jane Knodell, Department of Economics, University of Vermont, email correspondence with the author, May 13, 2012.

37. Geraldine Fabrikant, "Fewer Women Betting on Wall Street Careers," *New York Times,* January 30, 2010.

38. Ibid. Not unrelatedly, the proportion of women earning doctorates in the discipline of economics has been stagnating: about one-third of all American PhDs in economics in 1995 were women. That percentage remained the same seventeen years later, in 2012. Megan Woolhouse, "Despite Laurels, Progress Is Slow for Women in Economics," *Boston Globe,* May 14, 2012.

39. See Beatrix Campbell, *Iron Ladies* (London: Virago Press, 1987); Anna Coote and Beatrix Campbell, *Sweet Freedom,* 2nd ed. (Oxford: Blackwell, 1987; Kira Cochrane, ed., *Women of the Revolution: Forty Years of Feminism* (London: Guardian Books, 2012). For running British feminist analyses of the Thatcher government's policies and their gendered causes and effects, see also issues of *Feminist Review, Spare Rib,* and *Trouble and Strife,* 1979–1990.

40. James Kanter, "Britain Remains a Dissenter as Europeans Try to Set Capital Reserves for Banks," *New York Times,* May 3, 2012.

41. Richard Cracknell, *Women in Public Life, the Professions and the Boardroom* (London: House of Commons Library, March 9, 2012), p. 17.

42. Ruth Sunderland, "Revealed: Failure of Top UK Firms to Get Women on Board," *The Observer,* August 23, 2009.

43. Cracknell, *Women in Public Life,* 14–16.

44. Caroline Davies, "Poor Pay, Worse Jobs and Terrible Bonuses Too—Sexism in the City Lives On, Says Study," *The Guardian,* September 7, 2009.

45. "Women Face Hurdles at Senior Management Level," *Edge Online,* Institute of Leadership and Management, London, March 14, 2012, www.i-l-m .com/edge/Women_face_hurdles_at_senior_management_level.aspx, accessed March 22, 2012.

46. Ibid., 9.

47. Ruth Sunderland, "We Cannot Return to the Old Macho Ways," *The Observer,* February 15, 2009.

48. Caroline Lucas, "A Quota for Women in the Boardroom," *The Guardian,* July 19, 2009.

49. Ruth Sunderland, "After the Crash, Iceland's Women Lead the Rescue," *The Observer,* February 22, 2009; Inter-Parliamentary Union, "Women in National Parliaments," Inter-Parliamentary Union, December 31, 2006, www .ipu.org/wmn-e/arc/classif311206.htm, accessed May 7, 2012; Centre for Gender Equality in Iceland, *Gender Equality in Iceland* (Reykjavik: Centre for Gender Equality in Iceland, January 2012).

50. Ricardo Haussmann, Laura Tyson, and Saadia Zahidi, *The Global Gender Gap Report 2011: Ranking and Scores* (Geneva: World Economic Forum, 2012), p. ii, www.weforum.org/issues/global-gender-gap, accessed May 7, 2012.

51. Sunderland, "After the Crash, Iceland's Women Lead the Rescue."

52. Ibid.

53. Ibid.

54. Elra Sigurdardottir, "Nation-centric Masculinity Ideals and the Icelandic Bank Collapse," NIKK: Nordic Gender Institute, November 1, 2010, www.nikk. no/Nation-centric+masculinity+ideals+and+the+Icelandic+bank+collapse. b7C_wlfO3e.ips, accessed February 6, 2012; Inter-Parliamentary Union, "Women in Parliaments: World Classification," Inter-Parliamentary Union, December 31, 2011, www.ipu.org/wmn-e/classif.htm, accessed May 7, 2012.

55. Kristin Loftsdottir, "The Loss of Innocence," *Anthropology Today* 26, no. 6 (December 2010): 9–13; Jón Gunnar Ólafsson, "The 'Icesavior' Rises: A Media Narrative Featuring a Crisis and an Online Savings Brand in Starring Roles," in *Rannsóknir í Félagsvísindunn XII* (Reykjavik: Félagsvísindastofnun, October 2011), pp. 76–83.

56. Loftsdottir, "The Loss of Innocence," 11.

57. Janet Elise Johnson, "The Most Feminist Place in the World," *The Nation,* February 21, 2011, www.thenation.com/article/158279/the-most-feminist-place-world, accessed February 10, 2011.

58. Sunderland, "After the Crash, Iceland's Women Lead the Rescue."

59. Annadis Greta Rudolfsdottir, University of Iceland, email correspondence with the author, April 25, 2012.

60. Haussmann, Tyson, and Zahidi, *The Global Gender Gap Report 2011,* ii.

61. Quoted in Chrystia Freeland, "Canada's Great Escape," *Financial Times,* January 30, 31, 2010.

62. Ibid.

63. Alison Brewin, "Canada's Wrong Turn," *Ms. Magazine* (Winter 2011): 22–23.

64. Cynthia Cockburn, *Brothers: Male Dominance and Technological Change* (London: Pluto Press, 1991; reprint, Syracuse, NY: Syracuse University Press, 2000); Hugh Gusterson, *Nuclear Rites* (Berkeley: University of California Press, 1996); Carol Cohn, "Sex and Death in the Rational World of Defense Intellectuals," *Signs* 12, no. 4 (1987): 687–718; Anne Allison, *Night Work: Sexuality, Pleasure, and Corporate Masculinity in a Tokyo Hostess Club* (Chicago: Chicago University Press, 1994); Robin LeBlanc, *The Art of the Gut: Manhood, Power, and Ethics in Japanese Politics* (Berkeley: University of California Press, 2010); Nan Robertson, *The Girls in the Balcony: Women, Men and the New York Times* (New York: Random House, 1992); Lynn Povich, *The Good Girls Revolt: How the Women of Newsweek Sued Their Bosses and Changed the Workplace* (New York: Public Affairs, 2012).

65. Angelique Chrisafis, "France to Push Through New Sexual Harassment Law," *The Guardian*, May 19, 2012. As the charges against Dominique Strauss-Kahn continued to wend their way through the French court system, some French feminists called for a wide-open public discussion about the national "code of silence" that has enabled men in powerful positions—politicians, lawyers, judges, police officials, journalists—to engage in sexist and irresponsible (even if often not quite criminal) sexual behavior without it jeopardizing their careers or authority. Doreen Carvajal and Maia de la Baume, "Strauss-Kahn Says Sex Parties Went Too Far, But Lust Is No Crime," *New York Times*, October 14, 2012.

CHAPTER FIVE. WOMEN IN RECESSION

1. See, for instance, Seung-kyung Kim and John Finch, "Living with Rhetoric, Living Against Rhetoric: Korean Families and the IMF Economic Crisis," *Korean Studies* 26, no. 1 (2002): 120–39; Yasmin Husein Al-Jawaheri, *Women in Iraq: The Gender Impact of International Sanctions* (London: I. B. Tauris; Boulder, CO: Lynne Rienner, 2008).

2. Barack Obama, quoted in Randy Albelda, "The Macho Stimulus Plan," *Boston Globe*, November 28, 2008, www.boston.com/news/nation /articles/2008/11/28/the_macho_stimulus_plan, accessed June 8, 2012.

3. Cynthia Enloe and Joni Seager, *The Real State of America: Mapping the Myths and Truths of the United States* (New York: Penguin; London: University of California Press, 2011), pp. 38–39. In the 2008 presidential elections, CNN's election-day exit polls showed the following gender and race breakdowns: 96 percent of African American women and 95 percent of African American men voted for Obama; 68 percent of Latino women and 64 percent of Latino men

voted for Obama; 46 percent of white women and 41 percent of white men voted for Obama: CNN, "Election Center 2008," CNNPolitics.com, www .cnn.com/ELECTION/2008/results/polls, accessed October 30, 2012.

4. .U.S. Bureau of Labor Statistics, cited in Enloe and Seager, *The Real State of America*, 50.

5. Linda Gordon et al., "Letter from Women's Historians to President Elect Obama," Knitting Clio, December 12, 2008, http://hmprescott.wordpress. com/2008/12/12/letter-from-womens-historians, accessed May 1, 2012.

6. The following account is drawn from Heidi Hartmann, president, Institute of Women's Policy Research, email correspondence with the author, June 6, 2012; Albelda, "The Macho Stimulus Plan"; Linda Gordon et al., "Letter from Women's Historians"; Linda Gordon et al., "Actual Progress for the New Obama WPA?" Historiann, December 12, 2008, www.historiann. com/2008/12/12/actual-progress-for-the-new-Obama-WPA?, accessed June 8, 2012; Eileen Boris, Lisa Levenstein, and Sonya Michel, "Obama's Stimulus Plan Must Include Jobs for Women Too," News-record.com, January 4, 2009, www.news-record.com/content/2009/01/01/article/obama, accessed June 8, 2012; Eileen Boris and Lisa Levenstein, "Feminist Academics and the Stimulus Package: A Report from the Field," *Feminist Studies* 35, no. 1 (Spring 2009): 204–9.

7. Enloe and Seager, *The Real State of America*, 50.

8. Institute for Women's Policy Research, *Quick Figures* (Washington, DC: Institute for Women's Policy Research, May 2012), p. 1.

9. "As Austerity Bites, Pink Slips Roll in for Teachers and Cops," Editorial, *New York Times,* June 13, 2012.

10. Women's Scholars Forum, *Recommendations for Improving Employment in the Recovery* (Washington, DC: Institute for Women's Policy Research, September 2011).

11. Ibid.

12. See, for instance, Institute for Women's Policy Research, *The Gender Wage Gap by Occupation* (Washington, DC: Institute for Women's Policy Research, April 2012), briefing paper, p. 1.

13. Women's Scholars Forum, *Recommendations for Improving Employment in the Recovery.*

14. For instance, the Cameron government proposed an education plan that promoted the founding of additional local schools that are privately owned and run. Melissa Benn, a feminist journalist and public education advocate, warned that such a privatizing plan would seriously threaten

Britain's already underresourced state schools, as well as widen social inequalities and jeopardize the democratic accountability of the country's education system. Melissa Benn and Anna Wolmuth, "'Nineteenth-Century Inequalities in Shiny Classrooms': Melissa Benn on the Future of Schools," *Red Pepper,* January 2012, www.redpepper.org.uk/Melissa-benn-interview, accessed June 11, 2012.

15. Inter-Parliamentary Union, "Women in National Parliaments," Inter-Parliamentary Union, March 31, 2012, www.ipu.org/wmn-e/classif.htm, accessed June 10, 2012; Vikram Dodd and Amelia Gentleman, "UK Lags Behind in Cabinet," *The Guardian,* May 12, 2010.

16. Fawcett Society, *The Impact of Austerity on Women* (London: Fawcett Society, March 2012), p. 3, www.fawcettsociety.org.uk/, accessed May 10, 2012.

17. Ibid.

18. Gingerbread, "Statistics," Gingerbread, 2011, www.gingerbread.org.uk/content.aspx?CategoryID=365, accessed June 9, 2012. Gingerbread is an independent British research and advocacy organization for male and female single parents.

19. Fawcett Society, *The Impact of Austerity on Women,* 6.

20. Ibid.

21. "Public Sector Cuts Threaten Women's Employment," *Equal Opportunities Review* (May 2012): 5.

22. Ibid.

23. Ibid., 9.

24. Quoted in ibid., 15.

25. Mary-Ann Stephenson, "TUC Women and the Cuts, Coventry Women's Voices and the TUC," in *TUC Women and the Cuts Toolkit* (London: TUC, 2011), www.tuc.org.uk, accessed May 15, 2012.

26. Polly Toynbee, "'Calm Down, Dears'? Why It's a Bad Time to Be a British Woman," *The Guardian,* March 8, 2012.

27. Tanya Gold, "No Longer on Your Side," *The Guardian,* May 22, 2012. See also Gingerbread, "Statistics"; Gingerbread, *It's Off to Work We Go?* (London: Gingerbread, May 2012), www.gingerbread.org.uk/file_download.aspx?id=7690, accessed June 5, 2012.

28. Ailbhe Smyth, "Invited Talk to the Ireland Institute" (unpublished transcript, Dublin, January 2011). See also Mary Murphy, "A 'Ship of Men': Gender Equality as a Solution to This Man-Made Crisis" (lecture presented at the Feminist Open Forum, Dublin, 2010), available online from feministforum@gmail.com.

29. Smyth, "Invited Talk to the Ireland Institute."

30. Jane Fonda, Robin Morgan, and Gloria Steinem, "FCC Should Clear Limbaugh from Airwaves," CNN, March 12, 2012, www.cnn.com/2012/03/10 /opinion/fonda_morgan__steinem_limbaugh/index.html, accessed June 13, 2012. Jane Fonda, Robin Morgan, and Gloria Steinem are the cofounders of the Women's Media Center.

31. The following account of American feminists framing the Republican-backed legislative moves as a "war on women" is based on the following: National Organization for Women, "On International Women's Day NOW Calls for End to the 'War on Women,'" National Organization for Women, March 8, 2012, www.now.org/press/03–11/03–08.html, accessed June 12, 2012; EMILY's List, "War on Women Translates into Votes for Democrats," EMILY's List, March 8, 2012, http://emilyslist.org/news/releases/war_against_ women_translates, accessed June 12, 2012; NARAL Pro-Choice America, "NARAL Pro-Choice America Calls on Congress to End War on Women in Nation's Capital," NARAL Pro-Choice America, 2012, www.prochoiceamerica. org/media/press-releases/2012, accessed June 12, 2012; American Civil Liberties Union, "War on Women," American Civil Liberties Union, 2012, www.aclu. org/blog/tag/war-on-women, accessed June 12, 2012; MoveOn.org, "Top 10 Shocking Attacks from the GOP's War on Women," MoveOn.org, February 2012, http://pol.moveon.org/waronwomen, accessed June 12, 2012; Melanie Butler, "Occupy Wall Street Hold First Feminist General Assembly," *Ms. Magazine* Blog, May 18, 2012, http://msmagazine.com/blog/blog/2012/05/18/occupy-wall-street-holds-first-feminist-assembly, accessed June 5, 2012; Beth Baker, "Fighting the War on Women," *Ms. Magazine* (Spring–Summer 2012): 27–29. Loretta Ross, leader of the African American reproductive rights and health group SisterSong, spoke about the "war on women" in an interview on the radio program *Democracy Now*: "As Contraceptives Rule Enters GOP Race, Will Reproductive Rights Affect 2012 Election?" Democracy Now, February 8, 2012, www.democracynow.org/2012/2/8/as-contraceptives_rule, accessed June 6, 2012.

32. Susan Saulny, "On the Right, Santorum Has Women's Vote," *New York Times,* March 24, 2012.

33. Lindsey Kersker, quoted in ibid.

34. See, for instance, the speech by John Boehner, Republican Speaker of the House of Representatives: "Boehner Fired Up, Chastises Dems for Creating 'War on Women,'" *CBS News,* April 27, 2012, www.cbsnews.com/video /watch/?id=7406804n, accessed June 13, 2012.

CHAPTER SIX. MILITARISM, PATRIARCHY, AND
PEACE MOVEMENTS

1. Cynthia Cockburn, *Brothers: Male Dominance and Technological Change* (London: Pluto Press, 1983; new edition with afterword, London: Pluto Press, 1991); *The Space Between Us* (London: Zed Press, 1998), *From Where We Stand: War, Women's Activism and Feminist Analysis* (London: Zed Press, 2007); *Antimilitarism: Political and Gender Dynamics of Peace Movements* (London: Palgrave Macmillan, 2012).

CHAPTER EIGHT. EGYPTIAN WOMEN,
FEMINISM, REVOLUTIONS

1. I am indebted to Ngoc Du Thai Thi, Phuong Bui Tran, Karen Turner, Ximena Bunster, and Ayse Gul Altinay for their historically insightful suggestions for the Vietnamese, Chinese, Chilean, and Turkish feminist dinner guests. For more on the activism and analyses of women's advocates leading up to, during, and after revolutions, see Marie-Aimee Helie-Lucas, "The Role of Women in the Algerian Struggle and After," in *Women and the Military System,* ed. Eva Isaksson (New York: St. Martin's Press, 1988), pp. 171–89; Marie-Aimee Helie-Lucas, "Against Nationalism: The Betrayal of Algerian Women," *Trouble and Strife,* no. 11 (1987): 27–31; Lisa Baldez, *Why Women Protest: Women's Movements in Chile* (Cambridge: Cambridge University Press, 2002); Mala Htun, *Sex and the State: Abortion, Divorce and the Family Under Latin American Dictatorships and Democracies* (Cambridge: Cambridge University Press, 2003); Margot Badran, *Feminists, Islam and Nation: Gender and the Making of Modern Egypt* (Princeton, NJ: Princeton University Press, 1995); Nadje Al-Ali, *Secularism, Gender and the State in the Middle East: The Egyptian Women's Movement* (Cambridge: Cambridge University Press, 2000); Elizabeth Wood, *From Baba to Comrade: Gender and Politics in Revolutionary Russia* (Bloomington: Indiana University Press, 1997); Alexandra Kollontai, *Autobiography of a Sexually Emancipated Communist Woman* (New York: Herder and Herder, 1971); Louise Edwards, *Gender, Politics and Democracy: Women's Suffrage in China* (Stanford, CA: Stanford University Press, 2008); Tani Barlow, *The Question of Women in Chinese Feminism* (Durham, NC: Duke University Press, 2004); Christina K. Gilmartin, *Engendering the Chinese Revolution* (Berkeley: University of California Press, 1995); Karen Kampwirth, *Women and Guerrillas: Nicaragua, El Salvador, Chiapas, and Cuba* (University Park: Pennsylvania State University Press, 2002); Karen Kampwirth, *Feminism and the Legacy of Revolution: Nicaragua, El Salvador, Chiapas* (Athens: Ohio University Press, 2004); Margaret Randall,

Sandino's Daughters (Vancouver: New Star Books, 1981); Margaret Randall, *Sandino's Daughters Revisited* (New Brunswick, NJ: Rutgers University Press, 2004); Lorraine Bayard de Volo, "A Revolution in the Binary? Gender and the Oxymoron of Revolutionary War in Cuba and Nicaragua," *Signs* 37, no. 2 (2012): 413–39; Linda Kerber, *Women of the Republic: Intellect and Ideology in Revolutionary America* (Chapel Hill: University of North Carolina Press, 1980); Woody Holton, *Abigail Adams* (New York: Free Press, 2009); Hue-Tam Ho Tai, *Radicalism and the Origins of the Vietnamese Revolution* (Cambridge, MA: Harvard University Press, 1992); Karen Turner, with Thanh Hao Phan, *Even the Women Must Fight: Memories of War from North Vietnam* (New York: John Wiley and Sons, 1998); David Marr, *Vietnamese Tradition on Trial, 1920–1945* (Berkeley: University of California Press, 1981); Kumari Jayawardena, *Feminism and Nationalism in the Third World* (London: Zed Books, 1986); Yesim Arat, "Contestation and Collaboration: Women's Struggle for Empowerment in Turkey," in *Cambridge History of Turkey: Turkey in the Modern World*, ed. Resat Kasaba (Cambridge: Cambridge University Press, 2008), 4:388–418; Serpil Cakir, "Feminism and Feminist History Writing in Turkey: The Discovery of Ottoman Feminism," *Aspia* 1 (2007): 61–83; Ayse Gul Altinay, *The Myth of the Military-Nation: Militarism, Gender, and Education in Turkey* (London: Palgrave Macmillan, 2004); Sonia Kruks, Rayna Rapp, and Marilyn B. Young, eds., *Promissory Notes: Women in Transition to Socialism* (New York: Monthly Review Press, 1989); Seung-kyung Kim, *South Korean Feminists' Bargain: Progressive Presidencies and the Women's Movement, 1998–2007*, forthcoming.

2. Badran, *Feminists, Nation and Islam*.

3. Mette Erikson, "Women's Groups Relaunch Egyptian Feminist Union," *Egypt Independent*, October 18, 2011, www.egyptindependent.com/news/women's-groups-relaunch-egytian-feminist-union, accessed July 11, 2012.

4. UN Population Fund, "Indicators: Population and Development in Egypt," UNFPA Egypt, n.d., http://egypt.unfpa.org/english/Staticpage/54790f72–6e8b-4f77–99e2–4c5b78c20d5c/indicators.aspx, accessed June 20, 2012.

5. Mona El-Naggar, "In Egypt, Women Have Burdens But Not Privileges," *New York Times*, July 13, 2010.

6. Gehan Abu-Zayd, "In Search of Political Power: Women in Parliament in Egypt, Jordan and Lebanon," 2011, International Institute for Democracy and Electoral Assistance, 2011, www.idea.int/.

7. Megan Cornish, "Women Workers in Egypt Hidden Key to the Revolution," *Al-Jazeerah*, Opinion Editorials, April 11, 2011, www.aljazeerah.info/OpinionEditorials/2011/April/11, accessed June 25, 2012.

8. Global Attitudes Project, Pew Research Center, *Gender Equality Universally Embraced, But Inequalities Acknowledged* (Washington, DC: Pew Research Center, July 1, 2010), p. 2.

9. Ibid.

10. Laila Iskander, a Cairo-based organizer of garbage collectors, in conversation with the author, Cambridge, MA, April 7, 2011.

11. I am grateful to Paul Amar for first introducing me to this particular gender portrait of the Mubarak regime. See Paul Amar, "Why Egypt's Progressives Win," *Aljazeera English,* February 10, 2011, http://english.aljazeera.net/indepth/opinion/20112010103072622228.html, accessed February 12, 2011; Paul Amar, "Why Mubarak Is Out," *Jadaliyya,* February 1, 2011, www.jadaliyya.com/pages/index/516/why-mubarak-is-out-#comments, accessed February 14, 2011; Paul Amar, "Middle East Masculinity Studies: Discourses of 'Men in Crisis' Industries of Gender in Revolution," *Journal of Middle East Women's Studies* 7, no. 3 (Fall 2011): 36–70.

12. Fatma Khafagy, "Shadow NGO Report on Egypt's Fourth and Fifth Combined Periodic Report to the Committee on the Elimination of Discrimination Against Women," Alliance for Arab Women, Cairo, December 2009, distributed by the transnational feminist organization Women Living Under Muslim Laws, of which Marie-Aimee Helie-Lucas was a cofounder, www.wluml.org/sites/wluml.org/files/shadow%20NGO%20Report%20Egypt%20CEDAW.pdf, accessed June 18, 2012.

13. Joni Seager, *The Penguin Atlas of Women in the World,* 4th ed. (New York: Penguin, 2009), pp. 78–79, 118–19; UN Fund for Population Activities, "Population and Development in Egypt."

14. UN Women, *Progress of the World's Women: In Pursuit of Justice, 2011* (New York: UN Women, 2011), p. 51, http://progress.unwomen.org, accessed June 23, 2012.

15. Global Attitudes Project, Pew Research Center, *Gender Equality Universally Embraced,* 5.

16. Amnesty International, "Egypt: Military Pledges to Stop Forced 'Virginity Tests,'" Peacewomen, June 27, 2011, www.peacewomen.org/news_article.php?id=3857&type=news, accessed July 13, 2011; David D. Kirkpatrick, "Egyptian Military Court Acquits Doctor Accused of Performing 'Virginity Tests,'" *New York Times,* March 12, 2012.

17. Holly Kearl, "Egyptian Women Refuse to be Silenced by Assaults," *Ms. Magazine* Blog, June 12, 2012, http://msmagazine.com/blog/blog/2012/06/10/eyptian-women-refuse-to-be-silenced-by-assaults, accessed June 18, 2012.

18. Egyptian Center for Women's Rights, *Clouds in Egypt's Sky: Sexual Harassment: From Verbal Harassment to Rape* (Cairo: Egyptian Center for Women's Rights, 2010), http://egypt.unpfa.org/english/publication/6eeebo5a-3040–42d2–9e1c-2bd2e1ac8cac, accessed June 18, 2012.

19. Ibid., 16.

20. Ibid., 7.

21. Ibid.

22. Ibid., 16.

23. Margot Badran, "Women and the Uprising in Egypt: Analysis from an Eyewitness" (unpublished transcript of a talk presented at the Consortium on Gender, Security and Human Rights, University of Massachusetts Boston, March 28, 2011).

24. Ibid.

25. Quoted by Maxine Dovere, "A War with Roses: Women of the Protest in Cairo," Algemeiner, February 8, 2011, www.algemeiner.com/2011/02/08/a-war-with-roses-women-of-the-protest-in-cairo, accessed February 8, 2011.

26. Quoted in Chris McGreal, "Only Half the Struggle: Arab Women Fight to Keep the Gains Won on the Street," *The Guardian,* June 14, 2012. For a four-sided conversation about the implications of sexual harassment in Egyptian contemporary politics, see Omnia El Shakry, Terrell Carver, Cynthia Enloe, and Paul Amar, "Forum," *International Feminist Journal of Politics* 15, no. 1 (forthcoming, March 2013). The article that sparked this conversation is: Paul Amar, "Turning the Gendered Politics of the Security State Inside Out," *International Feminist Journal of Politics* 13, no. 3 (September 2011): 299–328.

27. Quoted in Kearl, "Egyptian Women Refuse to be Silenced by Assaults." For a description of an October 2012 public march by women from thirty-three women's groups calling on the newly elected government of President Mohamed Morsi to take forceful steps against sexual harassment, see "Women's Rights Groups March to Egypt Presidential Palace, Thursday," *Ahram Online,* October 4, 2012, http://english.ahram.org.eg/NewsContent/1/64/54786/Egypt/Politics-/Womens-rights-groups-march-to-Egypt-presidential-p.aspx, accessed October 5, 2012.

28. Coalition of Egyptian Feminist Organizations, "Egypt: Coalition of Egyptian Feminist Organizations Open Letter to Prime Minister," Cairo, March 14, 2011. An English translation of the letter is distributed online by the transnational feminist group Women Living Under Muslim Laws, www.wluml.org/node/7020, accessed March 16, 2011.

29. Anna Louie Sussman, "Prominent During Revolution, Egyptian Women Vanish in New Order," *The Atlantic* (April 2011), www.theatlantic.com /international/archive/2011/04/prominent-during-revolution-egyptian-women-vanish-in-new-order/237232, accessed April 15, 2011.

30. "Egypt: Regressive Calls for Repealing Personal Status Code and Children's Code," Cairo, April 7, 2011, distributed online by Women Living Under Muslim Laws, www.wluml.org/noce/7077, accessed April 16, 2011.

31. Yonna Mokhtar, "Arab Women's Association Forms Political Party," *Egypt Independent,* October 16, 2011, www.egyptindependent.com/news /arab-womens-association-forms-political-party, accessed July 11, 2012.

32. Laila Iskander, "Arab Spring" (public lecture, Bentley University, Waltham, MA, April 7, 2011).

33. "Global Short Takes: Middle East," *Ms. Magazine* (Winter 2012): 24.

34. Isobel Coleman, "Women and the Elections in Egypt," Council on Foreign Relations, January 12, 2012, http://blogs.cfr.org/coleman/2012/01/12 /women-and-the-elections-in-egypt, accessed January 25, 2012. See also Lourdes Garcia-Navarro, "In Egypt's New Parliament, Women Will Be Scarce," National Public Radio, January 19, 2012, http://minnesota.publicradio. org/features/npr.php?id=145468365, accessed Jan. 25, 2012.

35. Quoted in Coleman, "Women and the Elections in Egypt."

36. David D. Kirkpatrick, "Clinton Visits Egypt, Carrying Muted Pledge of Support," *New York Times,* July 14, 2012; Kareem Fahim, "After Meeting with Clinton, Egypt's Military Chief Steps Up Political Feud," *New York Times,* July 16, 2012.

CHAPTER NINE. CONCLUSION

1. Recently, I have learned a lot about how to think through these complex strategic choices from three determined progressive activist analysts, Madeleine Rees in Geneva, Rela Mazali in Israel, and Aaron Belkin in the United States. They each have made significant dents in official patriarchal mind-sets—on international peacekeepers' complicity in the trafficking of women in postwar societies, on private security guards being allowed to take home their guns, and on openly gay men and lesbians being banned from the military—by crafting thoughtful analytical agendas closely tied to policy campaigns that do not ignore deeper social distortions, yet engage with media and political elites in terms they can comprehend. For Madeleine Rees's central role in Sarajevo—as the Special Representative of the UN High

Commissioner for Human Rights—in blowing the whistle on low-ranking Dyncorp contract policemen and senior UN officials for their complicity in sex trafficking in post-1995 Bosnia, see Kathryn Bolkovac and Cari Lynn, *The Whistleblower: Sex Trafficking, Military Contractors, and One Woman's Fight for Justice* (London: Palgrave, 2011); Human Rights Watch, *Bosnia and Herzegovina Hopes Betrayed: Trafficking of Women and Girls to Bosnia and Herzegovina for Forced Prostitution* (Washington, DC: Human Rights Watch, November 2002); Elisabeth Prugl and Hayley Thompson, "The Whistleblower: Interview with Kathryn Bolkovac and Madeleine Rees," *International Feminist Journal of Politics* (forthcoming); Madeleine Rees, conversations with the author, Geneva, September 2011. The film closely based on Kathryn Bolkovac's and Madeleine Rees's experiences of whistle-blowing is: Larysa Kondraki, dir., *The Whistleblower* (Rotten Tomatoes Productions, 2011). For more on Rela Mazali and her coorganizers' efforts to make visible the causal connections between domestic violence against women and security guards' possession of guns, and to persuade Israeli officials to enforce the law making it illegal for private security companies to permit their employees to take home their guns, see Gun Free Kitchen Tables, *Gun Free Kitchen Tables Activity Report* (Tel Aviv: Isha L'Isha Feminist Center, December 2011) and their website: http://iansa/member/gun-free-kitchen-tables. For Aaron Belkin's detailed description of how he organized rigorous academic research that revealed the falseness of the central rationale for the U.S. Defense Department's 1994–2012 antigay ban, see his *How We Won: Progressive Lessons from the Repeal of "Don't Ask, Don't Tell,"* Huffington Post Media Group, 2012, http://howwewon.com, accessed July 20, 2012.

2. Michelle Bachelet, "Statement by Under-Secretary-General Michelle Bachelet to the UN Security Council on Women, Peace and Security," UN Women, New York, April 24, 2012, www.unwomen.org/2012/04/statement-by-the-under-secretary-general, accessed April 28, 2012.

3. The Kosovo Women's Network, *1325: Fact and Fables* (Prishtina, Kosovo: Kosovo Women's Network, 2011); Women in Black Belgrade, *Women, Peace and Security: Resolution 1325—10 Years* (Belgrade: Women in Black Belgrade, 2011); Sarai Aharoni and Rula Deeb, *Where Are All the Women? UN Security Council Resolution 1325: Gender Perspectives of the Israeli-Palestinian Conflict* (Haifa: Isha L'Isha—Haifa Feminist Center, 2005); NGO Working Group on Women, Peace and Security: www.womenpeacesecurity.org; Women's International League for Peace and Freedom, UN/New York office: www.peacewomen.org; WILPF International's headquarters, Geneva: www.wilpfinternational.org; Gender and Security Project of the Peace Research Institute Oslo: www.prio.no;

Women in Conflict Zones Network: www.yorku.ca/wicz; Consortium for Gender, Security and Human Rights, University of Massachusetts Boston: www.genderandsecurity.umb.edu. Pressed and coached by United States–based feminist peace groups, Secretary of State Hillary Clinton led a 2011 project to produce the U.S. National Action Plan for American implementation of 1325. See White House, "Executive Order—Instituting a National Action Plan on Women, Peace, and Security," White House, December 19, 2011, www.whitehouse.gov/the-press-office/2011/12/19/executive-order-instituting-national-action-plan-women-peace-and-security, accessed June 12, 2012. See also the four-part documentary film series, which aired in the United States on PBS, that explores diverse women's political activism in the midst of armed conflicts in Bosnia, Colombia, and Liberia in the years following the passage of 1325: Abigail E. Disney, Pamela Hogan, and Gini Reticker, *Women, War and Peace*, produced by THIRTEEN and Fork Films, New York, 2011.

BIBLIOGRAPHY

Abdulali, Sohaila. *Year of the Tiger.* New Delhi: Penguin, 2010.

Abu-Zayd, Gehan. "In Search of Political Power: Women in Parliament in Egypt, Jordan and Lebanon." International Institute for Democracy and Electoral Assistance, 2011, www.idea.int/.

Adams, Tim. "Testosterone and High Finance Do Not Mix: So Bring on the Women." *The Observer,* June 18, 2011, www.guardian.co.uk/world/2011/jun/19/neuoeconomics-women-city-financial-crash (accessed May 14, 2012).

Aharoni, Sarai, and Rula Deeb. *Where Are All the Women? UN Security Council Resolution 1325: Gender Perspectives of the Israeli-Palestinian Conflict.* Haifa: Isha L'Isha—Haifa Feminist Center, 2005.

Ahn, Christine, and Kavita Ramdas. "The IMF: Violating Women since 1945." Foreign Policy in Focus, May 19, 2011, www.fpif.org/articles/the_imf_violating_women_since_1945 (accessed May 24, 2011).

Al-Ali, Nadje. *Secularism, Gender and the State in the Middle East: The Egyptian Women's Movement.* Cambridge: Cambridge University Press, 2000.

Albelda, Randy. "The Macho Stimulus Plan." *Boston Globe,* November 28, 2008, www.boston.com/news/nation/articles/2008/11/28/the_macho_stimulus_plan (accessed June 8, 2012).

Alderman, Liz. "I.M.F. Chief to Face French Inquiry on '07 Dispute." *New York Times,* August 5, 2011.

Al-Jawaheri, Yasmin Husein. *Women in Iraq: The Gender Impact of International Sanctions.* London: I. B. Tauris; Boulder, CO: Lynne Rienner, 2008.

Allison, Anne. *Night Work: Sexuality, Pleasure, and Corporate Masculinity in a Tokyo Hostess Club.* Chicago: Chicago University Press, 1994.

Altinay, Ayse Gul. *The Myth of the Military Nation: Militarism, Gender, and Education in Turkey.* London: Palgrave Macmillan, 2004.

————. "Refusing to Identify as Obedient Wives, Sacrificing Mothers and Proud Warriors." In *Conscientious Objection: Resisting Militarized Society,* edited by Ozgur Heval Cinar and Coskun Usterci, 88–104. London: Zed Books, 2009.

Amar, Paul. "Middle East Masculinity Studies: Discourses of 'Men in Crisis,' Industries of Gender in Revolution." *Journal of Middle East Women's Studies* 7, no. 3 (Fall 2011): 36–70.

————. "Turning the Gendered Politics of the Security State Inside Out." *International Feminist Journal of Politics* 13, no. 3 (September 2011): 299–328.

————. "Why Egypt's Progressives Win." *Aljazeera English,* February 10, 2011, http://english.aljazeera.net/indepth/opinion/20112010103072628.html (accessed February 12, 2011).

————. "Why Mubarak Is Out." *Jadaliyya,* February 1, 2011, www.jadaliyya .com/pages/index/516/why-mubarak-is-out-#comments (accessed February 14, 2011).

American Civil Liberties Union. "War on Women." American Civil Liberties Union, 2012, www.aclu.org/blog/tag/war-on-women (accessed June 12, 2012).

Amnesty International. "Egypt: Military Pledges to Stop Forced 'Virginity Tests.'" Peacewomen, June 27, 2011, www.peacewomen.org/news_article .php?id=3857&type=news (accessed July 13, 2011).

Appelbaum, Binyamin, and Sheryl Gay Stolberg. "At I.M.F., Men on Prowl and Women on Guard." *New York Times,* May 20, 2011.

Arat, Yesim. "Contestation and Collaboration: Women's Struggle for Empowerment in Turkey." In *Cambridge History of Turkey: Turkey in the Modern World,* edited by Resat Kasaba, 4:388–418. Cambridge: Cambridge University Press, 2008.

"As Austerity Bites, Pink Slips Roll in for Teachers and Cops." *New York Times,* June 13, 2012, editorial.

Bachelet, Michelle. "Statement by Under-Secretary-General Michelle Bachelet to the UN Security Council on Women, Peace and Security." UN Women, New York, April 24, 2012, www.unwomen.org/2012/04 /statement-by-under-secretary-general-michelle-bachelet-to-the-un-security-council-on-women-peace-and-security (accessed April 28, 2012).

Badran, Margot. *Feminists, Islam and Nation: Gender and the Making of Modern Egypt.* Princeton, NJ: Princeton University Press, 1995.

Bair, Sheila. *Bull by the Horns: Fighting to Save Main Street from Wall Street and Wall Street from Itself.* New York: Free Press, 2012.

Baker, Beth. "Fighting the War on Women." *Ms. Magazine* (Spring–Summer 2012): 27–29.

Baldez, Lisa. *Why Women Protest: Women's Movements in Chile.* Cambridge: Cambridge University Press, 2002.

Barlow, Tani. *The Question of Women in Chinese Feminism.* Durham, NC: Duke University Press, 2004.

Barron, James. "After 40 Years, It's Still Ms. to Readers." *New York Times,* June 14, 2012.

Barton, Laura. "On the Money." *The Guardian,* October 30, 2008, www .guardian.co.uk/business/2008/oct/31/credit-crunch-gillian-tett-financial-times (accessed May 14, 2002).

Bayard de Volo, Lorraine. "A Revolution in the Binary? Gender and the Oxymoron of Revolutionary War in Cuba and Nicaragua." *Signs* 37, no. 2 (2012): 413–39.

Belkin, Aaron. *How We Won: Progressive Lessons from the Repeal of "Don't Ask, Don't Tell."* Huffington Post Media Group, 2012, http://howwewon.com (accessed July 20, 2012).

Benn, Melissa, and Anna Wolmuth. "'Nineteenth-Century Inequalities in Shiny Classrooms': Melissa Benn on the Future of Schools." *Red Pepper,* January 2012, www.redpepper.org.uk/Melissa-benn-interview (accessed June 11, 2012).

"Boehner Fired Up, Chastises Dems for Creating 'War on Women.'" *CBS News,* April 27, 2012, www.cbsnews.com/video/watch/?id=7406804n (accessed June 13, 2012).

Bolkovac, Kathryn, and Cari Lynn. *The Whistleblower: Sex Trafficking, Military Contractors, and One Woman's Fight for Justice.* London: Palgrave, 2011.

"Booklist Interviews Erin Duffy." Library Love Fest, January 1, 2012, http:// harperlibrary.typepad.com/my_weblog/2012/01/booklist-interviews-erin-duffy.html (accessed April 23, 2012).

Boris, Eileen, and Lisa Levenstein. "Feminist Academics and the Stimulus Package: A Report from the Field." *Feminist Studies* 35, no. 1 (Spring 2009): 204–9.

Boris, Eileen, Lisa Levenstein, and Sonya Michel. "Obama's Stimulus Plan Must Include Jobs for Women Too." News-record.com, January 4, 2009, www .news-record.com/content/2009/01/01/article/obama (accessed June 8, 2012).

Brewin, Alison. "Canada's Wrong Turn." *Ms. Magazine* (Winter 2011): 22–23.

Brooks, Ethel. *Unraveling the Garment Industry* (Minneapolis: University of Minnesota Press, 2007).

Bunster, Ximena. "Surviving Beyond Fear: Women and Torture in Latin America." In *Women and Change in Latin America,* edited by June Nash and Helen Safa, 297–326. South Hadley, MA: Bergin and Garvey, 1986.

———. "'Watch for the Little Nazi Man That All of Us Have Inside': The Mobilization and Demobilization of Women in Militarized Chile." *Women's Studies International Forum* 11, no. 5 (1988): 228–35.

Bush, Julia. *Women Against the Vote: Female Anti-Suffragism in Britain.* Oxford: Oxford University Press, 2007.

Butler, Melanie. "Occupy Wall Street Holds First Feminist General Assembly." *Ms. Magazine* Blog, May 18, 2012, http://msmagazine.com/blog/2012/05/18/occupy-wall-street-holds-first-feminist-general-assembly/ (accessed June 5, 2012).

Cakir, Serpil. "Feminism and Feminist History Writing in Turkey: The Discovery of Ottoman Feminism." *Aspia* 1 (2007): 61–83.

Campbell, Beatrix. *Iron Ladies.* London: Virago Press, 1987.

Carvajal, Doreen, and Maia de la Baume. "Strauss-Kahn Says Sex Parties Went Too Far, But Lust Is No Crime." *New York Times,* October 14, 2012.

Centre for Gender Equality in Iceland. *Gender Equality in Iceland.* Reykjavik: Centre for Gender Equality in Iceland, January 2012.

Chang, Leslie T. *Factory Girls: From Village to City in a Changing China.* New York: Spiegel and Grau, 2009.

Chrisafis, Angelique. "France to Push Through New Sexual Harassment Law." *The Guardian,* May 19, 2012.

"Christine Lagarde to 'Lower Testosterone at International Monetary Fund.'" News.com.au, June 8, 2011, www.news.com.au/business/breaking-news/christine-lagarde-to-lower-testosterone-at-international-monetary-fund/story-e6frfkur-1226071440139 (accessed May 9, 2012).

Cinar, Ozgur Heval, and Coskun Usterci, eds. *Conscientious Objection: Resisting Militarized Society.* London: Zed Books, 2009.

CNN. "Election Center 2008," CNNPolitics.com, www.cnn.com/ELECTION/2008/results/polls (accessed October 30, 2012).

Coalition of Egyptian Feminist Organizations. "Egypt: Coalition of Egyptian Feminist Organizations Open Letter to Prime Minister." Cairo, March 14, 2011. An English translation of the letter is distributed online by the transnational feminist group Women Living Under Muslim Laws, www.wluml.org/node/7020 (accessed March 16, 2011).

Cochrane, Kira, ed. *Women of the Revolution: Forty Years of Feminism*. London: Guardian Books, 2012.

Cockburn, Cynthia. *Antimilitarism: Political and Gender Dynamics of Peace Movements*. London: Palgrave Macmillan, 2012.

———. *Brothers: Male Dominance and Technological Change*. London: Pluto Press, 1983; new edition with afterword, London: Pluto Press, 1991.

———. *From Where We Stand: War, Women's Activism and Feminist Analysis*. London: Zed Press, 2007.

———. *The Space Between Us*. London: Zed Press, 1998.

Cohn, Carol. "Mainstreaming Gender in UN Security Policy." In *Global Governance: Feminist Perspectives*, edited by Shrin Rai and Georgina Waylen, 185–206. Basingstoke, U.K.: Palgrave Macmillan, 2008.

———. "Sex and Death in the Rational World of Defense Intellectuals." *Signs* 12, no. 4 (1987): 687–718.

Cohn, Carol, Felicity Hill, and Sara Ruddick. *The Relevance of Gender for Eliminating Weapons of Mass Destruction*. Stockholm: Weapons of Mass Destruction Commission, 2005.

Cohn, Carol, Helen Kinsella, and Sheri Lynn Gibbings. "Women, Peace and Security: Resolution 1325." *International Feminist Journal of Politics* 6, no. 1 (2004): 130–42.

Coleman, Isobel. "Women and the Elections in Egypt." Council on Foreign Relations, January 12, 2012, http://blogs.cfr.org/coleman/2012/01/12/women-and-the-elections-in-egypt (accessed January 25, 2012).

Confortini, Catia Cecilia. *Intelligent Compassion: Feminist Critical Methodology in the Women's International League for Peace and Freedom*. Oxford: Oxford University Press, 2012.

Coote, Anna, and Beatrix Campbell. *Sweet Freedom*. 2nd ed. Oxford: Blackwell, 1987.

Cornish, Megan. "Women Workers in Egypt Hidden Key to the Revolution." *Al-Jazeerah*, Opinion Editorials, April 11, 2011, www.aljazeerah.info/OpinionEditorials/2011/April/11 (accessed June 25, 2012).

Cracknell, Richard. *Women in Public Life, the Professions and the Boardroom*. London: House of Commons Library, March 9, 2012.

Davies, Caroline. "Poor Pay, Worse Jobs and Terrible Bonuses too—Sexism in the City Lives On, Says Study." *The Guardian*, September 7, 2009.

Democracy Now. "As Contraceptives Rule Enters GOP Race, Will Reproductive Rights Affect 2012 Election?" *Democracy Now*, February 8, 2012, www.democracynow.org/2012/2/8/as-contraceptives_rule (accessed June 6, 2012).

Disney, Abigail E., Pamela Hogan, and Gini Reticker. *Women, War and Peace.* Produced by THIRTEEN and Fork Films, New York, 2011.

Dodd, Vikram, and Amelia Gentleman. "UK Lags Behind in Cabinet." *The Guardian,* May 12, 2010.

Dominus, Susan. "Exile on Park Avenue: How the JPMorgan Chase Trading Fiasco Took Down the Most Powerful Woman on Wall Street." *New York Times Magazine,* October 7, 2012, 32–39, 54–55.

Dovere, Maxine. "A War with Roses: Women of the Protest in Cairo." Algemeiner, February 8, 2011, www.algemeiner.com/2011/02/08/a-war-with-roses-women-of-the-protest-in-cairo (accessed February 8, 2011).

Duffy, Erin. *Bond Girl.* New York: William Morrow, 2012.

Edwards, Louise. *Gender, Politics and Democracy: Women's Suffrage in China.* Stanford, CA: Stanford University Press, 2008.

Egyptian Center for Women's Rights. *Clouds in Egypt's Sky: Sexual Harassment: From Verbal Harassment to Rape.* Cairo: Egyptian Center for Women's Rights, 2010, http://egypt.unpfa.org/english/publication/6eeeb05a-3040–42d2–9e1c-2bd2e1ac8cac (accessed June 18, 2012).

———. "Egypt: Regressive Calls for Repealing Personal Status Code and Children's Code." Cairo, April 7, 2011. Distributed online by the transnational feminist group Women Living Under Muslim Laws, www.wluml.org/noce/7077 (accessed April 16, 2011).

Eichler, Maya. *Militarizing Men: Gender, Conscription and War in Post-Soviet Russia.* Stanford, CA: Stanford University Press, 2012.

El-Naggar, Mona. "In Egypt, Women Have Burdens But Not Privileges." *New York Times,* July 13, 2010.

El Shakry, Omnia, Terrell Carver, Cynthia Enloe, and Paul Amar. "Forum." *International Feminist Journal of Politics* 15, no. 1 (forthcoming, March 2013).

Elster, Ellen, and Majken Jul Sorensen, eds. *Women Conscientious Objectors: An Anthology.* London: War Resisters' International, 2010.

EMILY's List. "War on Women Translates into Votes for Democrats." EMILY's List, March 8, 2012, http://emilyslist.org/news/releases/war_against_women_translates (accessed June 12, 2012).

Enloe, Cynthia. *Bananas, Beaches, and Bases: Making Feminist Sense of International Politics.* London: Pandora Press, 1989; Berkeley: University of California Press, 1990.

———. *Does Khaki Become You? The Militarization of Women's Lives.* London: Pluto Press; Boston: South End Press, 1983.

———. *Ethnic Politics and Political Development.* Boston: Little, Brown, 1973.

————. *Ethnic Soldiers: State Security in Divided Societies.* London: Penguin, 1980.

————. *Globalization and Militarism: Feminists Make the Link.* Lanham, MD: Rowman and Littlefield, 2007.

————. *Maneuvers: The International Politics of Militarizing Women's Lives.* Berkeley: University of California Press, 2000.

————. *Nimo's War, Emma's War: Making Feminist Sense of the Iraq War.* Berkeley: University of California Press, 2010.

Enloe, Cynthia, and Joni Seager. *The Real State of America: Mapping the Myths and Truths of the United States.* New York: Penguin; London: University of California Press, 2011.

Erikson, Mette. "Women's Groups Relaunch Egyptian Feminist Union." *Egypt Independent,* October 18, 2011, www.egyptindependent.com/news/womens-groups-relaunch-egyptian-feminist-union (accessed July 11, 2012).

Fabrikant, Geraldine. "Fewer Women Betting on Wall Street Careers." *New York Times,* January 30, 2010.

Fahim, Kareem. "After Meeting with Clinton, Egypt's Military Chief Steps Up Political Feud." *New York Times,* July 16, 2012.

Fawcett Society. *The Impact of Austerity on Women.* London: Fawcett Society, March 2012, www.fawcettsociety.org.uk/ (accessed May 10, 2012).

Fonda, Jane, Robin Morgan, and Gloria Steinem. "FCC Should Clear Limbaugh from Airwaves." CNN, March 12, 2012, www.cnn.com/2012/03/10/opinion/fonda_morgan__steinem_limbaugh/index.html (accessed June 13, 2012).

Frank, Dana. *Bananeras: Women Transforming the Banana Unions of Latin America.* Boston: South End Press, 2005.

Freeland, Chrystia. "Canada's Great Escape." *Financial Times,* January 30, 31, 2010.

Freeman, Carla. *High Tech and High Heels in the Global Economy.* Durham, NC: Duke University Press, 2000.

Garcia-Navarro, Lourdes. "In Egypt's New Parliament, Women Will Be Scarce." National Public Radio, January 19, 2012, http://minnesota.publicradio.org/features/npr.php?id=145468365 (accessed Jan. 25, 2012).

Gibbings, Sheri Lynn. "No Angry Women at the United Nations: Political Dreams and the Cultural Politics of United Nations Security Council Resolution 1325." *International Feminist Journal of Politics* 13, no. 4 (December 2011).

Gilmartin, Christina K. *Engendering the Chinese Revolution.* Berkeley: University of California Press, 1995.

Gingerbread. *It's Off to Work We Go?* London: Gingerbread, May 2012, www.gingerbread.org.uk/file_download.aspx?id=7690 (accessed June 5, 2012).

————. "Statistics." Gingerbread, 2011, www.gingerbread.org.uk/content .aspx?CategoryID=365 (accessed June 9, 2012).

Gladstone, Rick. "Waiting in the Wings, a Survivor of Three Decades of Syrian Politics." *New York Times,* February 4, 2012.

Global Attitudes Project, Pew Research Center. *Gender Equality Universally Embraced, But Inequalities Acknowledged.* Washington, DC: Pew Research Center, July 1, 2010.

"Global Short Takes: Middle East." *Ms. Magazine* (Winter 2012): 24.

Gold, Tanya. "No Longer on Your Side." *The Guardian,* May 22, 2012.

Gordon, Linda, et al. "Actual Progress for the New Obama WPA?" Historiann, December 12, 2008, www.historiann.com/2008/12/12/actual-progress-for-the-new-Obama-WPA? (accessed June 8, 2012).

————. "Letter from Women's Historians to President Elect Obama." Knitting Clio, December 12, 2008, http://hmprescott.wordpress.com/2008/12/12 /letter-from-womens-historians (accessed May 1, 2012).

Green, Elna C. *Southern Strategies: Southern Women and the Suffrage Question.* Chapel Hill: University of North Carolina Press, 1997.

Gun Free Kitchen Tables. *Gun Free Kitchen Tables Activity Report.* Tel Aviv: Isha L'Isha Feminist Center, December 2011.

Gusterson, Hugh. *Nuclear Rites.* Berkeley: University of California Press, 1996.

Han, Suyin. *And the Rain My Drink.* London: Penguin, 1961.

Haussmann, Ricardo, Laura Tyson, and Saadia Zahidi. *The Global Gender Gap Report 2011: Ranking and Scores.* Geneva: World Economic Forum, 2012, www .weforum.org/issues/global-gender-gap (accessed May 7, 2012).

Helie-Lucas, Marie-Aimee. "Against Nationalism: The Betrayal of Algerian Women." *Trouble and Strife,* no. 11 (1987): 27–31.

————. "The Role of Women in the Algerian Struggle and After." In *Women and the Military System,* edited by Eva Isaksson, 171–89. New York: St. Martin's Press, 1988.

Hill, Amelia. "Front Pages Still Male-Dominated and Sexist—Report." *The Guardian,* October 15, 2012.

Ho, Karen. *Liquidated: An Ethnography of Wall Street.* Durham, NC: Duke University Press, 2009.

Holton, Woody. *Abigail Adams.* New York: Free Press, 2009.

Ho Tai, Hue-Tam. *Radicalism and the Origins of the Vietnamese Revolution.* Cambridge, MA: Harvard University Press, 1992.

Htun, Mala. *Sex and the State: Abortion, Divorce and the Family Under Latin American Dictatorships and Democracies.* Cambridge: Cambridge University Press, 2003.

Human Rights Watch. *Bosnia and Herzegovina Hopes Betrayed: Trafficking of Women and Girls to Bosnia and Herzegovina for Forced Prostitution.* Washington, DC: Human Rights Watch, November 2002.

Institute for Women's Policy Research. *The Gender Wage Gap by Occupation.* Washington, DC: Institute for Women's Policy Research, April 2012. Briefing paper.

———. *Quick Figures.* Washington, DC: Institute for Women's Policy Research, May 2012.

Inter-Parliamentary Union. "Women in National Parliaments." Inter-Parliamentary Union, December 31, 2006, www.ipu.org/wmn-e/arc/classif311206.htm (accessed May 7, 2012).

———. "Women in National Parliaments." Inter-Parliamentary Union, March 31, 2012, www.ipu.org/wmn-e/classif.htm (accessed June 10, 2012).

———. "Women in Parliaments: World Classification." Inter-Parliamentary Union, December 31, 2011, www.ipu.org/wmn-e/classif.htm (accessed May 7, 2012).

Isaksson, Eva, ed. *Women and the Military System.* New York: St. Martin's Press, 1988.

Iskander, Laila. "Arab Spring." Public lecture, Bentley University, Waltham, MA, April 7, 2011.

Jayawardena, Kumari. *Feminism and Nationalism in the Third World.* London: Zed Books, 1986.

Johnson, Janet Elise. "The Most Feminist Place in the World." *The Nation,* February 21, 2011, www.thenation.com/article/158279/the-most-feminist-place-world (accessed February 10, 2011).

Kampwirth, Karen. *Feminism and the Legacy of Revolution: Nicaragua, El Salvador, Chiapas.* Athens: Ohio University Press, 2004.

———. *Women and Guerrillas: Nicaragua, El Salvador, Chiapas, and Cuba.* University Park: Pennsylvania State University Press, 2002.

Kanter, James. "Britain Remains a Dissenter as Europeans Try to Set Capital Reserves for Banks." *New York Times,* May 3, 2012.

Kearl, Holly. "Egyptian Women Refuse To Be Silenced by Assaults." *Ms. Magazine* Blog, June 12, 2012, http://msmagazine.com/blog/blog/2012/06/10/egyptian-women-refuse-to-be-silenced-by-assaults (accessed June 18, 2012).

Kerber, Linda. *Women of the Republic: Intellect and Ideology in Revolutionary America.* Chapel Hill: University of North Carolina Press, 1980.

Khafagy, Fatma. "Shadow NGO Report on Egypt's Fourth and Fifth Combined Periodic Report to the Committee on the Elimination of Discrimination

Against Women." Alliance for Arab Women, Cairo, December 2009, distributed by the transnational feminist organization Women Living Under Muslim Laws, www.wluml.org/sites/wluml.org/files/shadow%20NGO%20Report%20Egypt%20CEDAW.pdf (accessed June 18, 2012).

Kim, Seung-kyung. *South Korean Feminists' Bargain: Progressive Presidencies and the Women's Movement, 1998–2007.* Forthcoming.

Kim, Seung-kyung, and John Finch. "Living with Rhetoric, Living Against Rhetoric: Korean Families and the IMF Economic Crisis." *Korean Studies* 26, no. 1 (2002): 120–39.

Kirkpatrick, David D. "Clinton Visits Egypt, Carrying Muted Pledge of Support." *New York Times,* July 14, 2012.

———. "Egyptian Military Court Acquits Doctor Accused of Performing 'Virginity Tests.'" *New York Times,* March 12, 2012.

Kollontai, Alexandra. *Autobiography of a Sexually Emancipated Communist Woman.* New York: Herder and Herder, 1971.

Kondraki, Larysa, dir. *The Whistleblower.* Rotten Tomatoes Productions, 2011.

Kosovo Women's Network. *1325: Fact and Fables.* Prishtina, Kosovo: Kosovo Women's Network, 2011.

Kruks, Sonia, Rayna Rapp, and Marilyn B. Young, eds. *Promissory Notes: Women in Transition to Socialism.* New York: Monthly Review Press, 1989.

Kulish, Nicholas, and Annie Lowrey. "German Leader and I.M.F. Chief Split Over Debt." *New York Times,* March 10, 2012.

Lang, Amy Schrager, and Daniel Lang/Levitsky, eds. *Dreaming in Public: Building the Occupy Movement.* Oxford: New Internationalist Press, 2012.

LeBlanc, Robin. *The Art of the Gut: Manhood, Power, and Ethics in Japanese Politics.* Berkeley: University of California Press, 2010.

Lewis, Jane, ed. *Before the Vote Was Won: Arguments for and Against Women's Suffrage, 1864–1896.* London: Routledge and Kegan Paul, 1987.

Loftsdottir, Kristin. "The Loss of Innocence." *Anthropology Today* 26, no. 6 (December 2010): 9–13.

Lucas, Caroline. "A Quota for Women in the Boardroom." *The Guardian,* July 19, 2009.

Marr, David. *Vietnamese Tradition on Trial, 1920–1945.* Berkeley: University of California Press, 1981.

Martinson, Jane. *Seen But Not Heard: How Women Make Front Page News.* London: Women in Journalism, October 2012.

McGreal, Chris. "Only Half the Struggle: Arab Women Fight to Keep the Gains Won on the Street." *The Guardian,* June 14, 2012.

McNicoll, Tracy. "Christine Lagarde Named New IMF Chief." *The Daily Beast,* June 28, 2011, www.thedailybeast.com/articles/2011/06/28/christine-lagarde-is-new-imf-chief.html (accessed May 9, 2011).

Meier-Pesti, Katja, and Elfriede Penz. "Sex or Gender? Expanding the Sex-Based View by Introducing Masculinity and Femininity as Predictors of Financial Risk Taking." *Journal of Economic Psychology,* no. 29 (2008): 180–96.

Mills, Mary Beth. *Thai Women in the Global Labor Force.* New Brunswick, NJ: Rutgers University Press, 1999.

Mokhtar, Yonna. "Arab Women's Association Forms Political Party." *Egypt Independent,* October 16, 2011, www.egyptindependent.com/news/arab-womens-association-forms-political-party (accessed July 11, 2012).

Morgenson, Gretchen, and Joshua Rosner. *Reckless Endangerment.* New York: Times Books and Henry Holt, 2011.

MoveOn.org. "Top 10 Shocking Attacks from the GOP's War on Women." MoveOn.org, February, 2012, http://pol.moveon.org/waronwomen (accessed June 12, 2012).

Murphy, Mary. "A 'Ship of Men': Gender Equality as a Solution to This Man-Made Crisis." Lecture presented at the Feminist Open Forum, Dublin, 2010, available online from feministforum@gmail.com.

NARAL Pro-Choice America. "NARAL Pro-Choice America Calls on Congress to End War on Women in Nation's Capital." NARAL Pro-Choice America, 2012, www.prochoiceamerica.org/media/press-releases/2012 (accessed June 12, 2012).

National Commission on the Causes of the Financial Economic Crisis in the United States. *The Financial Crisis Inquiry Report.* Washington, DC: Government Printing Office, February 25, 2011.

National Council for Research on Women. *Women in Fund Management.* New York: National Council for Research on Women, 2009.

National Organization for Women. "On International Women's Day NOW Calls for End to the 'War on Women.'" National Organization for Women, March 8, 2012, www.now.org/press/03-11/03-08.html (accessed June 12, 2012).

Ng, Cecilia, Maznah Mohamad, and Tan Beng Hui. *Feminism and the Women's Movement in Malaysia.* New York: Routledge, 2006.

Noyes, Gertrude E. *A History of Connecticut College.* New London, CT: Connecticut College, 1982.

Ólafsson, Jón Gunnar. "The 'Icesavior' Rises: A Media Narrative Featuring a Crisis and an Online Savings Brand in Starring Roles." In *Rannsóknir í Félagsvísindunn XII,* 76–83. Reykjavik: Félagsvísindastofnun, October 2011.

Pande, Rekha, ed. *Women's Studies Narratives.* Cambridge: Cambridge Scholars Publishers, forthcoming.

Peterson, V. Spike, and Anne Sisson Runyan. *Global Gender Issues in the New Millennium.* 3rd ed. Boulder, CO: Westview Press, 2010.

Povich, Lynn. *The Good Girls Revolt: How the Women of Newsweek Sued Their Bosses and Changed the Workplace.* New York: Public Affairs, 2012.

Pratt, Nicola, and Sophie Richter-Devroe, eds. "Critically Examining UNSCR 1325." Special issue, *International Feminist Journal of Politics* 13, no. 4 (December 2011).

Prugl, Elisabeth, and Hayley Thompson. "The Whistleblower: Interview with Kathryn Bolkovac and Madeleine Rees." *International Feminist Journal of Politics,* forthcoming.

"Public Sector Cuts Threaten Women's Employment." *Equal Opportunities Review* (May 2012): 5.

Puechguirbal, Nadine. "Discourses on Gender, Patriarchy and Resolution 1325." *International Peacekeeping* 17, no. 2 (2010).

———. "Peacekeeping, Peacebuilding and Post-conflict Reconstruction." In *Gender Matters in Global Politics,* edited by Laura Shepherd. London: Routledge, 2010.

Rai, Shirin. *Gender and the Political Economy of Development.* Cambridge, U.K.: Polity, 2002.

Randall, Margaret. *Sandino's Daughters.* Vancouver: New Star Books, 1981.

———. *Sandino's Daughters Revisited.* New Brunswick, NJ: Rutgers University Press, 2004.

Robertson, Nan. *The Girls in the Balcony: Women, Men and the New York Times.* New York: Random House, 1992.

Roose, Kevin. "A Hazing at a Wall Street Fraternity." *New York Times,* January 21, 2012.

Saulny, Susan. "On the Right, Santorum Has Women's Vote." *New York Times,* March 24, 2012.

Schwartz, Nelson D., and Jessica Silver-Greenberg. "JPMorgan Chief of Investments Is Set to Depart." *New York Times,* May 14, 2012.

Seager, Joni. *The Penguin Atlas of Women in the World.* 4th ed. New York: Penguin, 2009.

Shigematsu, Setsu. "Aftermath: Feminism and the Militarization of Women's Lives—a Dialogue with Cynthia Enloe and Eli Painted Crow." *International Feminist Journal of Politics* 11, no. 3 (September 2009): 414–28.

Shigematsu, Setsu, Anuradha Kristina Bhagwati, and Eli Painted Crow. "Women of Color Veterans: Dialogue on War, Militarism and Feminism." In *Feminism and War,* edited by Robin Riley, Chandra Mohanty, and Minnie Bruce Pratt, 93–102. London: Zed Books, 2008.

Sigurdardottir, Elra. "Nation-centric Masculinity Ideals and the Icelandic Bank Collapse." NIKK: Nordic Gender Institute, November 1, 2010, www.nikk.np/Nation-centric+masculinity+ideals+and+the+Icelandic+bank+collapse.b7C_wlfo3e.ips (accessed February 6, 2012).

Silver-Greenberg, Jessica, and Nelson D. Schwartz. "Red Flags Said to Go Unheeded by Chase Bosses." *New York Times,* May 15, 2012.

Smith, Greg. "Why I Am Leaving Goldman Sachs." *New York Times,* March 14, 2012.

Stalsburg, Brittany L. "Rape, Sexual Assault and Sexual Harassment in the Military: Quick Facts." Service Women's Action Network, April 2011, http://servicewomen.org (accessed February 2, 2012).

Stephenson, Mary-Ann. "TUC Women and the Cuts, Coventry Women's Voices and the TUC." In *TUC Women and the Cuts Toolkit.* London: TUC, 2011, www.tuc.org.uk (accessed May 15, 2012).

Story, Louise. "A Secretive Banking Elite Rules Derivatives Trading." *New York Times,* December 12, 2010.

Sunderland, Ruth. "After the Crash, Iceland's Women Lead the Rescue." *The Observer,* February 22, 2009.

———. "Revealed: Failure of Top UK Firms to Get Women on Board." *The Observer,* August 23, 2009.

———. "We Cannot Return to the Old Macho Ways." *The Observer.* February 15, 2009.

Sussman, Anna Louie. "Prominent During Revolution, Egyptian Women Vanish in New Order." *The Atlantic* (April 2011), www.theatlantic.com /international/archive/2011/04/prominent-during-revolution-egyptian-women-vanish-in-new-order/237232 (accessed April 15, 2011).

Taylor, Sarah, and Kristina Mader. *Mapping Women, Peace and Security in the UN Security Council: Report of the NGOWG Monthly Action Points, 2009–2010.* NGO Working Group on Women, Peace and Security, October 2010, http:// womenpeacesecurity.org/media/pdf-NGOWG_MAPReport_2009–2010. pdf (accessed February 13, 2013).

Tett, Gillian. *Fool's Gold.* Boston: Little, Brown, 2009.

Toynbee, Polly. "'Calm Down, Dears'? Why It's a Bad Time to be a British Woman." *The Guardian,* March 8, 2012.

Traynor, Ian. "EU-wide Quotas for Women in Boardrooms Rejected." *The Guardian,* October 24, 2012.

Turner, Karen, with Thanh Hao Phan. *Even the Women Must Fight: Memories of War from North Vietnam.* New York: John Wiley and Sons, 1998.

UN Population Fund, "Indicators: Population and Development in Egypt," UNFPA Egypt, n.d., http://egypt.unfpa.org/english/Staticpage/54790f72–6e8b-4f77–99e2–4c5b78c20d5c/indicators.aspx (accessed June 20, 2012).

UN Women. *Progress of the World's Women: In Pursuit of Justice, 2011.* New York: UN Women, 2011, http://progress.unwomen.org (accessed June 23, 2012).

U.S. Government Accountability Office. *Financial Services Industry: Overall Trends in Management-Level Diversity and Diversity Initiatives, 1993–2008.* Washington, DC: U.S. Government Accountability Office, May 12, 2012, https://docs.google.com/viewer?a=v&q=cache:s6xsUqGYw_U (accessed April 19, 2012).

———. *Homeless Women Veterans: Actions Needed to Ensure Safe and Appropriate Housing.* Washington, DC: U.S. Government Accountability Office, December 2011.

Waring, Marilyn. *If Women Counted: A New Feminist Economics.* San Francisco: Harper and Row, 1988.

White House. "Executive Order—Instituting a National Action Plan on Women, Peace, and Security." White House, December 19, 2011, www.whitehouse.gov/the-press-office/2011/12/19/executive-order-instituting-national-action-plan-women-peace-and-security.

"Women and Money." *Action Brief.* National Council for Research on Women, 2010, www.ncrw.org.

"Women Face Hurdles at Senior Management Level." *Edge Online,* Institute of Leadership and Management, London, March 14, 2012, www.i-l-m.com/edge/Women_face_hurdles_at_senior_management_level.aspx (accessed March 22, 2012).

Women in Black Belgrade. *Women, Peace and Security: Resolution 1325—10 Years.* Belgrade: Women in Black Belgrade, 2011.

"Women's Rights Groups March to Egypt Presidential Palace, Thursday." *Ahram Online,* October 4, 2012, http://english.ahram.org.eg/NewsContent/1/64/54786/Egypt/Politics-/Womens-rights-groups-march-to-Egypt-presidential-p.aspx (accessed October 5, 2012).

Women's Scholars Forum. *Recommendations for Improving Employment in the Recovery.* Washington, DC: Institute for Women's Policy Research, September 2011. Briefing paper.

Wood, Elizabeth. *From Baba to Comrade: Gender and Politics in Revolutionary Russia.* Bloomington: Indiana University Press, 1997.

Woolhouse, Megan. "Despite Laurels, Progress Is Slow for Women in Economics." *Boston Globe,* May 14, 2012.

Wyatt, Edward. "Bank's Lobbyists Sought Loophole on Risky Trading." *New York Times,* May 12, 2012.

Yi, Robin H. Pugh, and Craig T. Dearfield. *The Status of Women in the U.S. Media, 2012.* Women's Media Center, February 2012, http://wmc.3cdn.net /a6b2dc282c824e903a_arm6boK8.pdf (accessed February 14, 2012).

INDEX

Italicized page numbers indicate illustrations.